THE AFRICAN LINK

THE AFRICAN LINK

British Attitudes to the Negro in the Era of the Atlantic Slave Trade, 1550–1807

ANTHONY J. BARKER

FRANK CASS

First published 1978 in Great Britain by
FRANK CASS AND COMPANY LIMITED
Gainsborough House, Gainsborough Road,
London E11 1RS, England

and in the United States of America by
FRANK CASS AND COMPANY LIMITED
c/o Biblio Distribution Centre,
81 Adams Drive, P.O. Box 327, Totowa, N. J. 07511

ISBN 0 7146 3081 0

Printed in Great Britain by
Chapel River Press, Andover, Hants

CONTENTS

KEY TO ABBREVIATIONS IN THE NOTES

Accounts and Papers,
XXIV–XXVI, XXIX,
XXX, XXXIV.

Parliamentary Papers Printed by Order of the House of Commons from the Year 1731 to 1800. Vols. 82–84, 87–88, 92. The titles of individual papers cited are listed in the Bibliography under 'Official Publications'.

Astley

Thomas Astley (publisher), A New General Collection of Voyages and Travels, 4 vols. (1745–47).

Barbot

John Barbot, A Description of the Coasts of North and South Guinea... Churchill, V, 1–668. For Churchill, see below.

B.M., Add MS.

British Museum, Additional Manuscripts.

Bosman

William Bosman, A New and Accurate Description of the Coast of Guinea. 1705, new ed. with Introduction by J. R. Willis and notes by J. D. Fage and R. E. Bradbury (1967).

Churchill

Awnsham and John Churchill, A Collection of Voyages and Travels..., 8 vols. (1704–45).

Parliamentary History

The Parliamentary History of England from the Earliest Period to the Year 1803, Vols. XXI–XXIV, 1780–1800 (1814–19).

P.R.O.

Public Record Office

—C.O.

—Colonial Office Papers

—H.O.

—Home Office Papers

—T 70

—Treasury Papers: Records of the African Companies.

Note: all works cited were published in London, unless otherwise indicated.

PREFACE

The Atlantic Slave Trade has been a neglected chapter in the history of racial attitudes. No doubt this has been partly because the degradation and murder of millions of Africans amounted to racist exploitation on a scale so grand that more subtle attitudes and perceptions have seemed improbable or unimportant. Partly the neglect has come about because a majority of historians of racial prejudice have been mainly concerned with the consequences of the slave trade. For Americans the trade itself was no more than introduction to a story of prejudice which unfolded on the plantations and later in the ghettos of their own country. Thus the most eminent American historian of racial attitudes, Winthrop Jordan, looked closely at early images of Africa and the slave trade in tracing the origins of American chattel slavery, but found the sources of later attitudes almost exclusively within American society.

Those concerned with British history have not been preoccupied with significant domestic racial tensions. Nevertheless a major concern with the end of the slave trade—amongst both British social and Imperial historians—has encouraged generalized views about the racial attitudes of the preceding two centuries. For Eric Williams, arguing a famous economic interpretation of abolition, it was logical to see the relationships of the slave trade era in terms of human greed and cruelty rather than race. And even for those who deny the economic interpretation and continue to give priority to a genuine philanthropy it is logical to see the abolition movement as an assault on entrenched ignorance and indifference.

Certainly in the almost frantic search for factual information, first by abolitionists and eventually by officialdom, there is some support for the view that racial attitudes were as new as other facets of the "Negro problem" in the late eighteenth century. Nevertheless the research which has produced this book began with a tentative questioning of such assumptions. A trade so old, so lucrative, so central to British mercantilism might well encourage indifference to human suffering but was it likely that it fostered such ignorance? If accounts of Black Africa in the sixteenth

ix

century could provide rich source material for Winthrop Jordan,
might there not be equally valuable African evidence from a later
period to illustrate a British experience as much concerned with
the Negro in his own African cultural context as with the
brutalized chattels of the New World slave system?[1]

It did not take long for these questions to become more
confident assertions, as the extensive African sections of the
bibliography at the end of this study indicate. But the study of
racial attitudes demands as much attention to the oblique and
peripheral as to direct description. References to the Negro in
travel literature and propaganda must be seen in a context of
literary, scientific, and other intellectual orthodoxies. And
attempts must be made to balance the significance of a vicarious
British experience of Africa and the New World against the
Negro's presence in Britain as slave, servant, beggar, entertainer
and side-show curiosity. Assumptions and questions about these
perimeters and substrata of attitudes were less triumphantly
vindicated. There was, for instance, to be little confirmation of the
belief that the eighteenth century—the era of Enlightenment,
scepticism, and growing empirical inquiry—would promote
sustained investigation into the nature of racial difference or
undogmatic evaluations of non-European, non-Christian societies.
And it soon became apparent that indirect clues to social attitudes
in Britain—in such records as parish registers and legal
archives—were fragmentary in the extreme compared with the
published record of the Negro overseas.

Inevitably the heavy concentration on the published record has
meant that the attitudes discussed were primarily those of a literate
élite which was a mere fraction of the total British population. In
the absence of recorded comments from, for instance, the
Londoners who may have lived next door to Negroes, or seen
Negro skulls placed alongside those of the higher apes in a small
London museum, one can only make circumstantial and tentative
hypotheses about the attitudes of the "man in the street". In
assessing the attitudes of the élite one is of course looking at a
minority with immense responsibility, direct and indirect, for
decisions about slavery and the slave trade. It should, however, be
emphasized that this book is not concerned to argue causal
connections between racial attitudes and those momentous
decisions made by many individuals in the late eighteenth century
and ultimately by Parliamentary majority in 1807. Its division into
chronological sections may draw attention to that era of debate
and decision. But the central themes—that the slave trade had long
been widely reported, that Negro images were of Africans as well

as slaves—make it more clear than ever that the abolition movement must have emerged as the result of complex changes in economic and humanitarian attitudes rather than of sudden revelation about a sinister, hidden side of Britain's overseas experience.

Most of the research for this book was first undertaken in preparation for a doctoral thesis. In the early stages this research was supervised by Dr George Metcalf, then of King's College, London University, now of the University of Western Ontario, who was particulary helpful about the African end of the slave trade. In the no less difficult later stages I was fortunate to be supervised by Dr Peter Marshall of King's College, who was particularly helpful about everything. It gives me great pleasure to thank both of these gentlemen: they can claim considerable credit for the success of the thesis: they can in no way be held responsible for defects in this book which has been very extensively re-written in Perth. Neither can two colleagues here to whom I am nonetheless grateful: Mrs Penelope Hetherington for criticisms of one chapter and Dr Michael Louis for finding the time to read through the whole manuscript.

More indirectly but no less importantly I am indebted to recent students at the University of Western Australia and former senior colleagues at the University of Sydney. Of the former, Patricia Dodson, Lynne Eastoe, Peter Hopper, and Robert Stevenson have, by their contributions to honours seminars, helped me to re-assess some vital parts of the story. In Sydney Professor J. M. Ward and, especially, Associate Professor K. J. Cable were helpful in guiding me earlier to an M.A. degree on a related subject which still has echoes in the following pages.

Thanks also to Mrs Dianna Hollis and Miss Lee Carter for typing the manuscript with great competence.

Finally the usual thanks to my wife for her moral support must be supplemented by unusual thanks for much more vital financial support when things really mattered.

A. J. BARKER

University of Western Australia

Part I

**Public Awareness of the Negro in
the Era of the Slave Trade**

CHAPTER ONE

THE HISTORICAL BACKGROUND

From Classical and medieval geographers and from Arab contacts across the Sahara ideas about black Africa were circulating in Europe long before the Atlantic slave trade began. Britain's entry into that trade came relatively late. For two centuries before the Royal African Company was chartered in 1672 other Europeans had been establishing the basic patterns of the trade. With their Negro trading partners they had revolutionized Africa's lines of communication with the outside world. Previously these lines had stretched across the Sahara. West African slaves and gold were exchanged for European luxury goods and North African salt. The desert had been a barrier to mass movements of population but not to the movement of ideas and influences. Islam had penetrated widely if superficially into black animist Africa; and empires had risen and fallen in the savannah regions south of the desert partly as a result of contacts with the non-Negro world.

By the seventeenth century the ocean had been transformed from a barrier into a highway and its coastal states from insignificance to positions of power and influence. But it was still the interior regions, as they stood in the heyday of the trans-Saharan trade, which epitomized West Africa to the well-read seventeenth century Englishman. It was Timbuktu, Mali, and Gao, rather than the Gold Coast, Whidah, and Angola, which, with glimpses of African achievement, modified infinitely older images of a bizarre and repellent continent. The Africa of seventeenth century English geography was still a land of desert, burning sun, and exotic humanity, rather than one of green luxuriance, disease-ridden humidity, and hard commercial bargains.

British traders were soon to experience the reality of the coast and their attitudes to the Negro were inevitably shaped by the way they were forced to adapt to well established patterns of inter-racial contact as well as to the challenge of climate. At the same time the growing involvement in the slave trade awakened a more general British interest in its evolution, with the result that the eighteenth century Negro image was also influenced directly by historical accounts of its fifteenth and sixteenth century foundations.

These foundations had been laid by the Portuguese above all. Beginning in the fifteenth century, before the New World had been discovered and exploited to stimulate large-scale slave trading, they had seen African potential largely in terms of trade. Profits were made not by seizing the mineral resources of Africa but by invigorating existing African commercial systems. Colonization of the Cape Verde Islands was built on a cotton growing and textile manufacturing enterprise, in which Portuguese ships brought Negro slave labour and distributed its products in the neighbouring coastal regions. A slave trade to the Gold Coast was developed as part of another commercial network in which the Portuguese supplied labour for mining and porterage, as well as textiles from Benin, in return for gold dust.

In both these regions, while the emphasis was to turn to the export rather than import of slaves, the basic pattern of European-African relations was to survive the passing of Portuguese domination. English and other European successors were to find in the Senegambia regions the mulatto descendants of Portuguese traders acting as the main middle men in the slave trade. And on the Gold Coast they were to emulate the Portuguese example, first seen at Elmina, of establishing fortified trading posts, without improving the Portuguese dependence on powerful African middle men, whose small coastal states strictly curtailed the sovereignty of the forts.

The Slave Coast and Niger delta regions, which were to become important centres of the eighteenth century slave trade, were largely neglected by the Portuguese, as the main thrust of their activities centred on the Congo mouth and Angola and, still more, on the Indian Ocean. Despite an interlude of Dutch control, the trade of West Central Africa remained under their domination long after they had been supplanted elsewhere. But the different techniques—of colonization in the Congo and of sixteenth century conquest in Angola—were well known to British readers of historical and geographical literature. And the effects of this intrusive policy—both in terms of endemic warfare and the emergence of dimly understood interior African empires—came to be added to a general image of African depravity and instability which was to find particular emphasis in eighteenth century pro-slavery polemics.

The Portuguese slave trade had one other significant African centre—the island of São Tomé. At first an entrepôt for Portugal's African commercial operations it developed in the sixteenth century into a substantial market for slaves. Events were to show that the island's sugar plantations had been a useful laboratory for testing the slave system later perfected across the Atlantic. But the plantations were already in decline, beset by crop disease and slave revolts, before Brazilian sugar growing was developed in the second half of the sixteenth century. And in the same period the demand for slaves in Spain's New World possessions had seen the beginnings of the Atlantic slave trade. Increasingly São Tomé found a new role as victualling station for slave ships of many nationalities. With its enervating equatorial climate and its reputation for disease and interracial debauchery, it was to appear as a microcosm of West Africa's most unsavoury characteristics in the memoirs of many slave traders.

When Portuguese navigators began feeling their way down the West African coast in the fifteenth century their eventual maritime dominance of the region was far from certain. They were followed by Frenchmen and especially by Castilians. Rivalry with Castilians reached its height in the 1470s but continued in a lower key until Columbus's discovery of the New World in 1492. Papal Bulls in 1493 and the Treaty of Tordesillas divided the non-European world, giving Portugal a monopoly of Brazil, West Africa, and Asia, while Castile concentrated on the New World.

But although this division was to establish the first basic pattern of the slave trade, with Spain providing the overseas markets and Portugal the slaves, its terms were not recognized elsewhere in Europe. In the sixteenth century French and English merchants were increasingly active interlopers in the Portuguese West African trading network. But because English activities remained small privately financed expeditions, their participants gained little real insight into West African society. Their accounts—eventually published by Richard Hakluyt at the end of the century—showed the influence of legendary beliefs about Africa and some evidence of commercial activities and acumen among its inhabitants. But essentially fleeting English contacts could not give any indication of the importance the African slave trade was eventually to assume.

Even the famous slaving voyages by John Hawkins in the 1560s were more typical of the small private ventures of the period than of subsequent English involvement in the slave trade. Far from initiating a new enthusiasm for slaves the voyages were followed by a lengthy period in which Africa remained low on the list of English overseas priorities. Residual English interest centred more on Africa's mineral wealth than slaves. There was support for a Moroccan invasion in 1591 across the Sahara, which had considerable effects on African society without achieving its goal of capturing the sources of gold exports to North Africa. In the first half of the seventeenth century the same interior regions were far better known to the English public than the coastal areas of West Africa, thanks to the publication in 1600 of an English translation of Leo Africanus' *History and Description of Africa*. And in the same period a number of trading companies with African objectives revealed interest in a general exploratory economic activity rather than the slave trade. This was a time when English expansion was directed more towards the New World. Colonies were being founded in North America and the West Indies which were soon to stimulate the growth of the slave trade. But this was to come about only after further European innovations and influences.

The first European power seriously to challenge the Portuguese control of the slave trade was the Netherlands. With the union of the Portuguese and Spanish Crowns in 1580, the Dutch War of Independence from Spain, which had begun in 1572, soon assumed global dimensions. The Dutch West India Company, formed in 1621, succeeded first in winning naval supremacy over Spain in the Caribbean and then in conquering a large part of Portuguese Brazil. It was a desire to increase the profitability of Brazil's slave-based sugar economy which led the Dutch to seize control of the majority of Portuguese possessions in Upper Guinea, on the Gold Coast and in West Central Africa. Control of some of these acquisitions was short-lived, as Portugal, asserting her independence from Spain in 1640, launched a counter-attack on both sides of the Atlantic. But although they were expelled from Brazil, São Tomé, and West Central Africa by mid-century, the Dutch retained posts in Upper Guinea and a majority of the Gold Coast forts.

The loss of Brazil forced the Dutch to seek other markets for their slave cargoes. The rapid contemporary expansion of sugar plantations in the West Indies, which made these available, owed much to direct Dutch encouragement. But the Dutch maritime supremacy, which made them accessible, led to a more intensive European competition for the slave trade. By the mid-seventeenth century this supremacy was virtually world-wide and the Navigation Acts, which both England and France began to enact, reflected concern that national resources of precious metal would be drained away in payment for Dutch carriage of their trade with the outside world. These measures were part of an assault on Dutch trading dominance which had already led to the founding of national monopoly trading companies.

For the English the determination to exclude the Dutch from trade with the West Indies and meet the demand for slaves from within a national trading network led to the chartering of the Company of Royal Adventurers Trading into Africa in 1660 and, in 1672, to its successor, the Royal African Company. This was the effective beginning of the English slave trade and the manner of its inception said much about the existing pattern of race relations and implied much about the future influences on racial attitudes.

The use of monopolistic trading companies reflected more than a pervasive contemporary economic philosophy. It also was a response to the established African patterns of the slave trade, in which Europeans were confined to the coast and forced to trade with powerful African middle men, who in turn exchanged European goods for slaves in the interior. Spokesmen for the Royal African Company, in stressing the need for garrisoned and fortified trading posts, were to make much in the next few decades of the political and commercial vigour of the Africans. The interracial problems, which were cited to illustrate these arguments, were part of a much more complex international situation, especially on the Gold Coast. By the late seventeenth century the demand for slaves in the West Indies was sufficiently large to encourage other European powers to enter the slave trade, even though they did not share the French and English preoccupation with colonial self-sufficiency and Dutch maritime supremacy. Forts and factories flying the flags of Denmark, Sweden, and Brandenburg formed a subordinate factor in the major competition between Dutch and English on the Gold Coast. Even though the Portuguese never regained their lost positions and the French confined their attentions largely to Upper Guinea, conditions on the Gold Coast long remained unstable. Rival forts were in some cases very close together; irksome and unhealthy living conditions heightened tensions; and conflicts in Europe often, though not invariably, spread to Africa. Attitudes to African society were very much conditioned by this volatile situation in which the only stable factor was the indispensability of native contacts with the interior.

The only other regions in which the Royal African Company's servants found themselves directly in competition with another European monopoly company was at the mouth of the Gambia.

Here the French established a rival trading post at Albreda near the first of all English African forts, which had been erected on James Island as early as 1618. But this region was of subordinate importance to both national companies. While the English concentrated on the Gold Coast, the French, from bases on the island of St Louis and Gorée, made the Senegal their main focus of activity. From here in the early eighteenth century they penetrated some three hundred miles inland to Bambuk—much further than Europeans reached elsewhere in West Africa—before withdrawing in the face of strong competition from established African trading systems among the Mande and Fulani. French experiences in this region were known indirectly through English translations of major travel accounts before Britain temporarily occupied most French possessions in Senegal in 1763.

Elsewhere in West Africa the European side of the slave trade was in the hands of independent traders. There were English settlements on the Sierra Leone river and Sherbro island but the usual pattern of independent trade on the Windward Coast was to take slaves wherever they became available. A ship would move down the coast, responding to signals from the shore to move in and conduct negotiations at innumerable island and coastal rendezvous. These more transient contacts gave full rein to mutual mistrust between European and African, while giving less opportunity for European insight into African society than in more permanent trading posts. This was the case even more acutely to the south-east, on the Grain and Ivory Coasts, where heavy surf, difficult currents, and lack of suitable coastal anchorages led to a system of trading at sea from small native boats.

The private traders also made their presence felt on the Gold Coast. In the late seventeenth century, as far as the English were concerned, this was in defiance of the Royal African Company's monopoly. Without the expensive overheads connected with permanent posts such traders were able to compete on favourable terms with the companies. Resentment of this infiltration by the Company and criticism of the Company's monopoly were as potent factors in the reporting of the Gold Coast situation as international rivalries and produced equally revealing comments about native society.

Ultimately the relative failure of the Royal African Company, signalled by the end of its monopoly in 1698, represented a victory for the private traders. Fifteen years later Britain finally secured the *Asiento*—the right to supply slaves to the colonies of Spain—which had originally been held by the Portuguese and more recently by the French. But though this contract, signed at the Peace of Utrecht, represented an international victory for Britain, it proved of minimal importance in the history of British contacts with Africa. The South Sea Company, which secured the monopoly, owned no African bases but its demands were insufficient to revitalize the Royal African Company, since it found most of its cargoes in established slave societies in the West Indies. After an interlude of Anglo-Spanish war in the 1740s the *Asiento* was renewed in 1748 only to be relinquished two years later by Britain. The Royal African Company lingered on through the same period. The difficulties of its African-based servants in unhealthy and largely unprofitable circumstances continued to be reflected in the published accounts of West Africa. But in the eighteenth century it was through private traders that Britain developed and eventually dominated the slave trade.

The final dissolution of the Royal African company in 1750 was a mark of the private traders' success. Its replacement, the Company of Merchants trading into Africa, gave a formal role to the merchants of Liverpool, London, and Bristol instead of attempting to continue the losing fight against private trade. The new company was not concerned with trade in its own right but merely with creating the most favourable conditions for trade, especially by maintaining the forts and factories of the Gold Coast.

But although the eighteenth century slave trade continued to operate in this and other long established West African centres, from the late seventeenth century the private traders of many nationalities also moved into areas east of the Gold Coast previously either ignored or abandoned by the Portuguese. The area between the mouth of the Volta and Lagos rapidly earned the name Slave Coast and the Niger delta and areas around the shores of the Gulf of Guinea to the mouth of the Gaboon also became prominent.

The extension of the trade primarily reflected the still expanding demand of the West Indies. But the way it was conducted showed that Africans as well as Europeans were responding to lessons learned on the Gold Coast. African leaders refused to allow strong forts to be built in their midst and succeeded in maintaining even firmer control over the conditions of trade than had been achieved in the Gold Coast. These regions became such reliable sources of slaves, that even the private traders found there were advantages in maintaining permanent depots for storing trading goods and collecting slaves. But these bases were never more substantial than the moored hulks used in several Gulf estuaries or the mud and straw buildings erected in native towns on the Slave Coast.

The most important and frequently described of these towns was Whidah. Here, some miles inland from the safety of their ships, traders of many European nations operated within a system rigidly controlled by the African king. Resentment of this control produced many revealing comments about African personality and policy. But when the regime was overthrown in 1727 it was not by resentful Europeans but by Africans from Dahomey in the interior whose sudden irruption itself added new details to the European picture of West African society.

Although the instruments of Britain's eventual supremacy in the slave trade were private traders, the reasons lay in wider Anglo-French competition for world trade. Africa was rarely a major theatre of war compared with Europe, India, or North America. But trade with West Africa developed as part of a general British maritime success story. The climax of this process came at the turn of the century when, through fifteen years of war, British seapower entirely excluded the French from trade with West Africa. With most of continental Europe under French domination only Britain's ally, Portugal, and the neutral United States continued to take a significant share of the slave trade.

These trends meant that an increasing proportion of the writings about Africa was by British nationals. But this did nothing to produce a more homogeneous attitude. The more important the slave trade became the more the observations of its practitioners were distorted and supplemented by the special pleading of vested interests. Finally, in the period of virtual British supremacy, the debate over abolition led to conflicting extremes of fantasy, each equally remote from the available contemporary truth.

On the other hand, even in the eighteenth century the British relationship with Africa was not entirely a question of slave trading. West Africa continued to supply modest quantities of gold dust and ivory and—of importance to the textile industry—dyewoods from the Gambia and gum from Senegal. The Senegambia region was too thinly populated to be a major source of slaves comparable to the shores of the Gulf of Guinea and without the additional economic motive French and British might have been less continuously in conflict in the area. These local circumstances provided the motive and Britain's success in the Seven Years War the opportunity for an experiment in colonial rule which would have been both impossible and unnecessary in regions entirely devoted to the slave trade. The eventual failure of the experiment was equally the result of local events and wider international considerations.

It was almost ironic that Britain was embarking on colonial rule in Africa in the very period when the value of colonies first came under critical analysis. The end of the Seven Years War in 1763, which saw Britain initiate a provocative new Imperial policy for her expanded North American empire, also left her with all of France's possessions in Senegal, with the exception of Goreé. These were combined with British posts on the Gambia— previously controlled by the Company of Merchants—to form a new crown colony of Senegambia. The unsuccessful attempt to impose the institutions of colonial rule on people accustomed to an amalgam of French and African, rather than British, traditions gave extra dimensions to the usual picture of Negro society. By 1776, when Adam Smith published his *Wealth of Nations* and the American Declaration of Independence dealt a more tangible blow to the Old Colonial System, the Senegambia colony was already proving a failure. By 1783 when recognition of American Independence marked a definitive stage in British colonial history, France, as an American ally in the war, had recaptured most of her positions in Senegal and Britain's first experiment in colonial rule in Africa was abandoned. Its failure had been due to economic and commercial weaknesses as well as to French military and naval successes. But failure could also reinforce arguments about the intractability of problems of colonial rule among African Negroes.

Although the loss of its first major empire in America can be seen as a turning point in British colonial history, change came very slowly as various protected interest groups fought for more than half a century against the growing support for free trade policies. In the short term the loss of America actually sharpened colonizing interest in West Africa. The presence of large numbers of freed slaves from the American colonies in the streets of London led to the foundation of Sierra Leone in 1787. The problems of this struggling colony in the next few decades were to receive emphasis in the emerging argument over Negro capacities for civilization.

This argument was itself, of course, part of the wider debate over the slave trade which began almost abruptly in the 1780s. By then anti-slavery writing was at least a century old. But it was not until Thomas Clarkson published his *Essay on the Slavery and Commerce of the Human Species* in 1786 that a real movement for abolition gathered momentum. Clarkson's work was skilfully written and as comprehensive as anything previously penned on the subject. But it was originally a prize-winning Cambridge University essay written in Latin. And the reasons its English translation released a flood of support and opposition are to be found in a series of events and trends which had made the time ripe for intensified criticism of the slave trade.

Some of the underlying trends were extremely long term. David Davis has located the intellectual foundations of humanitarianism in important eighteenth century changes in the emphasis of theology and secular thought. Eric Williams has seen the abolition controversy as part of the wider conflict between advocates of a new free trade policy and the supporters of Britain's traditional mercantilist Old Colonial System[2]. Both these interpretations are valuable if used with caution. It was undoubtedly humanitarian agitation which began the controversy: it is unlikely ultimate success would have been possible without the support of vested economic interests. But it took a particular combination of factors to focus the critical attention of both humanitarian and economic interests on to the slave trade.

It was the West Indian planters who kept the slave trade going. By demanding a heavy preponderance of immediately useful adult male slaves; by insisting on rigorous labour; and by neglecting to provide adequate medical care, diet, and housing, they ensured that slavery could never be self-perpetuating. In their exploitation of land as well as labour the planters showed the same thirst for short-term profit. Smaller plantations were quickly swallowed up in most of the British islands but the larger units were not made more productive by innovations in methods nor consolidated by planned crop rotations. The relentless quest for quick profits was largely successful in the first half of the eighteenth century. Enormous fortunes were made and the returned planter, buying a country estate or even a seat in Parliament, became a familiar figure in English society. Ultimately this practice of regarding the West Indies simply as a means to social elevation in England exacerbated the other problems of the plantations. Absenteeism either led directly to neglect and decay or inhibited remedial action for accelerating agricultural and economic failure.

Such failure was not inevitable. Other West Indian islands, notably those belonging to France, were run more economically with smaller plantations, less absenteeism, and, at least according to contemporary critics of the British West Indies, a less exploitive slave system. The contrast between British and foreign islands became widely noticed in 1763, when a debate developed in Britain over whether to claim Canada or the French sugar island of Guadeloupe as spoils of victory in the Seven Years War. The retention of Guadeloupe might have made more sense in strict mercantilist terms; but such a decision would have been anathema to the British planters fearful of the competition of its superior productivity. The lobbying of the West Indies interests was only one of several reasons why the decision was made to keep Canada and not Guadeloupe. But from this time on, although for decades their defences of slavery were to stress national interest, the arguments of the West Indians were more and more transparently pleas for an economic system in decline.

If the lobbying in 1763 did little to quicken interest in abolition, there were other factors which did. The achievement of supremacy in North America provided Britain with problems of defence, administration, and expense which led to a new policy of more centralized control over long established seaboard colonies. The collision between Britain's reasonable demands and the colonies' equally reasonable aspirations eventually produced the American Revolution after more than a decade of trans-Atlantic friction. This was to have particular influence on the emergence of abolitionism in conjunction with events which were taking place in Britain in the same period.

West Indian planters had always been in the habit of bringing black servants with them on their return to England. Some of these had successfully absconded and others been recaptured in the past without arousing much attention. But in the 1760s circumstances brought a number of runaways to the doorstep of Granville Sharp, the philanthropist. In a series of test cases, culminating in the *cause célèbre* of James Somerset in 1772, Sharp and his friends challenged the right of slave owners to keep Negroes in bondage in England. Recent research has shown that the Somerset case provided a far from decisive victory for anti-slavery forces, with slavery continuing in England long after this particular individual was freed. But the issue had provided Sharp with a cause which had wider implications. And the interest with which the long drawn out proceedings were followed by the press showed that for some others too the whole question of slavery had been given an immediacy lacking in a century of intermittent academic debate.

These factors might alone have been insufficient to sustain humanitarian interest in the more remote problems of overseas slavery and the slave trade, if the American Revolution had not soon revived the issues. When the War of Independence began much of Britain's military hopes were pinned on success in the slave owning southern colonies. With some southerners making it plain they preferred to submit to Britain rather than enlist Negroes in their armies, slavery became an issue to be exploited to military and political advantage by Britain. Many slaves responded to British proclamations of freedom by joining the Loyalist ranks, while British observers were not slow to point out

the inconsistency between slavery and the Revolutionary libertarian rhetoric. This inconsistency worried Americans too. By the
time the freed slaves were making their presence felt in Britain
itself, by swelling the ranks of the Black Poor, several of the new
American states had abolished slavery. These were outside the
South, where such a decision would have massive economic and
social effects. But such important southern Revolutionary leaders
as Thomas Jefferson and George Washington were also critically
concerned about the continuation of slavery. The result was that,
at a time when Thomas Clarkson published his *Essay* and people
in London were being aroused to take notice of the problem of
the Black Poor, a contemporary abolition movement was already
being publicized in Britain. From these diverse attitudes and
origins there soon developed a comparable movement in Britain
too—and, in response, a pro-slavery lobby—which embraced
equally diverse attitudes to the Negro and his culture.

The literature of the debate soon became stereotyped after the
first exchanges in the mid-1780s. When the earliest abolition
motions were rejected by Parliament the prospects of an early
reassessment seemed politically favourable. But the French
Revolution and its attendant wars soon diverted the attention of
such sympathisers as William Pitt away from the issue. Soon the
French slave revolts, which produced the New World's second
republic in Haiti, added some extra ingredients to arguments about
both slavery and race. And at the turn of the century publication of
Mungo Park's *Travels* was a sign of a new interest in Africa
unconnected with either the slave trade or pressure for its
abolition. But despite these new details, the picture of the Negro,
in slavery or in Africa, in 1807 was substantially no newer than the
arguments which finally accompanied abolition of the slave
trade.

It is the sheer volume of these repetitive, stereotyped arguments
which commands attention. But neither this weight of evidence nor
the political importance of abolition should obscure the fact that
the Negro had been known by Englishmen as an African even
longer than he had been known as a chattel slave. And the extent
to which this older image had persisted or been modified cannot be
assessed simply by looking at the records of an era dominated by
propaganda. It is necessary first to consider how far the intimate
contact of a relative handful of Europeans with Africa had been
communicated to a wider British public.

CHAPTER TWO

THE MAKERS OF THE NEGRO IMAGE

The story of European contact with West Africa outlined in the previous chapter would have little relevance to racial attitudes if conventional assumptions about the slave trade were accepted. According to such assumptions, as sugar and tobacco grew from seventeenth century fads to eighteenth century necessities, Englishmen were dimly aware of the Negro labour which produced them and yet invincibly ignorant of the continent which provided the Negroes. The complex and varied European contact with Africa was a private experience as remote from Britain as the notorious cruelties of the Middle Passage. As a result, when the trade came under attack in the late eighteenth century, propagandists were able to invent their own images of Africa. At the same time, Negroes in Britain were being seen in ways which reflected and reinforced the underlying ignorance. They were so well known as flunkeyed servants or abject vagrants that individual Negroes could rivet the attention of fashionable society simply by doing something else.[1]

Although some of the details are irrefutable, this general argument is unacceptable. If some abolitionists challenged the slave trade with fantasies of African noble savagery, or showed excessive excitement when a Negro put pen to paper or bow to violin, many others put enormous stress on the descriptive record of African society compiled over the previous centuries. It is only relatively recently that the significance or even the existence of much of this material has been recognized. Before the 1960s more attention focused on the image of the Negro in abolitionist verse, drama, and fiction than on the evidence of his personality and culture in descriptive works. Eva Beatrice Dykes has produced a long catalogue of works to justify her title, *The Negro in English Romantic Thought, or a Study of Sympathy for the Oppressed*

(Washington, 1942). More provocative is Wylie Sypher's *Guinea's Captive Kings: British anti-slavery literature of the eighteenth century*.[2] Sypher's central theme is that the characteristic hero of anti-slavery writers was a noble Negro, cruelly torn from an earthly paradise in Africa, a primitive no less heroic than the savages extolled in the largely Continental cult of noble savagery. Sypher's analysis of imaginative literature is persuasive but tends to suggest that this mythical creation was virtually the only Negro image in eighteenth century Britain. The ignorance of the British about Africa, he argues, "liberated the fancy to roam the pseudo-Africa of verse and prose." To some extent this point is belied by the list of works he offers as "some of the chief sources of information about Africa available before the *Travels* of Mungo Park". Accounts such as that by John Barbot added a great deal to the picture of Africa in Richard Hakluyt's late sixteenth century anthology of voyages. And the detailed descriptions contained in Barbot's 668 double-column folio pages scarcely support Sypher's claim that "the usual voyage gives at best a vague notion of the Negro and Africa."[3] But, irrespective of the content of such works, Sypher fails to recognize the existence of a descriptive literature on Africa so vast as to render implausible his assertions of ignorance, especially among the educated classes who would read anti-slavery fiction.

More recent historians have recognized part of the scale of this travel and geographical *genre*. Philip Curtin, in his study of the image of Africa after 1780, points to the wealth of material published over a much lengthier period: Africa, he suggests, received more prominence than almost any other non-European region. David Davis, in his study of the intellectual background to anti-slavery thought, has also suggested that historians have "exaggerated Europe's long ignorance of the Dark Continent". James Walvin, too, points to the the proliferation of descriptive accounts before arguing the predominance of "mythological" beliefs. Winthrop Jordan, in the largest-scale study of seventeenth and eighteenth century attitudes, places some emphasis on the descriptive and synthesizing material in the late sixteenth and early seventeenth centuries. But as it is the essence of his thesis that by 1700 racial slavery dominated New World attitudes, his treatment of the eighteenth century necessarily depends very little on such evidence, since his main concern is the Negro image in America.[4]

Despite these re-appraisals, none of these writers—largely because they deal with different themes and periods—has recognized the full scale of the writing on Negroes, assessed its importance, or analyzed its content. It is on such published work that the main arguments of this book will be based. Many unpublished manuscripts of people involved in the slave trade or the New World slave system have been read. But these will be referred to only where they illuminate the public record. Most opinions about the Negro owed something to the specialized knowledge and vested interests of such individuals; but their private views are ignored where they did not make a contribution to the general awareness of the Negro which is the subject of this book. On the other hand, the same criteria demand consideration of numerous non-British views, where it is clear, by publication in Britain or from reference in contemporary works, that they contributed to knowledge and attitudes.

In first hand accounts of Africa there is a meaningful division between seventeenth and eighteenth centuries. For most of the seventeenth century the primary sources were the largely ephemeral contacts by early slave traders and voyagers recorded in Hakluyt; the more extensive description by Leo Africanus; and Richard Jobson's *Golden Trade* (1623). John Ogilby's *Africa* (1670), the basis of many secondary works in the next thirty years, was an inaccurate transcription of Olfert Dapper's *Beschreibung von Africa,* which was itself an uncritical amalgam of first and second hand information. One of ·Dapper's earliest critics was William Bosman, whose *New and Accurate Description of the Coast of Guinea,* translated into English in 1705, was the first significant literary result of the intensified Dutch slave trading activity in the late seventeenth century. At this period the English Royal African Company impinged on the public consciousness by engaging in a pamphlet war with critics of its finances and organization.[5] But it was some years into the eighteenth century before the late seventeenth century slave trade began to extend public knowledge of West African society. In 1704 the first four volumes of the celebrated Churchill *Collection* of voyages and travels, for instance, made their only contribution by including the first translations of several older foreign accounts. But the next four volumes, published in 1732, included the accounts of Thomas Phillips[6] and John Barbot, both of whom had been slave traders in the late seventeenth century.

The way in which Barbot's account—and William Smith's[7] a little later—contained many sections also in Bosman's shows that not every new work was completely original. Nevertheless, by any standards, this period before about 1760 was a fruitful one, yielding the most influential descriptions of Negro society of any in the eighteenth century. Apart from those of Bosman, Barbot, and

Smith, the works which were most often used by geographical popularizers and cited by abolitionists and pro-slavery writers were Francis Moore's description of trade in the Gambia region; William Snelgrave's account of the Gold and Slave Coasts;[8] and two works by John Atkins, a navy surgeon who provided one of the earliest relatively hostile accounts of the slave trade in Africa.[9] Almost as important was Michel Adanson's *Voyage to Senegal,* which was unique in presenting the views of a scientist visiting Africa for reasons unconnected with the slave trade, although in an area very much under its influence.[10] A relatively smaller number of reporters in the second half of the century added significantly to knowledge of Africa. Among the most important were John Matthews, with his account of Sierra Leone,[11] and Archibald Dalzel who, in the 1790s, added detail to the long-established reputation for bloodshed of the inland kingdom of Dahomey.[12]

Although virtually all these writers, as well as numerous less significant ones, shared a common experience in the slave trade, their attitudes, both to slavery and to Negro culture, were not monolithic. Paradoxically some of those most hostile to slavery—such as Atkins, the Reverend John Lindsay,[13] and Alexander Falconbridge,[14] a reformed late eighteenth century slave trader—provided less evidence of the cultural variety of west Africa than others, such as Bosman and Matthews, who combined a lack of moral misgiving and a frank sense of cultural superiority with valuable detailed information. On the other hand, not even slave traders wrote in isolation from the domestic British background of debate over the slave trade. The extent to which reporting could be a response to abolitionist pressure was revealed at its extreme by Archibald Dalzel in a purported royal Negro oration which smoothly articulated all the commonest pro-slavery arguments.[15] Yet while Dalzel wrote at the height of the abolition debate, James Houstoun's *Observations of the Coast of Guinea,* published in 1725, was scarcely less of a pro-slavery tract.[16]

It was indeed of some importance that for a much longer period before the abolition debate of the 1780s and 1790s than is generally recognized polemical works were also exerting an influence on British knowledge of the Negro. The generally accepted starting-point of American anti-slavery protest, the Germantown declaration of 1688, initiated the Quaker strand of American abolitionism, which was to have its major impact on British opinion in the works of Anthony Benezet, Ralph Sandiford, and John Woolman.[17] As David Davis makes clear, doubts about the morality of slavery dated from much earlier in Catholic Europe.[18] If these isolated protests of the early seventeenth century had no discernible influence and certainly no publication within Britain, strong anti-slavery sentiments did appear in Vincent Le Blanc's geographical survey, first published in English in 1660.[19] Aphra Behn's romantic novel attacking the slave trade, *Oroonoko,* was first published in 1688; and the dramatic version by Thomas Southerne, received the first of numerous performances, stretching through the eighteenth century, in 1695.[20] The equally romantic and equally long-lived story of Inkle and Yarico had appeared as early as 1657 and was repeated in the *Spectator* in 1711,[21] two years after an anonymous anti-slavery pamphlet appeared, purporting to be the speech of a free Negro at Guadeloupe.[22] In the next half century the publication of so many slave traders' accounts coincided with an extensive if sporadic output of anti-slavery writing. In addition to Sandiford's work, published in 1730, numerous protests appeared in the monthly journals, such as the *London Magazine,* and especially the *Gentleman's Magazine.*[23] Thereafter occasional books and pamphlets, such as J. Philmore's *Essay on the Man-Trade* (1760), kept the issues alive until Britain's own domestic debate over slavery, in the late 1760s and early 1770s, saw the emergence of the first notable abolitionist, Granville Sharp.[24]

This persistent anti-slavery refrain comprised many very different voices, each proclaiming different attitudes to the Negro. Many of these attitudes will be referred to in subsequent chapters. At this point it is appropriate to point out that they included opinions radically different from the romanticism which characterized the imaginative literature surveyed by Dykes and Sypher. Such romanticism held sway in a number of non-fictional works, of which Benezet's was the most notable, and in which Adanson's detached view of Negro primitivism was liberally quoted. But others, beginning with the speech of the Guadeloupe Negro, produced derogatory views, which were no less of a distortion, mainly through the application of natural rights principles to the question of African government.

From almost as early pro-slavery writing added its own distortions to images of the Negro. In the first half of the eighteenth century such essays were sometimes a response to anti-slavery criticisms, for example, in the minor debate in the *Gentleman's Magazine* in the 1730s. More often they were Christians' rationalizations of the moral dilemmas of slave-owning. Despite the strong religious element in abolitionism, a majority of theologians found no scriptural impediments to slavery. And a long line of them, beginning with the

Barbados-based Morgan Godwyn in 1680,[25] saw slavery as an evangelistic challenge and opportunity. Such men, with their implicit faith in the unity of mankind, often produced explicit defences of the Negro's character. But in the second half of the eighteenth century they were outnumbered in the pro-slavery ranks by writers with vested interests in the slave trade or the New World slave system. Later chapters will reveal crucial differences between the images of Negro Africa produced by these two broad groups of self-interested polemicists. The attitudes of those whose interests lay in the New World were, however, probably more monolithic than those of any other definable group of contributors to public knowledge. This was because they were overwhelmingly West Indian in background.

Echoes of North American pro-slavery attitudes were occasionally heard through travellers' reports and the London publication of such descriptive works as Hugh Jones' *The Present State of Virginia* (1724). But American society was large enough and sufficiently independent for its polemical pressures to be exerted internally. Moreover, by the period of intensive abolition debate America was independent in fact and in any case its slave system was assumed to be moribund. West Indians, by contrast, continued to regard themselves as expatriate Englishmen. They returned in considerable numbers to Britain, either in retirement or to play a role in public life; and their pressures were all exerted on British institutions and opinion. It was of some importance that British knowledge of racial slavery thus emanated from areas where that system was at its most rigid and pervasive.

This West Indian preponderance was not confined to propagandist works about slavery. The British public was presented with far more historical and geographical accounts of the West Indies than of North America. Some of these, particularly in the seventeenth century, said little about slavery. But as early as 1673 the second edition of Richard Ligon's *History of Barbados* offered evidence of the nature of slavery, revealed the prevalence of racial stereotypes and introduced West Indian generalizations about the savagery of Africa, all of which were to prevail till the end of the eighteenth century. These trends reached their furthest extreme in Edward Long's *History of Jamaica* (1774) and found somewhat more moderate expression in Griffith Hughes' mid-century work on Barbados and in Bryan Edwards' history of the whole West Indies (1793).[26] But this heavy weight of descriptive publication was less homogeneous than West Indian polemical works. In the early eighteenth century Hans Sloane provided a gory indictment of plantation cruelty,[27] which abolitionists were still quoting and slave-owners denouncing half a century later. And one of the most widely read, quoted, and plagiarized works of the eighteenth century was the Abbé Raynal's history of the East and West Indies, which presented unfavourable views of the Negro in a strongly anti-slavery context.[28]

The many influences on opinion discussed so far found full expression in a series of inquiries into the slave trade and West Indian slavery conducted by the Privy Council and then by Parliament in the late 1780s and early 1790s, as the question of abolition came to the fore. The published reports of the findings of these inquiries, the partisan pamphlet compilations they spawned, and the background ferment of newspaper comment and correspondence added some new details of information but scarcely any new philosophical influences to British awareness of the Negro. This mass of publication is important because it was presented at a time when the many aspects of the Negro question were a major preoccupation, rather than a minor backwater beside the mainstream of eighteenth century issues. As such it acts as an important standard by which to assess the plausibility of the most extreme racialist theories of the period. But in an assessment of attitudes over a much longer period these investigations were less important than an even more substantial body of publication, which had been distilled from the first-hand reports and propagandist stereotypes of the Negro by a long series of compilers and editors.

It is in such secondary works that one finds the most convincing evidence of prolonged interest in the non-European world. Whereas most of the major reports of Africa and histories of the New World were published only once, publication of so many précis and syntheses covering the same ground—and the frequent re-publication of many of them—indicates a widespread awareness of the Negro among the educated classes. Some works in this broad category were not strictly secondary. Several important first-hand descriptions achieved their only publication in collections of voyages and travels. But in many such anthologies the distinction between reporting and synthesis was blurred. Beginning with the notorious Samuel Purchas's *Pilgrimes* (1625)[29] probably a majority of collections of voyages were dominated by a heavy editorial hand. The process was not always as damaging as in Purchas's case. The collection published in mid-eighteenth century for Thomas Astley was, for instance, one of the most scholarly surveys, even though the accounts it used were summarized rather than reproduced in full, and subjected to a topical arrangement and frequent editorial comment.[30]

Although the Astley *Collection* and some more orthodox anthologies, such as the Churchill *Collection,* were extremely important, they were far outnumbered by avowed works of synthesis. For example, while the eighteenth century was to see many collections,[31] none appeared at all in the period between 1625 and 1704; yet in the last forty years of the seventeenth century there were at least eighteen new works containing significant descriptions of Africa and, frequently, of the slave system in the West Indies. Of these, many were reissued and six achieved at least four editions each.[32] The eighteenth century produced well over fifty new works of synthesis; and again most were reissued, some as many as twenty times.[33] In the eighteenth century, too, there were numerous monthly journals which, in reviews and précis of the geographical writings, added to public awareness of the Negro.

The works of synthesis fell into three broad categories. The first consisted of detailed descriptive surveys, often running to several volumes, in which it was common for Africa to occupy roughly one third of the space devoted to the non-European world. If their size made them heavy reading as simple entertainment, they performed an important role as works of reference. The largest of all, for instance, *The Universal History*[34]—which in its ancient and modern sections combined ran to 65 volumes—was frequently referred to in the later eighteenth century by both abolitionists and pro-slavery writers. From the late seventeenth century such detailed surveys were supplemented by a second category of more succinct reference material. Beginning with Edmund Bohun's *Geographical Dictionary,* which reached six editions between 1688 and 1710, there was a regular output of gazetteers, which contained, in a compact form, often quite detailed information about the Negro under appropriate geographical locations.

Many of the works in these two categories were especially influential in shaping opinion through their inclusion in educational curricula. Rigid classical bias meant that few seventeenth century grammar-schools taught geography.[35] In the eighteenth century, while the classics continued to predominate, geography was increasingly recommended by educationists, most often as an essential ancillary to history.[36] In some schools, notably Rugby, as well as figuring in the syllabus, geographical works were regarded as the most appropriate form of leisure reading, particularly for younger boys.[37] In dissenting and private academies, where the curriculum was less oriented to the classics, geographical studies played an even larger role.[38] At the same time contemporary advertisements, seeking and offering private tuition, showed that geography was a common ingredient of education outside the schools, not least for girls.[39]

Many schools and private tutors must have used the general surveys and gazetteers most frequently recommended by educationists. Of these Laurence Eachard's *Compendium*, for instance, achieved eight editions between 1691 and 1713: Patrick Gordon's *Geography Anatomiz'd* was in its twentieth edition in 1754; and William Guthrie's *Geographical Grammar* had also reached twenty editions by the end of the eighteenth century.[40] But in addition to such works there were also—in a period from late in the seventeenth century to the end of the eighteenth—about fifty instructional manuals, combining hints on practical geography with relatively condensed surveys of the world. Some of these were also reprinted more than once; *Geography for Children*, translated from the French of Pierre Nicolas Langlet du Fresnoy, had reached its twenty-second edition by 1800.

The detailed record of Negro life in the secondary geographical works will form a significant element of subsequent chapters. But certain general characteristics can be pointed out. For most of the seventeenth century these works were as much influenced by older descriptions such as that of Leo Africanus, as by slave trading contacts with West Africa. On the other hand, from mid-century the new British relationship with Negroes found many echoes in descriptions of West Indian slave society. In the absence of any strong moral doubts about slavery these sections faithfully reproduced the supremacist attitudes of the slave-owning class.[41] Yet the resulting tendency to present Negroes as insignificant beasts of burden was expressed in casual stereotypes rather than philosophical systems of inferiority. The major synthesizers in the period before Ogilby's *Africa* appeared in 1670—George Abbot,[42] Samuel Purchas,[43] and Peter Heylyn[44]—were all clerics, whose Christianity inhibited racialism even more surely than it promoted ethnocentrism.

Such conservatism remained characteristic of editors to the end of the eighteenth century. But the proliferation of information and propaganda about the Negro imposed strains on the editorial process which produced a much less homogeneous image. All summarized and plagiarized much the same group of authorities—such as Bosman, Barbot, Atkins, Smith, and Snelgrave on Africa, and Raynal on the West Indies—and they mostly opposed the slave trade. But although there was considerable plagiarism within the *genre*—with Fenning and Collyer's *New System*, for instance, containing many long extracts from the *Universal Modern History*[45]—these editors are much harder to categorize in their attitudes to the Negro than in their attitudes to slavery. The *Universal Modern History*[46] and the *Astley Collection*,[47] for example, both condemned the slave trade and both cited and analysed virtually every British and foreign account of Africa. Yet there was great contrast between the almost hysterical Negrophobia of the first and the balanced, often sympathetic, assessment of African culture in the second. In many cases editorial incompetence was as important as bias. Several works, which included diatribes against the slave trade in their African sections, continued to reflect the pro-slavery prejudices of many West Indian sources in their accounts of the New World.[48] Such works often presented evidence of the dehumanizing effects of slavery by providing a wealth of detail about the character of African society: but this was an involuntary result depending on the perceptiveness of the reader. Such inconsistencies also occurred in shorter surveys, such as educational text books, where the relative terseness of the descriptions gave little impression of the variations and complexities of West African life which, in the larger works, often redeemed the Negro image.

Although the published evidence about the Negro was usually presented in a tone which could only reinforce British feelings of cultural superiority, it was of some importance that the greatest repositories of information were geographical text books which also surveyed much wider areas of the non-European world. It would require many books to analyze fully attitudes to these many different races and cultures. But the succeeding chapters will briefly assess some of the most critical aspects of the Negro image in this wider perspective.

Although the images of Negro culture in Africa and Negro degradation in the New World were conveyed to significant numbers of British people only through publications, the slave trade indirectly brought Negroes to Britain in sufficient numbers for even the illiterate to be aware of their appearance and in sufficient concentrations in London for James Walvin to argue that prejudice was accentuated by group tensions. Closer analysis suggests however, that, while stereotypes of social and cultural inferiority were well established, the extreme antagonisms mentioned by Walvin were generated largely by expatriate West Indians rather than from within British society.

The broad outlines of the Negro presence in Britain in the seventeenth and eighteenth centuries have been sketched by a number of writers, most notably and recently Dr Walvin himself. It seems clear that deportation orders in Elizabeth I's reign did not rid the country of Negroes in the first half of the seventeenth century. By the later decades of the century the importation of Negro domestics from the West Indies was already under way. This was the major source of a probably increasing black population in the eighteenth century. While many remained in domestic service, others absconded or were granted freedom and formed a community in London sufficiently large to attract unfavourable comment some six years before the famous Somerset case in 1772. Dr Walvin has argued convincingly against the traditional belief that this case ended slavery in Britain. No doubt it was for this reason that there were no dramatic effects on black immigration. In the 1780s the favourite estimate of the number of London Negroes—15,000—was some 5,000 lower than it had been in the 1760s, while the only identifiable group of immigrants, the ex-sailors and soldiers who comprised the "Black Poor", numbered only a few hundred.[49]

It seems unlikely that research will ever produce an accurate assessment of the numbers of Negroes in Britain before 1800. The absence of any census statistics for the period or of any consistent policy of recording race in parish registers or other semi-official documents means that one is left with the impressions of contemporary observers. There seems little doubt that Negroes were present in sufficient numbers and sufficiently dispersed for most British people to be aware of their appearance. The *Universal Modern History* felt it unnecessary to describe a Negro because "evey man who has ever stepped beyond the place of his birth, has seen them. . . ."[50] Later in the century, an abolitionist, James Anderson, appealed to "the personal experience of every man in Britain" in arguing against unfavourable stereotypes produced by West Indian slavery.[51] The fragmentary evidence of newspapers and, occasionally, of parish records, supports such comments. Negroes were referred to fleetingly, not only in the obvious centres of London, Bristol and Liverpool, but also in Yorkshire and Northumberland, the Midlands, and such southern counties as Oxfordshire, Essex, Gloucestershire and Kent. Irish links with the slave trade made them well known in Dublin, while there were Scottish parallels to the English litigation over slavery, culminating in the case of James Knight, the Scottish Negro counterpart of Somerset.[52]

Attitudes to this alien presence contain an apparent paradox. While there were numerous hostile comments about threats to employment and the purity of the English race, many individual Negroes received privileged treatment and public acclaim. The paradox is explained by the fact that stereotypes about Negro inferiority were prevalent but that extreme hostility was unrepresentative of any substantial current of opinion.

One of the earliest of a succession of Negroes whose colour earned them special treatment in British society was Francis Williams. Son of a free Negro in Jamaica, Williams attended Cambridge University in the 1720s, was called to the bar and attracted the attention of the London intelligentsia.[53] A few years later Williams' mentor, the Duke of Montagu, extended his patronage to Job Ben Solomon, who had been redeemed from slavery in Maryland on the discovery of his claimed royal status and literacy in Arabic.[54] Later in the century Montagu's family were among the employers and patrons of Ignatius Sancho, whose literary works provided one of the period's most discussed publishing events.[55] At much the same time George Augustus Bridgetower, a black, ten year old violinist, was the subject of numerous press reports, as his recitals were received with ecstatic applause in the genteel salons of Brighton, London, and Bath.[56] Throughout the eighteenth century, too, a succession of Negro "princes" received hospitality in noble houses and public applause on visits to the theatre or concerts.

If such attention would have been impossible in a racially stratified society like the West Indies, it did not mean that Britain was devoid of prejudice. On the contrary, in many cases its patronizing character reflected all too clearly the prevalent connotations of blackness with cultural and social inferiority. The Duke of Montagu's promotion of Williams was said to have been a deliberate test of Negroes' capacity for education.[57] In the same way the enthusiasm for Job's Arabic translations and for Sancho's mediocre literary output reflected surprise at the evidence of Negro literacy.[58] It is probable that Bridgetower, who had studied under Haydn, was a musician of considerable skill.[59] Yet it was clear that the newspapers, which commented on his "extraordinary genius", regarded him as one of the "musical wonders of the Age" mainly because of his colour. They made much of the fact that he was "of the sable race, yet an extremely handsome youth considering his complexion". And they reported that he had been commended by the Prince of Wales—in whose private orchestra at Brighton he eventually found employment—"as an acceptable novelty to the admirers and lovers of music".[60]

It was typical of the period that Bridgetower's father—who was often portrayed weeping copiously in the background, while his son's playing created "general astonishment"—was invariably referred to as "the African prince".[61] The elevation to royal status of individual Negroes was often comparable to the ennoblement of the Negro character in the literature discussed by Wylie Sypher; only by such over-compensation could Englishmen differentiate individual Negroes from the predominant stereotypes.[62] If such status was suspect in many cases, it was wildly improbable when applied to "the surprising Negro, or African Prince", a contortionist whose postures baffled anatomists in the 1750s. The trend had been established—in slightly less ridiculous fashion—in the 1730s when Bullfinch Lambe, an English slave trader, emerged from a long captivity in the kingdom of Dahomey accompanied by a Negro named Tom, who had been his interpreter in Africa. To the officials of the Royal African Company, to whose care he was for a time entrusted, Tom was simply a "black servant".[63] But to London society, which staged plays in his honour, he was Prince Adomo Oroonoko Tomo.[64] His spurious status was challenged soon afterwards by William Snelgrave[65] and, at the end of the century, by Archibald Dalzel, who referred to the frequency of such attempts to impose on the credulity of "poor honest John Bull" with the remark that "we have had such black princes in abundance. . . ."[66]

There were other reasons, apart from fraud and romantic idealization, for according status and respect to certain Negroes. But implicit in their privileged treatment was the certainty that such men were foreign visitors neither wishing nor expected to be integrated into British society. In 1749 a performance of Southerne's *Oroonoko*—the title of which had no doubt inspired the middle part of Tom's name—was graced by the presence of William Ansah Sesarakoo, the "Prince of Annamaboe", who was moved to tears at the portrayal on the stage of a plight similar to his own recent experiences.[67] Ansah's royal credentials were viewed with scepticism in some quarters, to judge from a contemporary biography which went out of its way to counter such critics.[68] Yet, although not a prince, he was the son of John Corrente, one of the most powerful Negro slave traders on the Gold Coast. Recently redeemed from slavery, to which he had been sold by an English captain entrusted with conveying him to England, his treatment was symptomatic of one of the crucial factors influencing British attitudes to the Negro. While the slave trade consigned so many Negroes to a sub-human existence in the West Indies, it was conducted on an equal footing in Africa between European traders and influential Negroes such as Corrente. Ansah was merely one of the most notable of a succession of Negroes who, for political and economic reasons, were singled out for privileged treatment in Britain. At a time

when the French were making strenuous efforts to establish
themselves in Corrente's area, it was important for the English
company to have an influential ally, versed in the English language
and cognizant of English interests. Once the original plan to
educate Ansah in England had gone awry, with his sale into
slavery, it was even more important to placate his father. On his
redemption he was accordingly placed in the care of the Earl of
Halifax, a Commissioner of Trade and Plantations.[69] The
hospitality he received was indicated by press reports of his
frequent appearances in London society and by his own
subsequent expressions of gratitude,[70] contained in letters to
Halifax and the African Company, for whom he became a valuable
employee on his return to the Gold Coast.[71]

Equally practical motives underlay the privileged treatment of
other eighteenth century Negroes. The Society for the Propagation
of the Gospel—which had its own slave plantation in the West
Indies—made its only serious attempt to promote missionary
activity in West Africa by sponsoring the education of three young
Negroes in London in the 1750s.[72] One of these was the celebrated
Philip Quaque, who was ordained and returned to become one of
only two missionaries seen on the Gold Coast in the eighteenth
century. Late in the century the desire to consolidate their infant
colony led the Sierra Leone Company to provide an English
education for the son of King Naimbanna.[73] At much the same
time C. B. Wedstrom, the Swedish advocate of African
colonization, secured the redemption from slavery of the son of
King Peter of Mesurado and placed him in a school at
Mitcham.[74]

King Peter himself had been educated at Liverpool.[75] This was a
not uncommon practice. Late in the eighteenth century there was
said to be an average of fifty black children—and sometimes as
many as seventy—receiving the rudiments of English education in
Liverpool at any given time. Some were mulatto sons of English
traders resident on the African coast. But most were the sons of
Negroes prominent in the slave trade.[76] Dublin and perhaps Bristol
also entertained such youths from time to time.[77] They were no
doubt well treated since their education was part of a conscious
plan of fostering good relations with their parents. But it is
doubtful if their presence had a profound impact on English
attitudes. It may have helped to confirm the Negro's capacity for
civilization but even this is uncertain. The son of Naimbanna was
said to have "a very excellent understanding, a disposition earnest
in the pursuit of knowledge, and great facility in receiving
instruction".[78] This was in contrast to King Peter's son, who

attained only "tolerable efficiency" in reading and writing and—like many of the Liverpool children, according to John Matthews—"seems to retain an unconquerable propensity to return to his former habits of simplicity in his native country".[79] More important than this varying capacity and will for acquiring European manners was the fact that such youths were only temporary visitors. Even more ephemeral were the occasional visits of adult Negro traders and of free sailors, usually from the Gold Coast, who enlisted in English ships depleted by mortality and returned almost immediately to Africa.[80]

The visits of such free and sometimes privileged Negroes probably did little to break down the association between colour and lowly status. This and many other connotations of blackness, which were established even before Negroes appeared in Britain, will be analyzed in later chapters.[81] In the seventeenth and eighteenth centuries there were far more Negroes in servitude in Britain than enjoying the patronage of nobility or of institutions connected with Africa. In 1728, at a time when Francis Williams may well have been at the nearby inns-of-court, the *Daily Journal* carried an advertisement for a runaway servant wearing a collar with "Lady Bromfield's black in Lincoln's Inn Fields" engraved on it.[82] This was no new or isolated phenomenon. From the 1680s occasional newspaper advertisements for runaway Negroes or sales of Negroes offered evidence of more than simply menial status. References to brand-marks and the wearing of metal collars emphasized that, however ambiguous their legal condition, many Negro servants were regarded as chattels in Britain no less than in the New World.[83] That this role was widely familiar is also clear. Most of the evidence of the Negro's presence in many parts of Britain rests on advertisements for slave sales or for runaway Negroes. And even the occasional references to Negro baptisms and marriages almost invariably concerned family servants.

On the other hand, the extremely limited nature of such references makes it almost certain that nowhere except London were Negroes concentrated in sufficient numbers to be either a real or apparent social threat. By concentrating on such landmarks as the Elizabethan deportations and the "alarm expressed in England at the large numbers of Negroes settling in London in the last quarter of the eighteenth century", James Walvin presents a picture of considerable racial antipathy.[84]

Of these examples the one offering the most convincing evidence of prejudice against the Negro group was the first. Never again after the Elizabethan deportations was there an attempt to remove all Negroes from Britain; never again was there hostile action by government. But since these official actions came at a time when Englishmen considered themselves beset by hunger, poverty, and crime it is important to place them in the perspective of prejudice against other alien groups inspired by similar social fears. Throughout the sixteenth century the largest foreign groups entering England were Protestant refugees. Many were clothworkers importing valuable skills but also potential unemployment to a flagging industry. Anti-immigrant riots in London in 1593 and East Anglia in the 1570s reflected the hostility of the unemployed and the anxiety of trading competitors.[85] Laws demanding aliens' registration, segregation, and arbitrary re-settlement showed the same disquiet operating at an official level.[86] Official actions could encourage as well as reflect prejudice. In 1573 the Privy Council reversed its policy and ordered the dispersal of foreign communities in London because "moche infection grewe by reason that many families of the said straungers dwelt pestred up in one place."[87] In the same period Irish beggars were reviled and gipsies officially harassed in every southern county because they were readily labelled exponents of a considerable crime wave.[88]

These trends are of some significance also because in the late eighteenth century many similar preoccupations failed to produce any official action or mob activity against Negroes at a time when Walvin argues that prejudice was reaching new heights. In the period from 1785 to 1789, when unprecedented attention was focused on every aspect of the Negro question, there was widely expressed disquiet at the social problems of the metropolis. The same newspapers which carried numerous letters and paragraphs about the Black Poor and the abolition controversy also gave vast publicity to crime, vagrancy, and the prevalence of begging.[89] Yet, almost without exception, writers failed to use Negroes as scapegoats for these problems. The prejudice referred to by Walvin emanated not from people concerned with current social ills but almost exclusively from pro-slavery propagandists.

The trends are most obvious in the discussions aroused by the Black Poor. In 1785 and 1786, when black beggars were so conspicuous, there were numerous general discussions about vagrancy and begging.[90] Some writers proposed quite drastic solutions; beggars should be immediately apprehended and returned to their parishes, said one;[91] they should be discouraged by having their heads shaved, said another.[92] By contrast the plight of the black beggars—who had no parishes to support them—evoked general sympathy. Such sympathy was not universally bestowed on foreigners. In 1786 a paragraph in the *Public Advertiser* drew attention to a group of beggars who were neither English nor black, "for they speak French very fluently. . . . They ought to be taken notice of, and disposed of in some manner not injurious to the community."[93]

One of the interesting aspects of the phenomenon of the Black Poor was that in the early stages public references were entirely to Lascars rather than Negroes. In March 1785 "an old man just arrived from the country" professed himself "shocked at the number of miserable objects, Lascars, that I see shivering and starving in the streets."[94] After similar references through 1785[95] the humanitarian organization, which was soon to become the Committee for the relief of the Black Poor, introduced itself in January 1786 with a plan for public donations to relieve the distress of "many Asiatic Blacks . . . some of whom have absolutely expired in the streets."[96] In the following two weeks accounts of the public response to this appeal continued to refer exclusively to Lascars.[97] Eventually reports of the formal establishment of the Committee contained the first references to Negroes as well as Indians.[98] And soon the Committee's first active ministrations revealed the apparently surprising fact that out of 250 "Objects of the Charity . . . Thirty-five only are from the East Indies."[99]

This dawning awareness of the true racial proportions of the Black Poor is of importance to an analysis of attitudes. During the period when the Poor were considered to be Lascars there was considerable sympathy for their plight, which was, said one correspondent, "a reproach to us as a civilised country."[100] But some of this sympathy was dissipated by the belief that their difficulties were both surmountable and unnecessary. The captains who brought them over, wrote one man, were "obliged by law to provide for them till their return."[101] A wrangle developed as to whether the East India Company was culpable, with Company spokesmen claiming that they provided lodgings at Stepney and a shilling a day expenses for Lascars who came over in their service.[102]

By contrast the realization that most of the Black Poor were Negroes was accompanied by much less equivocal sympathy. There was general awareness that Negro beggars did not qualify by birth or residence for normal parish relief and that the circumstances which had brought them to London were altogether different from those affecting briefly visiting Lascars. The subscriptions for poor Negroes, wrote one correspondent, were proof of the "humane disposition of the British nation":

yet be it remembered, that many of these poor Blacks now in London, are part of the great numbers to whom, by Royal proclamation in Virginia, protection was promised, and who, contrary to every principle of justice and humanity, were afterwards abandoned . . .[103]

Another writer made the same point by explicitly comparing the condition of the two racial groups:

Among these poor sufferers, it should be remarked, that the *Lascars* and other *East Indian* mendicants demand our pity only; but that the *African* negroes have an actual claim on our justice:—*They,* or the greater part of them, have served Britain, have fought under her colours, and after having quitted the service of their American masters, depending on the promise of protection held out to them by British Governors and Commanders, are now left to perish by famine and cold, in the sight of that people for whom they have hazarded their lives, and even (many of them) spilt their blood.[104]

There is no evidence, as the Sierra Leone project was gradually formulated throughout 1786, that the solution to the problem of the Black Poor was conceived or interpreted as a desire to rid London of a group undesirable because of their race. Well before the colonization project was mooted the Committee reported generous public financial contributions, which can only be interpreted as further evidence of sympathy for a group whose status as military and naval veterans continued to be recognized.[105] At this time the only racial overtones lay in the assumption that Negroes would be more capable of supporting themselves in the African climate.[106] But this attitude is more plausibly explained in terms of the common, if ill-defined, belief—which will be discussed in a later chapter[107]—that Negroes and whites each functioned more efficiently in their native climates.

At the very end of 1786 and in 1787 the first hostile references to the Black Poor appeared. This partly reflected the fact that begging was no longer apparently necessary, with the opportunity of emigration to Sierra Leone and with charity providing regular food and medical care at centres in Mile End, Paddington and the City.[108] In January 1787 the *Public Advertiser* which had shown a sympathetic attitude to the Black Poor throughout the previous year, reported with satisfaction that the Lord Mayor had ordered the detention of all blacks still found begging: they were to be sent home or to the new colony. This, the paper considered, would be good riddance:

The blacks, especially those of the East Indies are naturally indolent; nothing but the utmost necessity will make them work; and the very thought of being subjected to that would soon reconcile them to the plan proposed by Government.[109]

Two other newspaper items in the same month showed how sympathy might have been eroded. The *Public Advertiser* referred to a plan to alleviate the misery of beggars, which made no reference to race or colour. Such plans, it suggested, were humane but misguided: there was no need for anyone to beg: most had the opportunity of shelter but refused, "knowing that they can earn more money by exposing sores, &c to the eyes of credulous men and women."[110] The next day *The World* printed a warning about two blacks who were continually in the Strand simulating illness but running away from those who offered to help them to hospital.[111]

But while such comments probably indicated a real change of attitude since the days, over a year previously, when blacks had been dying in the streets, it was probably of some importance that the fulfilment of the Sierra Leone project coincided with the start of intensive debate over abolition. It is impossible to identify the *Morning Post* correspondent who greeted the emigration of the Black Poor with a plea that no more Negroes should be admitted to Britain. But his argument was strongly reminiscent of the most extreme pro-slavery propaganda at the time of the Somerset case. His references to a French law prohibiting black immigration could well have been taken from the pamphlets published in 1772 by Samuel Estwick and Edward Long. And, alone among all who commented on the Black Poor, he referred to Negroes as "a lower link in the great chain of existence", a racialist theme which had been introduced by Estwick and greatly elaborated by Long.[112] No doubts, however, surround the motivation of James Tobin, who in 1787 made similar references to the French law in a comment on the Black Poor in his *Rejoinder* to James Ramsay's celebrated abolitionist essay.[113]

Other pro-slavery writers were to refer to the French law in the years ahead,[114] while Tobin himself had made the same point in 1785. On that occasion he was the only commentator to link the presence of the Black Poor to the crime wave which was causing general concern. He referred to large numbers of Negroes "who perish in our jails, or expire on our gibbets. . . ." His claim that three Negroes had recently died in Newgate on the same day, that two were under sentence of death, and that a third had been committed for a capital offence, is impossible to validate, since the *Newgate Calendar* did not record race.[115] In the voluminous newspaper reports of trials and sentences at the relevant period, however, only two criminals were identified as Negroes. One of these was transported for a series of apparently insignificant felonies and provoked no comment.[116] The other was a murderer,

John Hogan, whose case achieved sufficient notoriety to
undermine Tobin's general theme. It was a minor irony that
Hogan was employed as a porter,[117] for Tobin's warnings about
crime stressed Negro indigence; those Negroes who were not
servants were "thieves and mendicants". Had anyone, he asked
rhetorically, ever seen "a black porter, or chairman, in
London?"[118] Much more important, however, was the fact that
Hogan's case was widely publicized without provoking any
recorded racial prejudice. All the contemporary London
newspapers reported the case at length. But this unusual attention
was a reflection, not of Hogan's race, but of the singular brutality
of a criminal whose victim, a female servant, had died a lingering
death with a cut throat and multiple fractures and
disfigurements.[119] Not only did the reports fail to make any racial
generalizations but they did not invariably mention the murderer's
colour.[120]

Equally revealing were the boasts of abolitionists. James
Anderson made a point diametrically opposed to Tobin's. If
Negroes were as generally worthless as their West Indian
detractors claimed, their recent plight in London would have
driven them to crime:

> . . . these men, set free at once in such considerable numbers, must
> have become the most grievous nuisance to society. The gallows
> must have groaned under the load of the many blacks who would there
> have expiated their crimes, till the whole of that unhappy race had
> been utterly exterminated. . . . Has this been so? Every man can
> answer in the negative. . . .[121]

No one responded to the challenge of a "Free Negro" in 1788.
"Shew us," he demanded of pro-slavery opinion,

> that of the multitudes of negroes, who have within a few years trans-
> ported themselves to this country, and who are abandoned to them-
> selves, who are corrupted by example, prompted by penury and
> instigated by the memory of their wrongs to the commission of every
> crime: shew us, I say (and the demonstration, if it be possible,
> cannot be difficult) that a greater proportion of these, than of white
> men, have fallen under the animadversion of justice, and have been
> sacrificed to your laws.[122]

The fact that the only significant reference to Negro criminality
came from a West Indian propagandist is typical of the expressions
of prejudice to which Walvin refers. The vast majority of warnings
about unemployment, miscegenation, and less specified threats to
the social order came from similar propagandists. It is implausible
to see in the special pleading of this group any evidence of general
racial prejudice.

Even the crucial question of the size of London's black population is obscured by a polemical haze. Almost the only people to hazard an estimate were representatives of West Indian interests whose runaway servants are presumed to have formed the nucleus of the community. The only significant exception was the first estimate—of 20,000—which appeared in 1764 in an anonymous passage in the *Gentleman's Magazine*. Its theme was that Negroes were impossible to control in the liberal atmosphere of England: because they refused to regard themselves as slaves and insisted on their equality with whites, it was "highly impolitic to introduce them as servants here, where that rigour and severity is impracticable which is absolutely necessary to make them useful".[123] Although this was partly a criticism of West Indian importations, its strong pro-slavery tone makes it not impossible that it was written by a West Indian. Certainly within a few years many West Indians in Britain were prepared to deny themselves the luxury of black servants, when it became apparent that the litigation initiated by Granville Sharp might prevent their retaining such men as slaves.[124] And significantly the figure of 20,000 was quoted again in 1768 by the counsel for a West Indian slave owner in one of the early cases brought by Sharp.[125]

At the time of the Somerset case the estimate had become—and was to remain through the later abolition debate—some 15,000. And from this time those who cited it were all West Indians, such as Long and Estwick in 1772 and Tobin in 1785. Their aim was to stress the size of the existing black population before warning of even greater numbers who could be attracted to Britain if it was known they could thus win their freedom.[126] The arbitrary nature of the figure is shown by the casual way Long accepted it. At first he predicted various social ills from the Negro presence, while "admitting that there are only three thousand of them now in Great Britain. . . ." But in a postscript he revealed that he had since read Estwick's pamphlet and, in willingly accepting the much larger figure, he asked his readers to excuse his original low estimate made through "want of proper information on that head".[127]

Since abolitionists like Anderson also referred to large numbers[128] for very different polemical purposes—there can be little doubt that the black community was of considerable size. But if the figure of 15,000 was even approximately accurate, one can only conclude that this community had integrated with considerable success and that Negroes were not generally identified with social distress. Not only were references to a Negro problem trivial, in the perspective of current concern with social ills in general and alien groups such as the French in particular,[129] but the numbers of the most visibly distressed were a tiny percentage of the purported total black population. The highest figure given by the Committee for the Black Poor in detailed accounts of its activities was 460, of whom about ninety per cent were Negroes.[130]

Implicit in the criticisms by the West Indians was some evidence for a degree of harmony in race relations completely alien to the New World. Long, for instance, condemned the practice of sending the mulatto offspring of wealthy planters to England for education at public schools and refined ladies' academies in Chelsea, "for, however well this yellow brood may be received in England, yet here so great is the distinction kept up between white and mixed complexions, that very seldom are they seen together in a familiar way. . . ." Faced with discrimination in the West Indies the richer mulattoes tended to "withdraw to England".[131] If wealth smoothed the way for acceptance of such people, the most indignant West Indian criticisms attested to acceptance at lower levels of the social scale. Long referred to the way in which runaway Negroes associated with white servants and "the abandoned prostitutes of the town" before going on to condemn the prevalence of miscegenation: "The lower class of women in England, are remarkably fond of the blacks, for reasons too brutal to mention. . . ."[132]

Not everyone in Britain was happy about miscegenation. Their opposition ranged from Granville Sharp's concern that growing numbers of mulattoes would inherit the slave status of their parents to more overtly racist sentiments. Nevertheless all the most virulent statements came from West Indians. James Tobin and Thomas Atwood echoed Long in condemning the willingness of the English lower classes to inter-breed with Negroes. And John Scattergood, a merchant, joined other West Indians, such as Long, Samuel Martin, and Philip Thicknesse, in dire predictions about the tainted blood of future generations of Englishmen.[133]

Miscegenation was, of course, rife in the West Indies thanks, not least, to the philandering of the planter class now so outspoken on the British scene. But most British miscegenation concerned black men and white women and the West Indian indignation partly stemmed from this flouting of the most fundamental taboo of New World slave societies. The evidence that British attitudes were more liberal lies not only in the fulminations of the planters. A contemporary geographical work recounted the history of a Negro servant who had been sent to England by John Corrente, following the safe return of his son, William Ansah. The man had served the

Earl of Halifax for a time before residing in London, where he became known as the "Gentleman Black" and "married a white woman of considerable family, and some fortune, who broke her heart . . ." when he died. James Albert, a self-proclaimed Negro prince, told of a long life in humble circumstances in England married to an English-woman, who had proved a "blessed partner". Several people had attempted to prevent the marriage, not out of prejudice, but through solicitude for Albert because his wife was a widow in debt and with a child.[134]

None of this means that Britain was a paradise for blacks. Not even those few individuals—Olaudah Equiano, alias Gustavus Vassa, Ottobah Cugoano, alias John Stewart,[135] and Ignatius Sancho—who also stood out from the anonymous black ranks by writing books, revealed themselves as completely at ease in British society. The sense of alienation could well have been more acute among those who remained unprotected by the patronage of polite society and, in many cases, threatened by the continuation of slavery after 1772.

Nevertheless the crucial fact is that, however important it may have been to a Negro, slavery was an insignificant element in the total British social structure. In contrast to the West Indies, where the institution's fundamental importance was enshrined in elaborate and notorious slave codes, it has taken meticulous research into recondite evidence to reveal its continuing existence in Britain. The presence of Negroes was, after all, an interesting but minor aspect of British social history. It was an incidental by-product of major overseas events and situations and it is in the reporting of every facet of slavery and the slave trade that the more important evidence for British attitudes to the Negro lies.

Reports, on the other hand, have to be interpreted and it is in this area that the historian must be as concerned with Britain as with the outside world. In making judgements about the Negro—about his colour, his culture and even his "place in nature"—writers were influenced by a host of factors. Some of these were so individual and perhaps illogical that they defy analysis. But there were also intellectual traditions and even emotional and psychological reactions which were common to virtually everyone. The following chapter, in particular, is concerned to assess how far those who posed the most extensive and radical hypotheses about Negro racial inferiority were developing or challenging the basic assumptions of their contemporaries.

Part II

Attitudes Before 1780:
Sub-Humanity and Inhumanity

CHAPTER THREE

EDWARD LONG AND THE THEORY OF NEGRO INFERIORITY

Attitudes to racial difference may range anywhere between the extremes of complete acceptance and absolute rejection. On the one hand lies the argument that pigmentation and other physical characteristics are as superficial and meaningless as red hair; on the other hand that they are the mark of permanent inferiority—the black man is not fully human. In the eighteenth century there were public statements in support of both views of the Negro. At the period they were most frequent there were obvious polemical reasons for such opinions. But while it is relatively easy to identify propaganda, it is more difficult to establish the private thoughts lurking behind public proclamations. Could people be so indifferent to blackness that they believed without a moment's hesitation their assertions of equality? Could racists be so indifferent to the visible signs of the Negro's humanity that they could seriously place him among the higher apes?

Fortunately it is possible tentatively to separate belief from propaganda because the era of intensive debate began, after decades of desultory discussion, with relative abruptness. In the history of attitudes to the Negro—as distinct from attitudes to the slave trade—the early 1770s make a more useful dividing line than the 1780s. In this period for the first time men began to argue to the derogatory extreme about the Negro's place in nature. Among these Edward Long was the most important. His intellectual racism was elaborated at greater length than others' and incorporated in a monumental *History of Jamaica,* which enjoyed considerable contemporary respect. As a former planter and judge in Jamaica—and as a recent anti-Negro pamphleteer in Britain—Long's ulterior motives seem obvious. And yet there is just enough about the man and his work to raise doubts as to

whether his racism meant something more. He was in many ways
critical of the Jamaican plantocracy and he had no sympathy for
the barbarous cruelties of slavery. It may well be that, in much the
same way as his contemporary Thomas Jefferson,[1] he was a
humane man rationalizing his acquiescence in an inhumane
system. His extreme revulsion against interracial sex was
justifiable on his own terms of belief that the Negro was
sub-human. But it might well reflect deeper psychological
influences. The answer to such questions would be vital to a
biographer of Long. But in a study of the racial attitudes of a
whole period their mere formulation can serve to show that Long
was not simply a conventional plantocratic spokesman. The more
urgent question is whether his racism was in any way a
consummation of the thoughts and feelings of his British
contemporaries. Were attitudes of racial prejudice common before
Long wrote and before the intensified debate over the slave trade
and slavery gave new reasons for denial of the Negro's full human
status?

        *   *   *   *

The term 'race' was rarely used in the era of the slave trade. But
this does not mean that Europeans were indifferent to the obvious
marks of racial difference. Black skins, fleece-like hair, and even
the shape of the lips and noses evoked constant comment. The
Negro looked in so many ways as different from the white man as a
man could be that his appearance was inevitably the focus of
ethnocentrism. As the *Universal Modern History* put it, "it is
seldom that a people does not fix the standard of beauty among
themselves . . . ."[2] Such recognition of subjectivity, although by no
means unusual, did nothing to restrain its operation. A perennial
cliché was that Negroes deemed blackness and flat features
beautiful and painted the devil white.[3] Yet while some drew from
this observation the conclusion that there were no universal
standards of beauty, others portrayed Negro preferences as
perverse or amusing. Oliver Goldsmith referred to the Negroes'
"very extraordinary taste for beauty" before declaring:

> Of all the colours by which mankind is diversified, it is easy to perceive,
> that ours is not only the most beautiful to the eye, but the most
> advantageous. The fair complexion seems, if I may so express it; as a
> transparent covering to the soul . . .[5]

If Goldsmith's rationalization was unusual, his certainty that white
was aesthetically pre-eminent was shared by many. And the

corollary that Negroes were the ugliest of men was revealed in numerous discussions of other non-European peoples. In North America the juxtaposition of two non-European races produced many comparisons typified by Hugh Jones' assertion that the Indians "seem to be a different Breed from the *Negroes*, who are blacker, have uglier Faces and Bodies . . ."[6] Contemplation of the two racial groups in Madagascar and of Melanesian and Polynesian in the Pacific produced similar comparisons unfavourable to the blacker.[7]

As Hugh Jones' comment suggests, it was not only colour which set the Negro apart. William Macintosh enthused over the beauty of European women in the Isle of Bourbon "because it is a very singular circumstance, to find elegance of shape, delicacy of features, and bloom of complexion, in the torrid zone".[8] Several reports in which colour was seen to be the only impediment to beauty concerned the Negroes of Senegambia.[9] And several writers followed Michel Adanson in discarding all qualifications and describing these Negroes as beautiful.[10] Yet these admiring references only served to emphasize that Negroes in general were deemed ugly because their features were so far from European norms; the admired Wolof features, wrote the Comte de Buffon, "are not so disagreeable as those of other Negroes".[11] And while many reports publicized variations within the Negro ranks, others made it clear that "Negro" was much more than a general term for the dark-skinned inhabitants of Africa. Throughout the eighteenth century geographical writers echoed the sentiments of Job Ludolphus, who reported that, while Ethiopians were black, they were less ugly than Negroes with their "Blubber lipp'd and Flat Nos'd deformity".[12]

This ethnocentrism was largely an emotional process. Where it was reinforced by specific ideas, these tended to be fashionable and aesthetic criteria themselves entirely Europocentric in origin. Throughout the seventeenth and eighteenth centuries there was, for instance, a persistent cosmetic and artistic emphasis on the virtues of fair complexions and "classical" European features. In Elizabethan times foreign observers noted a determined copying of the sovereign's pale skin and fair hair among contemporaries.[13] Sir John Hayward recorded Elizabeth's physical appearance and moral qualities in a way which left no doubt about the gulf separating the Negro from this living criterion of excellence:

> Shee was a Lady, upon whom nature had bestowed, and well placed many of her fayrest favours . . . her haire was inclined to pale yellow, her forehead large and faire . . . But without good qualityes of mynde,

the gifts of nature are like paynted flowers . . . Now her vertues were such as might make an Aethiopian beautifull.[14]

In the eighteenth century—to judge from cosmetic advertisements in the newspapers[15]—the Negro appearance was just as remote from the fashionable criteria of beauty.

Negroes were indeed so very black that many modern writers would regard ethnocentrism as an inadequate label for more deeply rooted antipathies. The problem of colour prejudice has prompted psychiatrists to ponder history and historians cautiously to deploy the language of the psychiatrist. References have been made to the symbolic values of darkness and light, of dirt and defecation, and of childhood fears of the night. These basic reactions have been used to explain the identification of black with evil which has permeated many societies and in the process introduced cultural as well as psychological factors into the perception of racial difference. Black's identification with evil was deeply ingrained in Christian teaching for centuries. The same symbolism had a long association with English drama and pageantry, while the personification of the devil as the "Prince of Darkness" was common to every medium of literature.[16]

It is plausible to suppose, as many have argued, that this symbolism was important in the first encounters between Englishmen and Negroes. It may well have continued to be a factor in the era of the slave trade but, inevitably, it is one hard to document and must be put forward tentatively in the face of more obvious evidence for prejudice. By the eighteenth century—and probably long before—the Negro's appearance had acquired its own symbolic connotations. The relative degree to which this appearance symbolized slavery and cultural inferiority is a large part of the substance of this book. But, without anticipating the argument of subsequent chapters, it is clear that both these associations reinforced European ethnocentrism to such a degree that proclaimed indifference to colour required a conscious rejection of stereotypes.

In the late seventeenth century Thomas Phillips argued that the slaves he bought in Africa were "as much the work of God's hands, and no doubt as dear to him as ourselves; nor can I imagine why they should be despis'd for their colour, being what they cannot help . . . "[17] In 1763 a commentator, seeing colour prejudice as a threat to the success of Britain's Senegambian venture, asked "what is more unmanly, effeminate, or irrational than for a man to value himself on the colour of his skin?"[18] The trouble was that colour prejudice was indeed irrational and yet so entrenched that it was displayed involuntarily even by those who sought rationally to dismiss it. Sir Thomas Browne in the mid-seventeenth century attacked the theory that Negro colour was the result of the curse on Ham. He argued that there was no reason why blackness should be considered a curse and that there were no objective criteria of beauty. And yet, in the theological part of his rebuttal, he suggested that to accept the curse on Ham would "introduce a generation of *Negroes* as high as *Italy*; which part was never culpable of deformity, but hath produced the most magnified examples of beauty".[19]

In the eighteenth century the friends of the Negro confronted causal explanations which included polygenetic theories more derogatory than the Biblical curse on Ham. An army physician named John Hunter (not to be confused with the eminent surgeon of the same name) asserted the unity of mankind in terms of the scientific orthodoxy of fertile species: all races could interbreed, even at the greatest extremes, "let the one be a most beautiful Circassian woman and the other an African born in Guinea, as black and ugly as possible".[20]

*   *   *   *

If the friends of the Negro almost involuntarily cited him as the most extreme of human peculiarity, there were clearly going to be enemies who would push him completely out of the human family. When Edward Long did just this, he used the concept of gradation: the races of man were ranged in a fixed hierarchy—the "Chain of Being"—between God and the lower animals. This was such a familiar concept that some historians have been persuaded that Long's intellectual racism was virtually inevitable. As Winthrop Jordan has written, "an idea such as the Chain of Being can exert enormous leverage on social relationships and the way in which they are perceived." He suggests that the growing eighteenth century preoccupation with classification of the natural world combined with the concept of gradation to intensify Europeans' involuntary prejudices. The new methodology argued a division of humanity into categories based on physical appearance. And the availability of the Chain of Being led to the arrangement of these categories in a hierarchy in which Negroes inevitably occupied the lowest place, as the race physically most different from whites, who just as inevitably occupied the highest place.[21]

In practice, however important this process may have been in influencing the way men thought, it had little effect on the way they wrote. Hierarchical systems were far from dominant in classifications of racial difference. Many followed the pre-eminent classifier, Linnaeus, in adopting merely descriptive divisions. Richard Bradley, like Linnaeus primarily a botanist, described five human groups, based largely on colour, and explicitly argued against any hierarchical arrangement. With the exception of one reference to Negroes' fleece-like hair, Bradley's descriptions were notably free from value judgements.[22] In this he was certainly exceptional. But other classifiers tended rather to reveal underlying assumptions than to create intellectual systems of colour prejudice. The belated first English translation of Linnaeus' *Systema Natura*, for instance, incorporated Gmelin's proposed modification of the Swede's racial categories. This was at once both devoid of hierarchical arrangement and replete with prejudice, as it described Negroes' black complexions, frizzled hair, and flat features alongside white attributes "formed by the rules of symmetrical elegance and beauty . . ." In the same way Charles Bonnet, cited by Jordan as a leading exponent of gradation, denied that striking visible differences denoted any fundamental racial inequality. But he could not hide his aesthetic preferences, as he described the "flat faced African, with his black complexion and woolly hair" and the European "whose regular features are set off by the whiteness of his complexion".[23]

With the Negro so widely treated as if he were indeed a sub-human creature it was in many ways not a large step from aesthetic distaste to arguments of fundamental inferiority. But the way in which such arguments emerged with relative abruptness in the early 1770s suggests that there were nevertheless factors which restrained many Europeans from taking that step. These operated on many levels—ranging from the certainty of the sexual philanderer that he was not copulating with an animal to scruples based on religious dogma or intellectual training. Since Edward Long's theories were argued intellectually it is necessary first to consider the often expressed contention that they displayed sufficient intellectual respectability to make them more than crude propaganda. David Davis agrees that Long's "gross racial prejudice" was extreme but argues that he was expressing opinions "which were not only public ideology in Jamaica and South Carolina, but were apparently acceptable to an influential minority in Europe." Moreover, in assuming the "mantle of scientific philosopher" he was "not totally unrepresentative of his time." James Walvin, too, has referred to Long's scholarly credentials in favourable terms.[24]

These opinions would have pleased Long greatly because he took tremendous pains to conceal his opportunistic plagiarism in a cloak of respectable scholarship. As the ninth chapter of this book will show, his skill is to be measured in the way he in turn inspired plagiarism, emulation, and, in at least one instance, significant elaboration. But to say that Long, writing in and specifically for an atmosphere of controversy, pushed the argument about the Negro into new dimensions is quite different from arguing that his work was a consummation of the racial thought of preceding epochs.

Although, as Arthur Lovejoy has shown,[25] the Chain of Being was a key eighteenth century concept, its application to race was extremely rare until there were strong polemical reasons for declaring the Negro less than human. As far as can be ascertained, there were only three fleeting and speculative references of this kind before the 1770s. One of these was in an anonymous article in the London Magazine in 1750; one in a minor geographical work of 1766; and one in a tract of 1768 explaining the lack of baptisms among West Indian Negroes.[26] The extent to which these references had been inspired by similar unrecorded speculation is impossible to determine. But in the perspective of a vast amount of writing about Negroes, on the one hand, and about the Chain of Being, on the other, these three short passages in minor works do little to suggest that theories of racial gradation were a natural development of eighteenth century intellectual trends.

Analysis of Long's work reinforces this impression. He borrowed his central theme from a writer whose adoption of the concept of racial gradation can be traced with some precision to the debate over slavery in Britain in 1772. This was Samuel Estwick, assistant agent in London for Barbados. Estwick's Considerations on the Negro Cause, on its first appearance in 1772, argued simply that Negro slaves brought to England remained private property. But in a second edition, published in the same year, he supported the implicit corollary of this claim with a philosophical argument that Negroes were indeed not human beings in the same sense as Englishmen. It was well known that among animals there were many kinds, "each kind having its proper species subordinate thereto . . ." It seemed odd that man alone was universally the same:

> Does this not seem to break in upon and unlink that great chain of Heaven, which in due gradation joins and unites the whole with its parts? May it not be more perfective of the system to say, that human nature is a class, comprehending an order of beings, of which man is the genus, divided into distinct and separate species of men?

After surveying Negro barbarity, he concluded that the present state probably represented the summit of their potential, "as compleat, as that of any other race of mortals; filling up that space in life beyond the bounds of which they are not capable of passing, differing from other men, not in *kind,* but in *species* . . . ."[27]

Long began his section on Negroes with an unacknowledged extract from the *Universal Modern History,*[28] the most unfavourable, detailed contemporary account of Africa, before reproducing verbatim, and again without acknowledgement, Estwick's hypothesis about the Negro's place on the Chain of Being.[29] This basic argument he amplified with much more extensive references to Negro physical and cultural characteristics, and with arguments from natural history, anatomy, and philosophy. Despite his plagiarism, Long displayed a certain intellectual consistency and ingenuity. If a completely harmonic Chain of Being was a reality then there was a superficial consistency in arguing a minute gradation from animals to man and even within the ranks of mankind. At the same time, by arguing gradation even among the peoples of Africa, Long could disarm the potential criticism that not all Negroes were in an equal state of barbarity. Different groups might attain different cultural levels but even the highest point on the African scale was permanently below that of the lowest European.[30]

But this consistency does not mean that the application of gradation to racial difference was in any way intellectually inevitable. In the first place natural philosophers found the essential harmony of the chain impossible to apply in practice. The pre-eminent naturalist, Linnaeus, made no attempt to show a hierarchy in nature and simply arranged animals and plants in broad groups of similarity. Even this was not a decisive solution. Linnaeus was constantly re-arranging his animal classifications in successive editions of his great work. Thanks partly to the Swede's influence, and partly to independent discovery of the same practical difficulties, a large number of eighteenth century naturalists paid at most only lip service to the Chain of Being.[31]

Even among those who accepted the concept, the notion that the Chain was a completely harmonious hierarchy of minutely separated stages was far from predominant. Those who most intimately explored man's physical nature concluded by reaffirming the importance of intangible mental and spiritual qualities setting him far above the brute creation. In this field of comparative anatomy the decisive contribution came from Edward Tyson, who in 1699 published the results of his dissection of a chimpanzee. The fact that Tyson referred to his chimpanzee as an "Orang-Outang" in the title and a "Pygmie" in the text is indicative of a potentially ominous confusion among natural philosophers. And his opening statement contained a classic

outline of the Chain of Being, which also foreshadowed the
arguments of Long. But Tyson went on to dispel doubts and
disarm racialism. Despite its name, his pygmy was not a man.
Dissection revealed many similarities as well as some important
differences. But physical similarities merely emphasized the
intellectual and spiritual gulf between man and chimpanzee: the
"*Nobler Faculties* in the *Mind* of Man, must certainly have a
higher Principle; and Matter organiz'd could never produce
them . . . ."[32]

Tyson referred to the similar conclusions reached a year or so
earlier by anatomists in Paris.[33] These parallel French arguments
received some publicity in eighteenth century English works. But
it was Tyson's own thesis which was most influential over the next
eighty years. It was summarized in the periodical press; in works
by popularizers of natural history, such as Thomas Boreman and
Oliver Goldsmith; and by such respected naturalists as John Ray,
Richard Brookes, and George Edwards. In the late 1730s
Edwards had studied another chimpanzee imported into London.
His only qualification of Tyson's work was to point out that the
"Pygmie" was, like his own ape, in fact a chimpanzee.[34]

Edwards' conclusions were also mentioned in later works.[35] But
perhaps the major factor in giving Tyson's views general currency
was their acceptance by the influential French naturalist, the
Comte de Buffon. He praised the excellence of Tyson's dissection;
echoed his contention that the human soul was "totally distinct
from matter"; and outlined a Chain of Being whose minute
gradations stopped abruptly and at a distance from mankind;

> if man were of the same rank with the animals, there would be in nature
> a certain number of beings less perfect than man, and superior to any
> animal we are acquainted with; and those intermediate beings would
> descend imperceptibly from man to the monkey tribes. But no such
> beings exist. The passage is sudden from a thinking being to a material
> one, from intellectual faculties to mechanical powers, from order and
> design to blind impulse, from reflection and choice to ungovernable
> appetite.[36]

More abstract philosophers—not faced with problems of
classification—found it easier to refer to the absolutely harmonic
Chain of Being utilized by Long. And it was not uncommon to find
references in works published before Long's to barely perceptible
gradations from one species to another. According to John
Gregory, "Nature is a whole, made up of parts, which tho' distinct,
are intimately connected with one another. This connexion is so
close, that one Species often runs into another so imperceptibly,
that it is difficult to say where the one begins and the other

ends.''[37] But if Long's racialism was a logical development of such comments, it was also a perversion of the theories that embodied them. For remarks like Gregory's were invariably the prelude to arguments ultimately not very different from Tyson's and Buffon's.

The crucial difference between man and brute, it was argued, was between reason and instinct. Among many differing opinions about the degree of reason possessed by animals, was the consensus that Man had incomparably more.[38] Savagery was an animal-like existence because instinct appeared to dominate reason. But there was no tradition of permanent savagery in the years before Long wrote. While achievements in arts and sciences were universally recognised as the peculiar prerogative of humanity, most writers referred to fairly modest indications of aptitude in accepting the full human potential of savages. Many emphasized language as the most basic manifestation of reason. Charles Bonnet, for instance, provided a provocative outline of the Chain of Being, in which the ape was a "rough draught of man." But he concluded that "Man is endued with reason: he has ideas; he compares these ideas together; judges of their relations or oppositions; and acts in consequence of this judgment. He alone, of all animals, enjoys the gift of *speech* . . . .''[39]

For Bonnet and many others another crucial sign of reason was a religious sense: "The last mark of the greatness of man, and of his high exaltation above other animals, is the commerce he has with his CREATOR by religion." Some preferred to call this decisive human capacity a "moral sense". For John Gregory, imaginative faculties, science, art, and curiosity were all "peculiar to the Human Species. But above all the Moral Sense, with the happiness inspired by religion and the various intercourses of social life, is their distinguishing characteristic.''[40]

As long as savages had language and at least some traces of moral and religious sense, they were accepted into the ranks of mankind, not grudgingly, but with a recognition of their full potential for civilization. Some of the most sinister juxtapositions of man and brute in philosophical discussions of the Chain of Being were qualified by such references to the savage capacity for improvement. There was an "original difference in the Constitution of both Men and Nations", conceded Gregory, going somewhat further than most of his contemporaries,

> but this is not so great as at first view it seems to be. Human Nature consists of the same Principles everywhere.—In some people one Principle is naturally stronger than it is in others, but exercise and proper culture will do much to supply the deficiency.[41]

To some extent reiteration of the concept of a Chain of Being must have prepared the way for Long. It meant that comparisons between savage man and anthropoid animal were in no sense a shocking novelty. But there is even less doubt that the qualifications which invariably accompanied such discussions provided an obstacle to Long's theories which he could not easily surmount. His contention that Negroes were a separate and inferior branch of humanity may have been impelled by ulterior motives or even personal conviction. But it assumed its characteristic form because immutable savagery was so inconsistent with his chosen philosophical system. Estwick had shown a similar awareness of this system by arguing that the clinching proof of Negro inferiority was a lack of moral sense. Long attempted to sustain the case by denying any Negro cultural or political achievements which might depend on the exercise of reason.[42]

The extent to which Long's claims about Negro culture and Estwick's about morality were ridiculous or credible by eighteenth century standards can only be fully ascertained by analysis of the large weight of evidence about Negro life available to the British reading public. This assessment is embodied in later chapters.

But irrespective of the balance of opinion about African cultural and political potential, Long's attempt to apply the concept of gradation to racial difference was inherently implausible in its contemporary context. It demanded the assertion of easily refutable claims about the Negro's physical nature; it clashed with some of the dominant orthodoxies of social theory; and it put almost intolerable strains on the concept of gradation itself.

To all proponents of the Chain of Being its essential character was permanence. It was a static hierarchy, not an evolutionary process. The commonest way in which this was expressed was in the permanence and separation of species. In the animal sphere the long accepted criterion of species was the ability to produce fertile offspring; the mule's inability to reproduce was proof that the horse and ass were of different species.[43] To those who argued that nature was a harmonious hierarchy of minutely separated links this definition was particularly important. If different species could intermingle and reproduce at will, harmony would disintegrate. The belief that every part of nature was thus unalterably fixed for all time was, of course, what made the Chain of Being so attractive to Long: Negroes could go no further than fixed limits. Nevertheless his application of the concept to race left him in a position of precarious intellectual isolation.

It meant, in the first place, that he was forced to proclaim the infertility of mulattoes.[44] Philip Curtin argues that, while this was scarcely credible to those with first-hand knowledge of race mixtures in the West Indies, "most of his readers had no access to the evidence, and his specific argument was subtle enough to pass with people who might otherwise have known better."[45] This judgment seems to underestimate the Negro presence in Britain and to ignore the positive assertions by those who had observed miscegenation in many countries.[46] Indeed the alleged "subtlety" of Long's theory was probably a response to such reports. He agreed that mulattoes might reproduce by breeding with either Negroes or whites but insisted that two mulattoes could not breed together successfully; if they did have children, these would not survive to maturity. But this was a qualification of infertility which no reputable scientist applied to other hybrids. Much more typical of the period than Long's extremism was Buffon's amalgam of dogma and empiricism: so different in appearance were Negroes, Lapps and whites, that one would suspect that they were different species, "if, on the one hand, we were not certain, that one man only was originally created, and, on the other that the White, the Laplander, and the Negro, are capable of uniting, and of propagating the great and undivided family of the human kind."[47]

More generally, Long's theory implied equally implausible conclusions about other animal species. The implicit corollary of the application of gradation to race was a vast multiplication in the number of species below man. If, as Long argued, the races of men were different species, rather than varieties within species, then the same must be true of other animal groups. Long himself virtually ignored this problem, although he did refer to the dog "kind", which was his expression for a grouping of physically close but distinct species. But unlike his most notable successor, Charles White, he did not consider how the intermixture of canine breeds could be accommodated to the notion of mutually infertile species.[48]

By refusing to equate races with species other advocates of the Chain of Being could explain differences among dogs or other animals in terms of variations caused by climate and environment.[49] Thus Long, in insisting that races were species, was isolating himself from one of the dominant social theories of his time. Scarcely less important was his isolation from theology. A wide range of literature reveals a reluctance to jettison scripture in the face of awkward discoveries in science and geography. While voluminous treatises grappled with the chronological problems created by fossils or by the claims to antiquity of Asian civilizations,[50] nothing showed more clearly the tenacity of theological orthodoxy than the attempts by polygenists to accommodate their theories to the Old Testament.

Isaac de la Préyère in the mid-seventeenth century and the anonymous *Co-Adamitae* of 1732 attempted to prove polygenesis from the internal evidence of the scriptures. The same was true of the anonymous essayist in the *London Magazine* who had foreshadowed Long's arguments in 1750. The idea of gradation among the races of men would be attractive, he said, "if it were permitted by our religion." Philip Curtin has referred to the shock to orthodox Christians occasioned by the "fully fledged polygenist theory" of Lord Kames. Yet Kames, too, was an intellectual contortionist who attempted to base his radical theory on Old Testament authority. He was persuaded that there was "an original difference" between Negroes, Hindus and Europeans. It seemed that there were different races of men, like plants, fitted for different climates:

> But this opinion, however plausible, we are not permitted to adopt; being taught a different lesson by revelation, viz. that God created but a single pair of the human species. Tho' we cannot doubt of the authority of Moses, yet his account of the creation of man is not a little puzzling . . .

The answer to the puzzle, he decided, was that different racial characteristics had been bestowed, not through polygenesis, but by a later divine intervention at the time of the Tower of Babel.[51]

Long's reliance on the Chain of Being isolated him not only from the most orthodox but also from the most radical theories. One of these was a minority scepticism about the permanence of species. Winthrop Jordan has shown how John Locke suggested that species might not exist, except as arbitrary categories in men's minds. And he has also shown that Linnaeus toyed with the idea of hybridization of species in a manner fraught with derogatory implications for the Negro. Accepting the existence of hybrid plants, and noting reports of hybridization in the animal worlds, Linnaeus recoiled in dismay, as he realized that the "most frightful conclusions could in fact be drawn from this; as far as mankind is concerned one would have reason to think that the Moors (i.e. Negroes) had a rather strange origin—something that I for my part, however, am unwilling to ascribe to them."[52]

Long of course was only too willing to ascribe strange attributes to Negroes. Moreover he had made much out of the supposed copulation between Negroes and apes reported by many travellers.[53] But because he insisted so rigidly on the separation of species, he was not able to carry Linnaeus' suppositions to their logical conclusions. Copulation with apes confirmed Negro lechery; it emphasized the narrowness of the dividing line between species; but such liaisons could not be fruitful; the Negro, though lower than Europeans, was not an ape.

By the same criteria Long could not adopt the arguments of Lord Monboddo who, far from shrinking from the possibility of ape-human procreation, accepted it as the clinching proof of his theories. Long borrowed many illustrations of the anthropoid appearance and habits of "orangs" from Monboddo.[54] But he had to insist on an impassable division between "orangs" and even the lowest of men, whereas Monboddo's whole case was that certain apes were men in a primitive stage of development.

Monboddo had one significant precursor. Jean-Jacques Rousseau argued that some of the higher apes might in fact be savage men. Combining current anatomical beliefs with travellers' reports of rudimentary social behaviour in certain species, he contended that speech was a socially acquired attribute. Monkeys were not human, partly because they could not speak, but more fundamentally because they did not have the "faculty of Improving" which distinguished man from brute. But "it does not appear that the same Experiments have been made with the *Pongos* and *Orang-Outang* carefully enough to afford the same Conclusion."[55]

This was basically Monboddo's case. But his illustrations were more far-fetched than Rousseau's and supported only by isolated writers no less gullible than himself. For instance, he laid some stress on a report by a seventeenth century Swedish traveller, Keoping, of tailed men in the East Indies.[56] The only other eighteenth century writer who accepted Keoping's report at face value was the Frenchman, Benoît de Maillet. His *Telliamed* has received some attention from historians of evolutionary thought because of his theory of the marine origins of animal life. De Maillet did not suggest a protracted evolution of organisms but argued the abrupt emergence from the ocean of familiar terrestrial species. As such his theory was as absurd by eighteenth century standards as by those of evolutionists. Its application to the human species demanded the reassertion of archaic beliefs about mermaids and sea-monsters and uncritical acceptance of contemporary reports of beast-like men. It not only reproduced Keoping's report but also referred glibly to the "little man" dissected by Tyson. The preface of *Telliamed* showed that even its author saw this theory as no more than a "Conjecture formed by a warm Imagination", a conclusion which English reviewers shared wholeheartedly.[57]

To point out the intellectual shortcomings of those who placed the Negro outside the human family is more than a form of historical literary criticism. It helps to explain the paucity of similar theories and to estimate the reactions of an intelligent readership. On the other hand, racial attitudes operate on many other levels than the rigorously intellectual. However insistent scientists and theologians might be about the distinction between ape and man, in the popular mind the similarities—whether observed in a zoo or accentuated in travel literature—could well seem uncomfortably numerous. Edward Long illustrated his pseudo-intellectual arguments with travellers' tales from Africa, while among modern scholars Winthrop Jordan has placed considerable emphasis on the same kind of anecdotes to argue the persistence of popular beliefs in Negro affinity with apes. Jordan makes much of Africa's reputation, established since Classical times, as the home of monsters and of men apparently part-brute. Almost as old, and persisting into the eighteenth century, were the reports of ape-Negro sexual intercourse, which both Monboddo and Long used to the full. Jordan does not argue that any significant number of people believed that Negroes were apes or even that ape-Negro copulation might produce fertile offspring. His theme is that the constant reiteration of the ambiguous Classical ethnology and, in particular, of the reports of copulation, formed a vigorous tradition of Negro-ape affinity which no theoretical system could obliterate: on the contrary, it was a tradition which the Chain of Being concept nourished rather than undermined.[58]

In many ways Jordan's argument is convincing. There can be no serious challenge to his appraisal of Classical ethnology nor to his contentions about the frequency of reports of copulation. And it is not implausible that the prevalence of the idea of gradation helped to focus attention on the relationships between the most savage of men and the most anthropoid of animals. On the other hand, there are ways in which the scholarly Jordan is as selective in his use of African sources as Long himself.

Until late in the seventeenth century the causal explanation of African monsters mentioned by Jordan—the production of hybrids through the mingling of species at Africa's rare water-holes—recurred in most geographical surveys available to English readers.[59] But in this same period human monsters were already unacceptable to a theologically-based ethnology.[60] And by the eighteenth century monsters of any kind were rejected as the notion of fixed and separate species permeated into popular works of natural history and geography. Geographical editors could no more accept the water-hole explanation for the strange appearance of the giraffe than they could admit that Negro-ape sexual intercourse could ever produce fertile offspring.[61]

The eighteenth century also—thanks largely to Tyson—firmly rejected an apparent Classical confusion about the distinction between apes and mankind. Jordan argues that Tyson's work "did nothing to weaken the vigorous tradition which linked the Negro with the ape". But he refers only to the dissection of the chimpanzee and its accompanying conclusions about "the close relationship and the non-identity of ape and man."[62] Tyson's more influential contribution to this question was his "Philological Essay concerning the Pygmies, the Cynocephali, the Satyrs and Sphinges of the Ancients", appended to his account of the chimpanzee. After this closely argued demonstration that all the most ambiguous and brutish groups in Classical ethnology had been in reality apes, no eighteenth century editor was prepared to exhibit the credulity of Samuel Purchas in the early seventeenth century. Purchas had accepted Diodorus Siculus' description of an African "people", who "feede on the tops of twigges and leap[ing] on the trees and from bough to bough with incredible agilitie."[63] After Tyson scepticism even overreached itself, to the extent that for the whole eighteenth century the African pigmies were unanimously dismissed as either an ancient fabrication or a confusion of man and ape.

Rejection of Africa's fabulous ethnology did nothing to silence the reports of sexual intercourse, which Jordan regards as a more important factor in the popular association of Negro and ape. But again his view is insufficiently analytical of the literature in which such reports found currency. In the first place, he sees the strength of the tradition, in part, in terms of a centuries-old image of Negro sexual depravity which ante-dated any significant English contact with Africa. But he does not adequately consider the ways in which two centuries of such contact might have modified the original image by mid-eighteenth century.[64] Jordan mentions only the way in which the old image was confirmed by the promiscuity of interracial settlements in West Africa. He does not consider the extent to which these greater contacts also purveyed to eighteenth century readers criticisms of the corrupting role of Europeans or more rounded descriptions of African society, in which polygamy, public prostitution and even wife-lending could be seen as a form of social control rather than sexual abandon. Such insight, together with the evident appreciation of the attractions of African women, could serve to restrain rather than accelerate the Negro-ape association.[65]

More generally, it must be emphasized that reports about

Negroes and apes were given little prominence in accounts of Africa. For the reading public to be aware of them it was necessary for them also to read much lengthier descriptions of African society, which emphasized only too clearly the human status and cultural potential of Negroes. And for most of the century the public was offered no short cuts to racialist conclusions by the selectivity or distortions of editors. Those whose opinions were formed by educational works were innocent of the ape-Negro association. School text books protected young minds from both moral and intellectual shock by ignoring the sexual anecdotes and the concept of racial gradation. Negroes were widely depicted in such works as ugly and culturally backward but their savagery was presented in terms no different from that of numerous non-African groups. Adult readers found Negro-ape associations mentioned only rarely in geographical texts and popular surveys of natural history, and then only briefly and without any racialist emphasis.

The most provocative evidence for popular belief in ape-human affinities lies outside the literature discussed by Jordan and on the seedy fringes of eighteenth century "show business". Exhibitions of animals—whether permanent like that at the Tower of London—or temporary collections in public halls and fairgrounds were matched in popularity by freak shows displaying animal-like human beings and man-like animals. The public display of Negroes in such exhibitions was generally of little significance, since they were invariably chosen for characteristics which marked them out from the rest of their race. Albino Negroes exercised the same fascination as gigantic children, limbless men, and bearded women. And there was no particular racial lesson to be drawn from a poster advertising a "Grand Menagerie", which concluded a list of seventeen assorted birds and beasts with the intelligence that "the Spotted Negro attends from 11 till 7 in the evening".[66]

But posters and newspaper advertisements for similar entertainments sometimes seemed to foster a vagueness about the dividing line between man and animals which reflected on the Negro. A decade after Tyson and the French anatomists had argued the differences between man and "orang-outang" an exhibition of animals at a Fleet Street public house included "Two Wood-Monsters" from Africa, which were advertised solely in terms of their similarity to "humane Nature", as well as a "Little Black Man but three foot high, 31 Years of Age. . . ."[67] And through the century, while Tyson's conclusions continued to dominate works on natural history, a succession of apes was presented to the public in terms which blurred the distinction between human and beast. These included "a young Oronuto Savage from Africa", which "walks upright, does Soldiers Exercise, drinks Wine, takes the Money and pays for it, like a rational Being", and a "man-Tyger" from Angola, which "comes the nearest human Nature of any Animal in the World."[68]

Although such exhibitions were a threat to the Negro more than to any other racial group, they must be seen in perspective. Not all the anthropoids were billed as natives of Africa. At the same time, the London public which perhaps flocked to such exhibitions were people who, more than any other English contemporaries, had daily experience of the human attributes of Negroes. From their ranks came those who, according to West Indian extremists like Long, were indecently prone to interbreed with Negroes and those who had been prepared to assist slaves in their bids for freedom prior to 1772. And amid all the doubts which surround the question of what Englishmen actually thought of Negroes in the early 1770s there is one certainty. This is that the two men who suddenly declared the Negro sub-human—Samuel Estwick and Edward Long—were incensed by the human freedom to which West Indian slaves in England were now aspiring.

CHAPTER FOUR

THE BURDEN OF SLAVERY

In one very obvious sense Samuel Estwick and Edward Long were carrying British attitudes to the Negro to a logical conclusion. For two centuries British people, especially in the West Indies, had treated Negroes as if they were indeed animals rather than human beings. The attitude was declared not simply in the brutal drudgery inflicted on the plantation gang but in the legal definition of chattel status. In an age of judicial violence and widespread social cruelty it was this denial of the opportunity for human fulfilment which most clearly marked the racist exploitation of the Negro slave. With no security of family life, no freedom of movement, no choice of occupation, and, above all, no mechanism for earning manumission, the slaves in Britain's New World colonies enjoyed the rights of cattle rather than men.

It may be that this most simple aspect of racial attitudes is also the most important. But it is an aspect which has been frequently described.[1] The questions which are more pertinent to the present study are concerned with the relevance of this racism to opinion within Britain. How well known were the details of slavery before intensive debate in the late eighteenth century produced intensive publicity? How far had the inhumanity of slavery either reflected or encouraged a belief in the sub-humanity of the slave?

The answers to these questions are not clear cut: as with the Chain of Being they operate at several levels of perception. New World slavery was sufficiently well known for "slavery" and "Negro" to become almost interchangeable terms. Slavery accentuated belief in Negro inferiority. And slavery even produced explicit arguments that only Negroes could be used as slaves in hot climates. But the arguments connecting the Negro with slavery were invariably generalizations and empty slogans unsupported by either contemporary scientific belief or the observations of those who described slavery to the British reading public. And the interests—sometimes the very individuals—who made special pleas about natural slavery also put forward a contrary polemic stressing the human potential and, involuntarily, the intractability of the Negro in slavery.

*　　　*　　　*

By the late eighteenth century—and probably much earlier—there was no question but that slavery and blackness were virtually synonymous. Most British people may not have shared the prejudices of West Indian planters. But when one of the planters' critics proclaimed that the ideas of "blackness, and slavery, are so blended, so twisted together in their minds that they may be supposed as utterly incapable of separating them",[2] he was describing a universal truth. As James Dunbar was to remark despairingly in an attack on slavery, Negro "features and complexion, regarded as the natural badges of inferiority, seem to mark them out for slavery . . ."[3]

Although the English were slow to enter the slave trade, the long established servile status of Negroes in the Spanish and Portuguese empires was well known. By the late seventeenth century slavery in the New World and English involvement in the slave trade had made the association of racial appearance and status unequivocal. It was revealed in comments on the ethnic divisions of Africa. Herman Moll's influential *Geography* was not alone in contrasting the black, robust, and "altogether servile" Negroes with the free tawny North Africans.[4] In the late eighteenth century a discussion of the two racial groups of Madagascar probably drew more on this stereotype than on objective analysis:

> they differ considerably in bodily constitution; those on the western coast have short and curled hair, and are strong and vigorous. Those who occupy the centre of the country have long and flat hair, features of a European cast; and their women are handsome; but this race, though much more sagacious and dextrous than the Coeffers, are feeble in make, and incapable of bearing hard labour.[5]

Comments about particular Negro groups illustrate the same association. The Negroes of Senegal, cited by Michel Adanson as temperamentally suited to "bearing fatigue", were, he added, of the "deepest black". John Lindsay, in praising the same Negroes, revealed other facets of the stereotype: "they have not that thickness of the lip and the flatness of the nose, that common slaves are always found to have . . ." According to Hugh Jones,

Negroes were not only blacker and uglier than American Indians but "of a more servile Carriage and slavish Temper . . ."

Isolated examples of admiration for the Negro appearance must be considered in the context of this association with slavery. Thomas Phillips showed how the rigid colour-based hierarchy of the West Indies might already be influencing slave traders' judgements in the late seventeenth century. Negroes from one part of the Gold Coast, he wrote, "are esteemed the worst and most washy of any that are brought to the West Indies; why I know not, for they seem as well limb'd and lusty as any other Negroes, and the only difference I perceiv'd in them, was, that they are not as black as the others . . ."[6]

In the eighteenth century these West Indian perspectives on colour were well known in Britain, as geographical text books listed in detail the different degrees of colour and their social significance and planters imported attitudes into Britain along with their slaves. A newspaper advertisement, offering a ten year old Negro boy for sale at Lichfield in 1771, stressed that he was "for Colour an excellent fine Black".[7]

Accompanying the almost automatic connections made between servile characteristics and racial appearance was the persistent argument that only Negroes were capable of the tropical labour demanded by slavery. Pervasive though this claim was, it never became more than a vague generalization. All Negroes were black; all slaves were Negroes; yet only a tiny handful of writers associated the widely proclaimed immunity to heat with this definitive skin colour. Of these all but one confined themselves to the observation that Negro skins blistered less easily than those of whites. Only Lord Kames attempted to explain this difference. Negroes were "protected by nature against the violence of the heat. Their skin is to the touch remarkably cooler than that of a European . . ."—to be precise two degrees fahrenheit cooler. The lack of other explanations may partly have been because the connection between colour and immunity to heat was taken for granted by people well aware of different susceptibilities to sunlight even among the British population. Thus only one traveller to West Africa explicitly made the observation—which must have been obvious to all—that Europeans "of a light or sandy complexion" were more affected by the heat than those who were swarthy.[8]

But there were other reasons for the vagueness. In the eighteenth century the notion of different racial constitutions clashed with a vogue for environmental explanations of physical and cultural characteristics which dominated contemporary writings. In ways which will be analysed more thoroughly in later pages Negroes in Africa were seen as lazily succumbing to tropical heat rather than as superhuman labourers. Despite their flourishing in the white man's graveyard of West Africa, they were not customarily seen as people especially equipped with racial traits enabling them to cope with the tropics. They were black because Africa had made them so, not because God or providence had first equipped them with skins which would not burn. Thus Lord Kames' claim was not only overshadowed but eventually refuted by a resourceful American cleric, Samuel Stanhope Smith, armed with environmental theories and a thermometer.[9]

In general, however, the contention that Negroes were natural slaves was not advanced by intellectuals like Kames. It was the product of propaganda. It was significant that nearly all writers either flatly accepted or rejected the stereotype. In the period before the major abolitionist debate only one essayist argued that aptitude for tropical labour depended on acclimatization. The dangerous dependence on black slaves in the West Indies could be avoided by importing poor children from Britain and Ireland. These would become "as much seasoned to the sun, and at least as hardy, as any negroes that can be found in Africa". Mature white servants, on the other hand, had always been found unfit for labour in the tropics.[10] The failure of others to follow suit reflects the fact that propaganda demanded bold assertions rather than reasoned explanation.

On the other hand, the polemical imperatives were less simply pro-slavery than the one major controversy about racial constitutions in the first half of the eighteenth century might suggest. This concerned Georgia, where Negroes were at first excluded by the founders in the 1730s as a threat to the colony's twin aims of providing a bulwark against the Spanish in Florida and a haven for English poor. Later the authorities gave in to demands that Negroes must be used to undertake the heavy labour of clearing land and planting a rice crop. Winthrop Jordan regards this Georgia debate as revealing "with striking clarity the social and economic pressures behind development of the climatic theory". He notes that "no one . . . linked the supposed differences between Negroes and whites to specific physiological features . . ." And he makes the valid point that, underlying the settlers' claim that only Negroes could do such killing work in a hot climate, was the attitude that "they preferred killing Negroes to killing themselves". This point is no less valid for similar claims by slave owners in the West Indies and South America.[11]

But accurate though Jordan's analysis is in itself, the Georgia debate did not fully represent the division of opinion about the Negro's tropical constitution. For the notion was adopted almost as frequently as an attack on slavery as it was used in its defence. As Ralph Sandiford complained in 1730, one of the great injustices of the slave trade lay in taking Negroes to "unnatural climates which is hard for them to bear whose Constitutions are tendered by the Heat of their Native Country; for God that made the World, and all Man of one Blood, that dwell upon the Face of the Earth, has appointed them Bounds of their Habitations . . ."[12]

Although the idea of divinely ordained racial zones suited particularly well the purposes of those wishing to denounce European interference in Africa, one might have expected West Indian interests, at least, to defend the slave trade on the grounds that their islands were part of the same broad climatic zone as tropical Africa. In fact only Long made much use of the argument. In his prediction of growing numbers of Negro servants in England in 1772, he argued that these would quickly become parasites, as they had been removed from their natural climate and would be unable to work efficiently in the English one. He also referred to the constitutions of Negroes as "by nature and the Divine Will" appropriated to hot climates. But it was an anti-slavery tract, the *Plan for the Abolition of Slavery in the West Indies*, published in the same year, which provided the fullest propagandist elaboration of this broad interpretation of racial zones. Its theme was that Negroes' unique ability to function in tropical heat should be the basis of a scheme to settle colonies of emancipated slaves in Florida.[13]

This proposal emphasizes that motives for opposing slavery were more varied than simple humanitarianism. Similar schemes focussed attention on West Africa. An anonymous *Plan for Improving Trade at Senegal*, published in 1763, argued that it was stupid to transport Negroes to the West Indies and employ them under a wastefully coercive system. They would be far more productive as free labourers in Africa. And only they could develop the economic potential of this newly acquired region, since Europeans were unable to work in the tropics.[14] On the other hand, the most prolific early advocate of such schemes, Malachy Postlethwayt, argued to the contrary in his efforts to minimize the effects on the West Indies of ending the slave trade. West Indian planters did not need Negroes. European paupers could do their work just as well if not overworked, as the Negroes were.[15]

An even more potent factor in undermining the plausibility of the climatic justification of slavery lay in the way a significant minority of West Indies slave-owning interests agreed with Postlethwayt. As early as 1736 one essayist argued that slavery was a necessity forced on the West Indies, not by climate, but by British policies and interests. With the mother-country demanding sugar on the one hand, and refusing to transport white convicts on the other, the planters had no alternative but to accept the Negroes foisted on them by avaricious slave-traders. But the first thirty years of settlement in Barbados and the Leeward Islands had shown that white labour was capable of doing the work.[16]

While propagandists provided such contradictory conclusions about the Negro's racial capacity for slavery, medical science implicitly rejected the notion. The weight of such evidence was formidable but, in an age before Edward Long had offered his pseudo-intellectual provocations, there was little need for anyone to marshal it. Indeed in a period when Negroes were conspicuously failing to survive in the West Indies there was little chance that pro-slavery spokesmen would even attempt a reasoned analysis of the alleged superiority for tropical drudgery. Accounts of the diseases of the West Indies must have reinforced this reticence. Since some of them were designed to assist the efficiency of the plantations, they were doubtless read by slave-owners. If so the planters were understandably reticent about stressing the information they gleaned. Whites were seen to be at risk in the tropics, not through a racial susceptibility to heat, but through a gluttonous self-indulgence, in which their digestive systems were overpowered with meat and their mental faculties with alcohol. Even Long was eventually to agree with Richard Blome's seventeenth century diagnosis that most disease in Jamaica was caused by "Surfeits, Slothfulness, or excessive drinking . . ."[17] At the same time medical evidence was revealing blacks as normal men with resistance to disease lowered by the rigours of slavery.

References to "Negro" diseases have led Philip Curtin to argue that medicine encouraged a belief in racial peculiarity even as it presumably exploded the belief that Negroes flourished as tropical slaves.[18] Yet the major "Negro" diseases located in the West Indies were described in terms which emphasized the inhumanity of slavery rather than the sub-humanity of the slave. Patrick Browne, an historian of Jamaica, who was also a doctor of medicine, referred to Negro diseases "of a peculiar nature". But he also said:

> When we consider the inconveniences under which these creatures labour, the toils they are obliged to undergo, the vicissitudes of heat and cold, to which they are exposed, and the grossness of their food in general; we ought not to be surprised if they had been still more

slothful and sickly than they are commonly observed to be; or if the diseases to which they are obnoxious, had differed more apparently from our own . . .[19]

Charles Leslie, in his *Account of Jamaica* (1740), reported that Negroes were subject to all white diseases plus some others, "which no doubt their coarse way of Living very much occasions."[20] Among these was yaws, which, however, whites also occasionally contracted. Edward Bancroft offered a more detailed explanation. Yaws consisted of pus-filled lumps usually covered with flies "through the indolence of the Negroes." He believed it was passed on by flies and noted that no one seemed to catch it whose skin was whole, "for which reason the whites are rarely infected; but the backs of the Negroes being often raw by whipping, and suffered to remain naked, they scarce ever escape it."[21]

Many others regarded yaws as a venereal disease. This meant that discussions of its prevalence helped to reinforce images of the Negro's sexual looseness. But at least some authorities made it clear that, where this looseness was shared by the white slave owners, so was the so-called Negro disease. Fenning and Collyer's mid-eighteenth century synthesis claimed that the disease, unknown in America till the introduction of Negroes, had been passed on by sexual intercourse and was now hereditary in many white families in the Carolinas.[22]

At the same time the prevalence of various parasites affecting the feet and of tetanus was explained in terms of the mode of life of the slave. It was recognized that whites who went barefoot were as liable as blacks to contract these diseases. Tetanus, as William Hillary, M.D. pointed out, was a great scourge of Barbados slaves because they normally went barefoot and frequently had open wounds from the nature of their labour.[23]

Hillary was one of very few contemporaries to mention elephantiasis and leprosy, two "Negro" diseases mentioned by Curtin. Elephantiasis, he reported, had been introduced by Negroes into the West Indies, "where it is now but too frequent among them, and among the white people also, who are not exempted from it." He also outlined a similar history for leprosy in the West Indies; it affected many Negroes "and I may add several white People also . . ." Richard Towne placed some stress on how "utterly unknown" elephantiasis was in Europe, but he concluded that:

Sometimes *white People*, whose unhappy Circumstances have reduced them to Hardships but little inferior to what the *Blacks* are obliged to undergo, have given us Proof that this *Disease* is not limited to one *Colour* . . .[24]

Eighteenth century attitudes to smallpox probably best illustrate
how little scientific backing there was for the barriers which slavery
erected between whites and blacks. In the West Indies and
America those who debated the efficacy and morality of
inoculation shared the assumption that Negroes were no different
from other men, and it was an "Essay on Smallpox", published in
1757, which most clearly summed up the anti-racialist trend of
contemporary medical opinion:

> There is scarce a climate upon the face of the globe that does not
> produce its peculiar endemic distemper; so that, when a foreigner
> happens to reside where any new disease (unknown to him before)
> reigns, he will be in great danger of contracting it; and from hence,
> we learn why the Europeans dealing with the Africans are subject
> to the same diseases with the negroes, etc. which diseases, in a general
> way, are not seen or known in England.
>
> What I would infer from the foregoing reasoning is this, viz. All
> animals are subject to particular distempers, peculiarly incident to this
> or that species of animals; and hence we see, that the distemper, lately
> so violent among the horned cattle, was not communicated to horses
> or other animals.[25]

*   *   *

Even though the academic evidence was so clear cut, Negroes,
especially in the West Indies, were being treated as if they were as
different from whites as horses are from horned cattle. This form
of racism might reflect genuine belief—operating at a different
level from the rigorously intellectual—that Negroes were indeed
natural slaves. Occasionally the comments of pro-Negro writers,
such as Morgan Godwyn in seventeenth century Barbados,
indicated that planters, free from the shackles of intellectual or
theological convention, were arguing privately that Negroes lacked
souls and other definitively human attributes.[26] And from the same
early period the processes which established automatic
associations between racial appearance and slave status made it as
likely that such sentiments were effects rather than causes of racist
exploitation. It was not uncommon for early geographical text
books to describe Negroes in terms reminiscent of the cattle
market. Admiration for the straightness and strength of black
limbs was recorded alongside a recurring slogan: "if you would
have a Negro to serve you well, you must give him enough to eat,
enough to work, and beat him often."[27] In the mid-eighteenth
century, when such simplistic labels were no longer in vogue, there
were none the less occasional visitors to the West Indies who
voiced opinions which in later more controversial decades, were to
form a minor part of the pro-slavery case. Negroes, they said, did

not suffer physical and especially emotional pain to the same degree as whites. Their bodies might bear the mark of the whip but their minds were unscarred by the deprivations of slavery.[28]

Such opinions may have been genuinely held. They may well have reflected both an involuntary response of individuals seeing plantation slavery for the first time and the private thoughts of planters and overseers corrupted by their own tyranny. But whatever they indicate about the attitudes of those who saw slavery, they are quite unrepresentative of the picture of slavery conveyed to the remote metropolis by all the media of publication.

The amount of information published about New World slavery grew enormously through the eighteenth century. But consistently, from its seventeenth century inception, it came across as a system to be judged by normal human criteria. If it were possible for an individual to read only a handful of pro-slavery tracts, he might be convinced that the institution was benign. If he read more widely, he would find looming in the background of even the pro-slavery case recognition of the way it was built on the systematic suppression of human aspirations, a message naturally conveyed with far more force by the more numerous anti-slavery writings of the eighteenth century.

Very soon after slavery was introduced in British America its essential characteristics were being reported in geographical surveys. The differences between Negro slavery—perpetual and hereditary—and short-term white indentured servitude were made clear. Reports differed as to whether this meant that Negroes were treated worse in other ways. But the claim that perpetual bondage made them valuable assets to be cherished was clearly a response to criticisms which were already being reflected in the same *genre*. Several early surveys followed comments about the poor food given to slaves by strictures on the complete absence of a spiritual diet. Not for the last time one of West Indian slavery's few redeeming features—the break from plantation work each Sunday—was presented as a planters' failure to "convince the Negroes of the necessity they lye under serving their Creator."[29]

From the same early period until the end of slavery there were in other *genres* published affirmations of the Negro's potential for Christianity and, in the publications of the Society for the Propagation of the Gospel, some reports of modest success in providing Negroes with the education necessary for Protestant conversion.[30] To judge from the recurrent themes of the would-be evangelists' writings most objections to conversion were based, not on ideas of racial incapacity, but on fears that baptism might undermine slavery. Slave-owners were constantly being reassured that baptism made no difference to the legal status of slaves and that Christianized Negroes would be more, not less obedient.[31] Significantly, the writer who came closest to arguing a racial incapacity for conversion concluded with an explicit affirmation of Negro human integrity. An anonymous pamphleteer suggested that only a simplified version of Christianity should be presented to Negroes and claimed that he had never known any Negro show the least interest in conversion. But he admitted that "with some Care and Culture they may be made to come pretty near us in point of Skill, and consequently that they must be the same species of Creatures that we are in every respect but Colour . . ."[32]

Whatever their private thoughts, it was this potential for improvement which planters publicly emphasized. In the first half of the eighteenth century the stock defence of the slave trade as a rescue operation emerged. This contrasted the barbarity and depravity of Africa with a New World situation which raised Negroes to a condition comparable with the peasantry of Europe. While most merely implied Negro capacity for civilization, Griffith Hughes was one pro-slavery writer who said explicitly that Negroes were not inferior but merely brutalized by social conditions. And he concluded by suggesting that the slave trade was justified if only a few of those saved from "savage and barbarous Guinea" were brought to a "better Knowledge of their Duty to God and man."[33]

This period had also seen the emergence of the West Indian claim—frequently advanced in the later eighteenth century—that one Creole slave, born in the West Indies, was worth two "salt-water Negroes" fresh from Africa. John Oldmixon produced one of the most uncompromising pro-slavery statements of the early eighteenth century. But he emphasised the great difference between new slaves and those born in the West Indies, who "are every way preferable. . . ." And his conclusion confirmed the innate ability of their race: "Some of these Wretches are very ingenious, and others of them as stupid. Indeed such of them as are dull, are so to Brutality; and such as are ingenious are as apt to learn as any People."[34]

In the decade or so before Long and Estwick introduced their radical hypotheses, these themes were continued. The argument that the slave trade was a means of giving Negroes opportunities denied them in Africa reappeared in an anonymous pamphlet on the Peace of Paris of 1763,[35] and in Samuel Martin's *Essay on Plantership*, which achieved five editions between 1765 and 1773.[36] In a work published in 1760 Thomas Jefferys made the same contrast between African and Creole Negroes as John Oldmixon. An anonymous *Soldier's Journal,* sympathetic to slavery, saw the Creole and African Negroes of Guadeloupe as forming two quite distinct social groups. The Creoles were said to have assumed their masters' social *mores* and some lived in modest affluence, even sharing in the management of plantations, or working as skilled carpenters, joiners, and coopers. Others had been able to save enough money to buy their freedom and "follow any branch of business they think proper."[37]

Despite his sympathy for slavery the author of this work provided glimpses of its realities which planters were normally prone to dismiss as anti-slavery fantasies. He wrote of punishments for theft which were severe for first offenders and, for recidivists, sadistic even by the standards of eighteenth century justice: "sometimes they are chained by the middle to the fire-places at the boiling and baking houses, where they remain night and day for months and years together."[38]

Inevitably other travellers condemned a system which could allow such cruelties. Andrew Burnaby, in remonstrating against the "cruel and oppressive" slave system of Virginia, put most emphasis, not on actual cases of torture, but on the virtual absence of legal restraints which made torture possible. The slave's human status might be legally ambiguous but in practice courts always emphasised the master's rights over his property, rather than his obligations to the Negro's moral being. The same point was made by the Swedish traveller, Peter Kalm, who nevertheless said that Negroes in North America were treated more mildly than those in the West Indies. This conclusion found its way into a number of surveys of Britain's mid-eighteenth century Empire. In William Burke's treatise it was extended with dogmatic finality: Negroes in the British West Indies "endure a slavery more compleat, and attended with far worse circumstances, than what any people in their condition suffer in any other part of the world, or have suffered in any other period of time."[39]

With so much evidence confirming what anti-slavery critics had been saying in lurid detail for decades, it would have been far simpler for West Indians to deny that the Negro was fully human than to defend the institution as humane. Yet although Edward Long's writings in this sense largely broke new ground, in another sense they were typical of a more liberal strand of plantocratic opinion which tried to find a middle way by reforming slavery. While the mainly anonymous hacks of the West India interest inserted articles and paragraphs in the press and published the occasional pamphlet defending slavery as it existed, a handful of writers were suggesting that the institution could only survive in practice—and justify its survival philosophically—if it made more concessions to the human dignity of the Negro.

The two most notable of this school were James Grainger and Samuel Martin who, in the mid-1760s, published works which were essentially guides to good planting. Each argued that cruelty was both unwise and immoral. To deny Negroes adequate clothing and shelter was, in Martin's words, as "repugnant to the master's real profit" as to "the laws of humanity". While Martin was able to support such arguments with details of his own success story as one of the few planters to rely on natural increase rather than slave imports, Grainger emphasized how far the general current practice fell short of his ideals:

> How shocking to philanthropy is it, to think there are human beings, who are made to act from motives of fear only! Surely were Negroes instructed in the practical principles of Christianity, they would be rendered much better servants . . .[40]

In the same work in which he rejected the assertions of such as Grainger and Martin about the Negro's essential humanity, Edward Long developed their major reformist theories. In condemning cruelty and the associated mortality rates which kept the slave trade going he was probably genuinely repelled by conspicuous brutality. But above all he was obsessed by the fear which lurked in the background, and often intruded into the foreground, of every justification of slavery: the danger of insurrection. Long's prescription embraced a tightening of defensive vigilance but a relaxation of slavery's cruelties, so that the institution might become self-perpetuating and end the dangerous dependence on wild, unbroken savages. Long was careful enough to reconcile his criticisms with his racist theory: while accepting the usual West Indian comparisons between Creole and African Negroes, and even some of the familiar argument about rescuing Negroes from Africa, he stressed that there were strict limits of attainment beyond which they could not pass.[41]

For all previous writers such twisted logic was irrelevant to a situation which was frightening precisely because slaves were human beings. Whether they believed the dangers should be minimized by humanizing slavery or making it ever more coercive, all writers shared the assumption that security was a more complex problem than confining wild animals. To abolitionists the cruelty which was reported in graphic detail from the late seventeenth century was part of a systematic attempt to deprive Negroes of human rights and dignity, and every example of revolt, whether it took the form of suicide, truancy, insolence, or bloody insurrection, was a triumph for human sensibility in inhuman circumstances.[42]

If some of the celebrations of revolt were stylized and romanticized, the underlying assumptions of slavery's critics were shared by its apologists. The author of the *Soldier's Journal* concluded his catalogue of incredible tortures with the comment: "these punishments, however severe, are said to be very requisite, for if the planters did not keep them under great subjection, they would reap no great advantage from them, and be also exposed to daily insurrections." Edward Bancroft, commenting on slave insurrection in Guiana, argued that slavery could only survive if the spirit of the slave was systematically broken. In arguing—and approving—the notion that white security and even the happiness of the slave depended on "annihilating every hope of liberty", Bancroft was accepting the same psychological premises as the author of the *Plan for the Abolition of Slavery In the West Indies*. "It is shocking," wrote the latter,

> to think that those unhappy victims must, from the nature of the thing, become more wicked, dangerous, and refractory, in proportion to the natural greatness and generosity of their minds. A brave ingenuous, principled slave, is indeed a monster, and not included in the general economy of nature.[43]

Pro-slavery propaganda was rarely as frank as sympathisers like Bancroft. It often saw revolt as a lingering manifestation of African savagery rather than a sign of indomitable human will.[44] But other sympathizers implicitly countered this argument by seeing the issue of slavery in Britain in the 1760s and 1770s primarily in terms of a potential libertarian contagion which might topple West Indian slavery by raising the aspirations of the slaves. Sir John Fielding urged planters not to bring slaves to Britain because there was reason to believe that it was Negroes educated in Britain and returning to the West Indies who had caused recent insurrections.[45] Such arguments may have convinced some readers. Black importations from North America were much less common and the incidence of slave revolt there was far less. The weekly and monthly news columns, as well as books and pamphlets, made it clear how the prevalence of revolt, actual and feared, was a constant feature of West Indian life to a far greater degree than in North America.

But for more careful readers it was clear that West Indian revolt was often a spontaneous combustion of local ingredients rather than a manifestation of either perverse savagery or humanitarian contamination. While slavery was institutionally similar in most

British colonies, it was in the West Indies that the ratios of blacks to whites were most extreme. Those who wished to preserve slavery by reforming it made much of the problems of absenteeism, including the brutalities of overseers and the neglect of laws designed to balance the black majority with fixed percentages of white servants.[46]

Local circumstances varied within the West Indies but never sufficiently to reduce the published awareness of an ever-present fear. Barbados was said by some to be too small and flat for successful revolt, yet attempted revolts were reported from this first British slave colony from mid-seventeenth century.[47] From the same period, when the British took over Jamaica, they confronted a situation in which a mountainous interior was already in the hands of Negroes who had successfully escaped slavery. The role of these Jamaica Maroons, in the history of the island and in British images of the Negro varied over the next century and more until they were finally removed to Nova Scotia and hence to Sierra Leone. For long an inconvenience to the British; sometimes a real threat; and always to the Negro slaves a living sign of their deprivation, the Maroons in the eighteenth century were successfully bought off by the colonial authorities. By hunting down absconding slaves they now preserved an institution they had previously threatened. But whether they were heroes or villains to observers, they were always there as a living contradiction of the equations between blackness and slavery.[48]

Even those who remained slaves preserved shreds of human individuality and, collectively, of their African cultural background. The very factors—large plantations, absenteeism, hugh black populations—which encouraged the brutality of West Indian slavery diminished its homogenizing, de-humanizing effects. By encouraging slaves, for reasons of economy, to grow some of their own produce in their own free time, planters were involuntarily encouraging vestiges of independence which would have otherwise been obliterated by the coerced labour of the plantation. By employing retinues of black rather than white domestic servants they were preventing the growth of a balanced European society which might have supplanted African cultural values by example as well as force. By refusing to permit Christian conversion they were encouraging the preservation of African religious beliefs and rituals.

These tendencies did not go completely unnoticed. But, until the enquiries launched by Parliament in the last two decades of the eighteenth century, they were largely unstressed. The combination of polemical motives and a pervasive ethnocentrism meant that the evidence for African survivals and adaptations, which has fascinated modern historians and sociologists, was largely ignored or condemned. To the anti-slavery writer Negroes triumphed over the brutalities of slavery by magnificently futile gestures of revolt or revenge, rather than by preserving their African heritage. Such critics could point to black harems and mulatto children in planters' households in order to counter the more extreme charges about Negro sexual debauchery. They could mention the heavy preponderance of male over female slaves and the inadequacy of medical care against the plantocratic argument that slavery failed to sustain itself because Negro women were rendered infertile by venereal disease and sexual excess. But, whether for or against slavery, virtually all writers would agree in dismissing African cultural traces as corrupt and licentious.[50]

Griffith Hughes was an exception in regarding Negro dancing as an integral part of religion. There was no admiration in his depiction of tenacious addiction "to the Rites, Ceremonies, and Superstitions of their own Countries, particularly in their Plays, Dances, Music, Marriages, and Burials." But few others, in echoing his report of "unseemly and wanton dancing", placed this activity in the wider framework of even a despised traditional culture: it was simply one of many manifestations of an uncontrollable sexual urge. "Love of women," wrote Thomas Jeffreys, "is their prevalent passion, and dancing their favourite diversion . . . attended with gestures which are not entirely consistent with modesty." Hans Sloane, who provided text book editors with irresistible descriptions of castrations, amputations, and other plantocratic cruelties, was nevertheless contemptuous of Negro music in much the same way as Jefferys: "the *Negroes* are much given to Venery, and although hard wrought, will at nights, or on Feast Days Dance and Sing: their Songs are all bawdy and leading that way."[51]

Where they were not censorious, writers were too preoccupied with diverting the Negro's musical talents to approve of them. John Wesley plagiarized the arguments of the Reverend Samuel Davis who saw in music a device for fostering Christianity; despite the neglect of baptism by many slave owners there were examples of Negroes attending church and learning to read the Bible, "and I cannot but observe that the Negroes, above all of the human species I ever knew, have the nicest ear for music. They have a kind of ecstatic delight in psalmody." The same viewpoint was expressed by a spokesman of the Society for the Propagation of the Gospel and eventually mentioned in the Church of England's published *Instructions for Missionaries to the West India Islands* in 1795. The Abbé Raynal, on the other hand, saw music as a means, profitable to the planters, of ameliorating the effects of slavery:

> So strong an inclination for music might become a powerful motive of action under the direction of skilful hands. Festivals, games, and rewards might on this account be established among them. These amusements, conducted with judgment, would prevent that stupidity so common among slaves, ease their labours, and preserve them from that constant melancholy which consumes them and shortens their days.[52]

Despite the prejudices, distortions, contradictions, and omissions, which disfigured the reports of slave society, one common theme came across strongly. The Negro—with his anguish, his perversity, and his varied techniques of resistance—was no more amenable to the regimentation of slavery than any other man. The associations which had grown up between "Negro" and "slavery" were clearly, by all the evidence of the eighteenth century, a commentary on the exploitive nature of slavery rather than the natural subservience of the Negro.

Part III

Attitudes Before 1780: African Savagery in Theory and Practice

CHAPTER FIVE

INTELLECTUAL PERSPECTIVES

African cultural inferiority was an essential part of the racial justification of slavery launched in the 1770's. There were some precedents for seeing savagery as a product of racial incapacity. Belief in the unique oddness of black Africans could be traced back to speculation about the exotic fringes of the Greek and Roman world. And in the eighteenth century David Hume briefly raised the possibility that Negroes were naturally inferior to whites because of Africa's cultural barrenness. Inevitably exploited by the West Indian racists, these precedents have also impressed historians. They have emphasized that fantasies about Africa persisted through the Middle Ages into the period of new maritime contact in the sixteenth century. And they have given prominence to Hume's brief and casual remark because of his eminence as a philosopher.[1] But emphasis on these precedents is misplaced because it ignores the existence of a social theory by which Englishmen explained to their own satisfaction the physical and cultural characteristics of non-European peoples.

This theory is not to be found in considered statements by Enlightenment intellectuals as famous as Hume. It has to be reconstructed piecemeal from the writings of largely forgotten contemporaries who were responsible for the mass of published comment about the human condition in all parts of the world. The rarity of Hume's comment is symptomatic of a pervasive apathy about problems of racial and cultural difference among the more innovative thinkers of the period. With clergy continuing to play a role in geographical editing, which they had dominated since Hakluyt's day, and with education equally the province of ordained schoolmasters, this apathy meant that conservative theories, often theologically reasoned, largely held sway. This clerical influence was not monolithic nor were all clerical theorists circumscribed by theology. Environmental theories—centuries old but newly refined and popularised by the disciples of Montesquieu—fitted in well enough with scriptural orthodoxy about the unity of mankind. The conservatism of the period was revealed less in the continuing virility of dogma than in an absence of challenging hypothesis or empirical inquiry.

None of this meant that the Negro's savagery was viewed with anything but disdain. Indeed, both scriptural and environmental explanations of cultural difference can be seen at least partly as rationalisations of ethnocentric assumptions about European superiority. It is in this sense alone that the new West Indian racism was in the mainstream of eighteenth century thought. Edward Long, in claiming that Negro backwardness was permanent, and Samuel Estwick, in declaring that Negroes had degenerated to a point of no return, were attempting to exploit a general feeling that savagery was deplorable. But they were defying the logic which made it so: savagery was widely condemned because the savage was demonstrably failing to realise his full human potential. Long and Estwick were also exploiting a tradition of colour prejudice in new ways. Blackness had come to symbolise savagery just as much as slavery. But it had also become common to see blackness as a result of the savage condition.

*   *   *   *

Long before the Negro was a New World slave, he occupied a dubious position on and beyond the fringe of European knowledge and acceptance. For centuries Europeans filled a vacuum of ignorance about sub-Saharan Africa with ethnological and zoological fantasies. Association with legendary monsters and images of ferocious equatorial heat could make strange black men seem even stranger. An influential medieval astronomer, Sacrobosco, had, on the one hand, described this zone as uninhabitable and, on the other, described the black men who lived there. In the early sixteenth century, with the notion of a fiery barrier girdling the earth finally discredited, Sir Thomas More had yet implied that only people fundamentally different from Europeans were capable of living there.[2]

Christian orthodoxy prevented men of this period from extending these passing comments into more elaborate hypotheses about racial difference. And soon the work of Leo Africanus provided some modest improvement in the Negro image. But even though Pory's 1600 translation provided glimpses of political strength and cultural achievement in the sub-Saharan savannah regions, it did not seriously undermine the association between the Negro and cultural inferiority. In seventeenth century geographical texts, the broad ethnic divisions of Africa distinguished the sub-Saharan peoples not only as blacker and more servile, but also as "blacker and less politic".[3] If these stereotypes were partly ancient legacy, they also reflected the ethnocentrism of the Africanus translation. The "wretched" people of Casena—"extremely black, having great noses and blabber lips"—lived in "most forlorn and base cottages", while those of Agadez "are all whiter than other Negroes; and their houses are stately built after the fashion of Barbarie".

Soon the geographical text books were to reflect the experiences of traders dealing with the coast rather than the interior and generally too knowledgeable to express their distaste for the Negro in quite such terse generalisations.[5] But even while such contacts were producing a depth and breadth of knowledge which displaced classical stereotypes, old associations between blackness and savagery were in another sense being strengthened as men grappled with the problem of why the Negro was black. Many historians have surveyed the various causal theories of blackness which held sway from medieval times until the dawning of current wisdom about natural selection. This is not the place to provide still further documentation for the currency of theories about the Biblical Curse of Ham or the Mark of Cain. However frequently such theories were advanced—or embellished by such new refinements as Lord Kames' references to the Tower of Babel—they were far more often refuted, not least because the Bible simply did not make the references to race and colour which were being claimed. The most revealing aspect of such theories was their assumption that blackness was in some way derogatory, a disability if not a curse. This was an assumption shared by the proponents of environmental theories, whose dominance was the main reason for the relative insignificance of all other hypotheses. And in the prevalence of environmental theories lay a major reason for a continuing association between blackness and savagery which was sometimes at odds with expanding knowledge of Negro societies.[6]

There was nothing novel about environmental explanations of racial and cultural characteristics. Classical and medieval writers, who saw the equatorial zone as an uninhabitable ring of fiery heat, inevitably had extreme views about climatic effects on those who lived nearest to this zone. According to Pliny, Solinus, and Strabo, the heat made Africans black and forced them to live underground like animals. In the thirteenth century, Bartholomaeus Anglicus, described the brutish social habits of Negroes, their "horribly shapen" faces, and the ferocity of a sun which "roasteth and toasteth them" to blackness. And Robert Gainsh, who imported the first Negroes into England in mid-sixteenth century, referred in medieval fashion to Africans as "a people of beastly living without a God, law, religion, or common wealth, and so scorched and sered with the heat of the sunne, that in many places they curseth it when it riseth".[7]

This association between appearance and savagery was in no way diminished by the fact that from this period greater knowledge of colour variations on similar latitudes made men sceptical that Negroes were merely sunburnt. Indeed, the need to find new explanations strengthened the association. The old theories had depicted Negroes as hapless victims; both savagery and appearance were the result of climate. New theories tended to argue that appearance, though still linked to climate and environment, was itself partly the result of savagery.

The core of most environment theories rested on geography and topography. Colour variations depended on ways in which the heat of the sun was affected by height above sea level, proximity to oceans and land masses, prevailing winds and similar factors. But there remained puzzling juxtapositions of skin colour which did not fit easily into these patterns, with the result that most theorists also paid attention to cultural factors. Such theories could be crudely simplistic. According to J. R. Forster, among many reasons for Negro blackness was nakedness. In contrast the Tahitians "go almost constantly dressed and covered". They were the fairest of Pacific Islanders because, unlike some other groups, they washed regularly.[8]

Although Forster's opinions were quoted with approval by many contemporaries, eighteenth century theories were usually more complex. The Reverend Samuel Stanhope Smith, for instance, stressed lack of hygiene, the use of "coarse and filthy unguents", and parental neglect in exposing infant Negroes to the sun. But he also introduced a socio-medical argument based on equally derogatory assumptions about Negro behaviour. Skin colour was affected by the bile, which was "shed through the whole mass of the body". the primary causes of a "surcharge of bile" were such social factors as fatigue, hardship, vapours from stagnant waters in badly cultivated regions, and "poverty and nastiness" in general. Savages, he concluded, "will always be discoloured", even in cold climates.[9]

Stanhope Smith also referred rather cryptically to the thicker skin produced by the savage's exposure to the elements. Here he was probably influenced by John Hunter, the army physician, who combined current environmental theories with Newtonian optics: the savage way of life roughened and thickened the skin, resulting in the same intensification of darkness achieved by increasing the number of dark optic plates in the laboratory. This was an unusual hypothesis only in its attempt to define precisely the causal connection between savagery and colour. While no one else referred to the science of optics and few mentioned that Negro skin was unusually thick, many other writers would have accepted Hunter's assessment of the significant factors in savagery, without explaining how they operated physiologically. Hunter's stress on exposure to sun and air was only slightly more commonplace than his references to diet and soil. He could have been citing one of many contemporaries when he explained that savages, even in cool climates, were brown because "they lead a most wretched life, their food consists of fish and wild beasts. For bread, they dig up roots out of the earth". Most influentially, Buffon returned again and again to this theme. The different racial colours in Africa were probably due to diet, just as in Europe white and black hares flourished according to different feeding patterns.[10]

Buffon also argued that diet contributed to other physical traits: "Coarse, unwholesome, and ill-prepared food, makes the human species degenerate. All those people who live miserably are ugly and ill-made." But although this argument was accepted by Stanhope Smith, it did not achieve great prominence, mainly because more explicit causal explanations equally related to savagery were available. Buffon himself argued that "peculiarities in features depend much upon the customs which take place among different nations . . ." And there was abundant contemporary corroboration of his contention that Negro noses were artificially flattened. So old were reports of Negro babies having their features depressed by being parcelled on their mothers' backs, that they already formed a stereotype in seventeenth century works on Africa. While this practice was the most popularly attributed cause, there was no lack of evidence in support of Buffon's claims about deliberate deformity. The Astley *Collection,* the *Universal Modern History,* and Salmon's *Universal Traveller* all gave currency to reports of this nature by such observers as Francis Moore.[11]

Collectively, for all their aspersions on Negro culture, environmental theories formed an even more decisive bulwark against pseudo-scientific racism than the specific rebuttals of gradation discussed in an earlier chapter. For while the environmentalists both assumed and accentuated the Negro's social inferiority they emphasised his essential humanity. In many instances this emphasis was explicit. A majority of theorists discussed the Negro, not in isolation, but as a not particularly unusual example of world-wide tendencies. The reports of artificial deformity were, for instance, placed in the perspective of similar eccentricities among other racial groups.

Occasionally, as in references to Chinese foot-binding, these reports were accurate. More often they were as inaccurate as the African ones. American Indians were said to have flattish heads through being swaddled on boards as infants, while the Caribs had noses "crushed down by their mothers, at the time of their birth . . ." It is true that James Dunbar concluded a global survey of such customs by nominating Africa as the "principal seat of the enormity . . ." But such a grading was no more typical than John Gregory's suggestion that the flattening of Negro noses was comparable to the shaping of an Englishwoman's figure by corsets and stays.[12]

In the same way, Buffon's theory of the relationship between diet and "deformity" emphasised differences within Europe as well as between races. He claimed important physical differences between rural and urban populations and between inhabitants of high and low ground, whose food was affected by different qualities of soil. And in his evaluation of other influences of savagery he contrasted the colours of Tartars and Europeans, and discussed the bleaching effects on the Chinese of more polished lives than their neighbours. Buffon's opinions influenced Stanhope Smith and Goldsmith and probably also J. R. Forster, who referred to the swarthiness of labouring Europeans' and who mentioned Negroes only as incidental illustrations in his environmental explanation of the physical differences between Melanesian and Polynesian. Discussions specifically concerned with Negroes were no less emphatic about the superficiality of racial difference. According to John Hunter, Europeans in the tropics remained white because they never adopted the customs which led to blackness, while the unfortunate Negroes were "never able to enjoy that easy kind of life, by which whiteness is greatly brought about."[13]

One might expect that these environmental theories would be undermined by the failure of whites and Negroes to change colour in alien climates and altered circumstances. As early as the mid-seventeenth century, Robert Boyle pointed out that Negroes had not grown lighter after many generations in America. If this exaggerated the testing period when they had been in the cooler latitudes of North America, a century later writers could make the same point with more conviction. By this time, too, white people in the West Indies, especially, had a vested interest in proclaiming their own hereditary immutability.[14]

With this commitment and the first-hand experience of interracial societies, it is hardly surprising if such opinions were, as Jordan claims, predominant in the New World. But thanks to the ability of arm-chair theorists to overlook reports incompatible with their arguments, opinion was heavily weighted against the proposition of permanent colours among the writings available to an English audience. The eighteenth century might not be able to accept the assurances of earlier writers, like Matthew Hale and Morgan Godwyn, that complete reversals of colour would ensue after a few generations. But J. R. Forster went much further than most of similar views when he suggested a time span necessary for change longer than recorded history. Buffon, for instance, argued in terms of ten or twelve generations in ideal conditions.[15]

Although he recognised that miscegenation would produce the same effect much more quickly, Buffon was one of a large number of contemporaries who were prepared to overlook this factor in arguing that environmentally induced changes had already taken place. Easily the most popular example concerned the black "Portuguese" traders of Sierra Leone and Senegambia. As early as 1623, Jobson had described these scattered groups: all had wives from among "the country blackwomen, of whom they beget children . . ." Several of the leading eighteenth century geographies, probably influenced by Francis Moore's similar observations, reiterated that the original Portuguese had long since merged with the indigenous population.[16] But these opinions were set on one side, while such as George Forster and Goldsmith postulated that Europeans had, in Forster's words, "gradually degenerated through nine generations (three hundred years) to their present hue". The main influence on Forster and a host of others, was Cornelius de Pauw's *Recherches Philosophiques.* Forster withheld complete acceptance; but he had noticed, on visiting the area, that these peoples were already darker than de Pauw had described them; and he was impressed by a climatic argument supported by "so able and judicious an investigator of nature as Count Buffon".

Other affirmations rested on equal superficiality. An anonymous critic in the *Monthly Review* raised the question of miscegenation but found himself persuaded by the analogy of the Jews that whites had probably turned into Negroes. Despite rigorous exclusivity the English Jews were whiter than those in Portugal or the Levant. Buffon was equally prone to confuse race and culture: Ethiopians were obviously of Arabian descent because of their customs, so the fact that they were darker than the Southern Arabians must be due to long residence in a more southerly latitude. Claims that Negroes had grown lighter were also made. Stanhope Smith, writing in North America, was as willing as commentators on Senegambia to overlook miscegenation in describing the lighter complexions and less Negroid features of domestic slaves, as opposed to field labourers.[17]

To explain why environmentalism prevailed even with such suspect arguments is to demonstrate once again the unsuitability of eighteenth century thought as a vehicle for the pseudo-intellectual racism of an Edward Long. A pervasive conservatism underlay the reluctance of nearly all commentators to jump to conclusions which would see race as a cause of cultural difference and inferiority. Despite the characteristics of scepticism which are so often bestowed on the era of "Enlightenment", traditional beliefs in the unity of mankind were strengthened rather than threatened by contemporary science during the eighteenth century.

The most clear-cut scientific definitions of Negro skin colour were a by-product of microscopic investigations by the Italian, Marcello Malpighi, in the second half of the seventeenth century. Previously anatomists had divided the skin into two layers, an exterior cuticle and an interior cutis or derma, the "true skin". Malpighi defined a third layer, a fine membrane between these other two sections. In the late seventeenth century this innovation was only imperfectly absorbed into English text books as the location of racial colours.[18] But Thomas Gibson in 1682 and, decisively, James Keill, in 1698 in a treatise which was to run to twelve editions in the next half century, both accepted Malpighi's findings.[19]

Through the eighteenth century this new division of the skin was the dominating orthodoxy and its accompanying re-location of racial colours was often mentioned in works otherwise unconnected with the Negro. It achieved passing comment in most anatomical text books and a full exposition by William Hogarth in an instructional work on painting.[20] Beginning with the Astley Collection in the 1740's the Malpighian layer was also accepted by a majority of geographical works referring to skin colour in different parts of the world.[21] This acceptance was not universal. Several works in English discussed the views of a Frenchman, Pierre Barrere, who upheld the old theory that the outer cuticle was the seat of colour. At the same time the Universal Modern History was driven to scepticism of both theories through contemplation of the unpigmented soles and palms of Negroes.[22]

Neither theory of skin structure carried with it connotations of Negro peculiarity. By locating colour in a stratum so fine that it could be detected only by a microscope, each theory implied that racial difference was slight. In most eighteenth century works on anatomy the only reference to Negroes was in a single sentence describing the Malpighian layer. Anatomists accepted that in doing this they had described the only significant difference between races. As James Drake put it, in his text book of 1707, "they differ in no other Circumstances . . . but in this particular".[23] Non-medical works gave these views wider currency. Griffith Hughes, still accepting the two-tier structure of the skin in 1750, stressed that "blackness reaches no deeper than the outward Cutis . . ." Thomas Bacon, writing in the same year, accepted Malpighi's version, but emphasised that colour "affects no more than the Skin". Both underlined the triviality of colour by referring to the whiteness of scars and blisters on Negro skins: "like the Colour of our own Flesh", said Bacon. This kind of observation was not uncommon. John Oldmixon in 1708 even produced an improbable anecdote of a Negro so blistered by a shower of boiling sugar as to qualify for the clothing of a white servant. Significantly Hughes, Bacon, and Oldmixon were all supporters of slavery.[24]

Although anatomy merely described the limits of racial differences without explaining causes, contemporary science also offered direct support to environmentalism through its genetic theories. As Jordan points out, all theories were doomed to failure, "until development of the idea of natural selection operating over an unbelievably long period of time." As he also says, the common eighteenth century assumption was that acquired characteristics could be "transmitted to progeny". Buffon, summing up his own argument, concluded that changes wrought by climate, diet and "ways of living" had been transmitted through generations like diseases. Stanhope Smith argued that the various effects of the savage way of life influenced subsequent generations "for the same reason, whatever that may be, that other resemblances of parents are communicated to children."

Jordan points out that only two contemporary naturalists, Pierre Louis Moreau de Maupertuis and Henry Baker, came "close to detecting the true importance of accidental variation in an hereditary trait". Both men, after studying human deformities, saw that an accidental abnormality might become the source of an entire race bearing the same characteristics. Jordan rightly sees these men as exceptions to the rule of eighteenth century genetic thought. Only George Edwards among British writers made even

passing reference to the suggestion of Baker, an American, that
here might be the reason for the Negro's distinctive appearance.[25]
The only other theory to consider accidental mutation did so in
terms of an ancient folk superstition which was yet as near to the
mainstream of contemporary racial thinking as the scientific
research of these pioneers.

Thomas Browne mentioned, among many hypotheses of colour
change, "the Power and Efficacy of Imagination". Referring to
Hippocrates' account of a woman who had borne a Negro child
after gazing intently at a picture, Browne suggested that this or a
similar accident might have been the origin of a race. A century
later Goldsmith, rejecting the majority opinion that Negro
features were artificially deformed, suggested that perhaps they
may have originated as a deformity inherited by later generations.
But on the question of colour, he revived Browne's speculation
before rejecting the imagination in favour of his environmental
argument. While the power of the mother's imagination was never
universally accepted, it received sufficient credence, even in
intellectual circles, to stand as an important illustration of the
contemporary   willingness   to   accept   dramatic   genetic
transformations. In 1689 an orthodox text book on anatomy
explained how an image imprinted on the mother's brain was
communicated, via the "Animal Spirits" and the blood to the
"matter of the Seed . . ." In the first half of the eighteenth century
there was a minor but prolific pamphlet debate on the subject,
mainly between two medical practitioners, Daniel Turner and
James Blondel. The theory was rejected by Buffon, but one of its
adherents was the English classifier of mankind, Richard Bradley.
In explaining how "juices" circulated from the brain to the foetus,
Bradley did not mention Negroes. But the Hippocrates story and
some modern counterparts were among the favourite illustrations
in other works, including Turner's and various geographical
surveys.[26]

The most ambitious application of the theory came from the
Universal Ancient History, which suggested that the earliest
inhabitants of hot climates must have grown so sunburnt that their
tawny colour might have become an object of national pride:

The men might begin to value themselves upon this complexion, and
the women to affect them the better for it; so that their love for their
husbands, and daily conversation with them, might have a considerable
influence upon the fruit of their wombs, and make each child grow
blacker and blacker, according to the fancy and imagination of the
mother; the force of which is evident from many instances . . .by such
degrees it is not improbable that people of the fairest complexion,

when removed into a very hot climate, may, in a few generations, became perfect negroes.[27]

Apart from the important positive contributions in anatomy and genetics British scientific circles supported environmentalism through a general apathy about racial difference. It was significant that the only purported anatomical investigations of the Negro were undertaken outside Britain. The researches of Barrere and of a German contemporary, Johann Friedrich Meckel, were known in Britain, but their claims were untranslated and ignored in text books on anatomy and they failed to stimulate any parallel research. Numerous fleeting references in the *Transactions* of the Royal Society concerned, not the general characteristics of the race, but albino Negroes, mottled Negroes, and Negroes who changed colour—freaks of nature exercising the same fascination as bearded babies and hermaphrodites.[28] Jordan claims that the great interest, both popular and scientific, aroused by albino Negroes helped to confirm impressions that the Negro race was unique.[29] Such an attitude did not emerge in Britain. Over a long period, Lionel Wafer's description of the albino Indians of Panama received as much publicity as reports of albino Negroes.[30] Belief in the genetic power of maternal impressions made it possible for men to accept that black babies might be born to white parents.[31] And by the end of the century albinism was widely recognised as either a disease or an hereditary deficiency which occurred in many races.[32]

The failure to undertake more basic research revealed late eighteenth century attitudes less different from those of the early seventeenth century than might be imagined. Seventeenth century writers like Purchas, Heylyn, and Abbot had denied any need to find causal explanations for the Negro's colour, which could be referred "wholly to God's secret pleasure". But they had all gone on to review such current explanations as the curse of Ham, the heat of the sun, or the colour of sperm. John Hunter, on the other hand, began his eighteenth century thesis with exasperation at the way theology inhibited the spirit of inquiry when it dismissed the causes of racial difference as the "will of God". But he ended with pious bewilderment about the transmission of colour through procreation:

> . . . the Creator has hidden the business of generation in the deepest recesses of nature, and has kept all its processes sunk and overwhelmed in the deepest darkness, never perhaps to be brought to mind. And therefore to explain things depending on such a cause would be a vain and idle undertaking.[33]

Underlying this complacency was a ubiquitous certainty that

Negroes must be part of the human race. The strained, inconclusive, often contradictory theories of the environmentalists were partly the result of an unwillingness to contemplate any alternative to monogenesis. This was seen particularly in their ignoring many reports which contradicted assertions about the transformation of Portuguese into Negroes. Yet in other ways the reporters themselves showed the same disregard for facts in propagating ideas which minimised racial difference. A common contemporary opinion was that Negro babies were born white, achieving their full colour only after some weeks and a degree of exposure to the air.[34] While it is probably true that Negroes are lighter in colour at birth, the blunt assertions undoubtedly overstated the case. Yet this belief, which fitted the environmentalist theories so well, rested on the reports of voyages, slave traders, and other passing observers, and on the compilations of geographical editors, none of whom had elaborate intellectual systems to uphold.[35]

In the eighteenth century, particularly, the underlying belief in the unity of mankind was sustained by miscegenation, by scientific definition of species, and by observation of the human attributes of Negroes. But even in this period there is strong evidence that the single most important factor was the persistence of scriptural monogenesis. The extent to which even polygenists attempted to give their theories scriptural respectability has already been noted in an earlier chapter. Apart from the formulators of elaborate racialist theories, one of the few eighteenth century writers to consider polygenesis as an explanation of the Negro's colour was John Atkins, writing in 1735. Yet even he conceded that his idea was "a little Heterodox". "This", rejoined the editor of the Astley Collection, "is not to be a little heterodox, but in a great degree so; since that Doctrine cannot subsist but in the Destruction of the Mosaical Account . . ."[36]

*   *   *   *

It may not be entirely paradoxical that Atkins, who was willing to regard Negroes as fundamentally different from whites, was a commentator unusually sympathetic towards Negro social practices which normally aroused ethnocentric scorn. His unprejudiced views of African religion and his strenuous defence of Negroes against contemporary charges about cannibalism and human sacrifice, deserve more discussion in later chapters on the reporting of the African scene. Whether Atkins' sympathy was intellectually based or not, there is no question but that it challenged the same scriptural orthodoxies affronted by his polygenetic theory. Orthodox contemporary thought rejected savage and barbarous cultures even as it upheld the human status of the savage and barbarian. In this rejection above all—but also in the ethnocentrism underlying environmental theories—lay some major reasons why the Noble Savagery of literature was a relatively insignificant ingredient of racial theories.

The seventeenth and eighteenth centuries produced numerous eulogies of the noble savage, especially South Sea Islanders, but also Negroes in Aphra Behn's *Oroonoko* and the abolitionist poetry surveyed by Wylie Sypher and Eva Dykes. But these were largely Utopian criticisms of European decadence or, in the case of the abolitonist literature, of the inhumanity of the slave trade. From the earliest days of contact with the non-European world, such eulogies competed not only with less favourable reports of repellent naked primitives, but, more crucially, with theoretical principles which saw Christian civility as the fulfilment of divine purposes.

As H. N. Fairchild has pointed out, the embryo of noble savagery took shape in the earliest days of the European voyages of discovery, when men identified New World savages with the tradition of an earthly paradise. The islands of the Caribbean seemed to some voyagers to combine beneficent climate and savage innocence in the way tradition decreed. The Caribs emerged in sixteenth century travel literature favourably associated with a delightful climate and accredited with social virtues.[37] According to the translations of Richard Eden, the islands were "rich, fruteful and pleasaunt regions" untroubled by either "outragious heats or sharpe coulde". All property was said to be held in common; and, individually and collectively, they were "contente with soo lyttle" that

> they seeme to lyve in the goulden worlde, without toyle, lyving in open gardens, not intrenched with dykes, dyvyded with hedges, or defended with waules. They deale trewely one with another, without lawes, without bookes and without Iudges. They take him for an evyll and myschevous man, which taketh pleasure in doinge hurte to other.[38]

But while noble savagery found expression in sixteenth century Britain, the concept could be no more than a literary device. To see people living innocently in an earthly paradise, reminiscent of the Garden of Eden, was to challenge the Old Testament version of the peopling of the earth. Savages could not be innocent and at the same time the descendants of Adam and Noah. Not even the most favourable English accounts took this large step towards heresy.

Francis Drake produced an account of the Californian Indians which in many ways matched the early European depictions of the Caribs. The Californians welcomed him as a god; they crowned him their king. They were an admirable people "of a tractable, free, and loving nature, without guile or treachery". But the significance of this was that it showed they might "by the preaching of the Gospel, be brought to the right knowledge and obedience of the true and everliving God."[39]

A contemporary offered a similar qualification to one of the rare favourable accounts of the more northerly Algonquins:

> Doubtless yt is a pleasant sighte to see the people, sometymes wadinge, and goinge sometymes sailinge in those Rivers . . . free from all care of heapinge opp Riches for their posteritie, content with heir state, and living frendlye together of those things which god of his bountie hath giuen unto them, yet without giunge hym any thankes according to his deserte. So sauage is this people, and depriued of the true knowledge of god.[40]

In the early seventeenth century such savages might still be regarded as blamelessly ignorant of Christianity. But this ignorance did not justify either their heathenism or their incivility. The doctrine that established that all men were the progeny of Adam also established that the fundamentals of religious truth and civilised behaviour were available to them. Adam's sin, said Samuel Purchas, "did not wholly deprive us of the Image of God, whereunto we were created. A remainder and stumpe thereof continued". The Anglican theologian, Richard Hooker, argued similarly that "by force of the light of Reason, where-with God illuminateth every one which cometh into the world, men being enabled to know truth from falsehood, and good from evil, do thereby learn in many things what the will of God is".[41]

This concept of natural reason had found continuous expression since the earliest days of the Christian church.[42] Like Hooker, comparatively few theologians who discussed it were concerned with non-European savagery. But the concept gave a particular force to the observations of early voyagers and colonisers. It was no doubt a formative influence on some as they studied uncivilized peoples. But even if these men were not actively hunting for traces of religious awareness, their reports provided the data for theorists to whom the concept was second nature. Nearly all late sixteenth and early seventeenth century geographers—Hakluyt, Purchas, Heylyn, Abbot—were, after all, clerics. Such editors found that non-Europeans did have glimmerings of "divine light". Even naked savages, said Purchas, had some religion, "showing it easier to put off ourselves, than to put the Principles of Religion out of our selves." "So natural", said Peter Heylyn, "is the knowledge of the Soul's immortality, and of some *Ubi* for the future reception of it, that we find some trace or other of it in most barbarous Nations". Even in the later seventeenth century John Ogilby's *Africa* reported that some inland Negroes had anciently worshipped a single God from "Instinct and the meer dictates of Nature". But usually the traces of religion were so slight that they were creditable only in that they confirmed descent from Adam. By rejecting monotheism and lapsing into idolatry savages almost everywhere were demonstrating their blindness to God's truth. "The wandering generations of Adams lost posteritie", wrote Roger Williams of the New England Indians, "having lost the true and living God their Maker, have created out of the nothingness of their own inventions many false and fained Gods and Creators".[43]

Blindness to the divine light was not confined to savages. English theorists agreed with John Calvin that it could be induced by superstition, blinding the intelligence, or by sin, corrupting the senses; and sin and superstition had descended generally on mankind with the Fall of Adam. But blindness could also be the result of the continuing activity of the devil who had led man into sin originally. It was the devil, argued Roger Williams, who encouraged Indian religious perversions, "as he doth all false worships".[44] Devil-worship, and diabolic interventions, were perhaps the most widely reported aspect of the newly encountered non-European societies in the early seventeenth century. From the Lapps and Samoyeds, to the Hottentots and Indonesians, from the American Indians to the Chinese and Japanese, there was no society, north, south, east or west, which was not labelled by some Englishmen as actively under diabolical influence.[45] For many who reported devil-worship on only superficial acquaintance the allegation was probably an imprecise description of the strange and grotesque. But for theorists who pondered their reports this was a crucial cause of savagery. This was the only way George Abbot, geographical editor and Archbishop of Canterbury, could understand the condition of the American Indians:

> But that in all ages it hath appeared, that Satan uses ignorance as one of the chiefest meanes whereby to encrese Idolatry, and consequently to enlarge his kingdome; it were otherwise incredible, that any who have in them reason, and the shape of men, should be so brutishly ignorant of all kinds of true Religion, devotion, and understanding.[46]

The "divine light" obscured by sin or the activities of Satan revealed more than the existence of God. It showed also how men should behave towards one another. Sir Walter Raleigh was both a first hand observer of savagery and a reflective geographer and historian who asserted the universality of natural reason as a guide to morality. Christians might have an advantage in that God had provided them with the written law of the Ten Commandments. But the Gentiles of the Old Testament had, in St. Paul's words, done "by nature those things contained in the law", even though they "had not the law". Each commandment, though God-given, was, Raleigh demonstrated at length, consistent with "the impression of Gods divine light on men". Even if men had not been given the Commandments they would have been impelled to follow the principles in them. These principles were a "blessing", which ensured that "wee might liue the liues of reasonable men, and not of beasts; of free-men and not of slaves; of civill men, and not of savages". Thus it was "by a nature blinded and corrupted", said Raleigh:

> that by the lawes of Lycurgus it was permitted to men to vse one anothers wife, and to the women to choose them others besides their husbands, to beget them with child: which law in those parts hath lasted long, and is not forgotten to this day.
> The Scythians, and the people of both *Indies,* hold it lawfull to burie with them the best loued wives: as also they have many other customes . . . against nature and right reason.[47]

Every aspect of savagery was "unnatural", in this fundamental sense of the word. Man's most important duty, said Richard Hooker, was to honour God. But this was impossible without the organisation and skills developed by civil societies:

> inasmuch as righteous life presupposeth life; inasmuch as to live virtuously it is impossible except we live; therefore the first impediment, which naturally we endeavour to remove, is penury and want of things without which we cannot live. Unto life many implements are necessary; more, if we seek (as all men naturally do) such a life as hath in it joy, comfort, delight, and pleasure. To this end we see how quickly sundry arts mechanical were found out, in the very prime of the world.[48]

Yet increasingly reports showed that these elementary principles were neglected by savage nomads like the Lapps, American Indians, and Tartars, who were seen to have no settled residence and no "arts or sciences"; and by Negroes and others who risked starvation by sowing inadequate crops. Thus the frequent allegations of brutish behaviour could rest on theory as well as descriptive analogy; savagery was a negation of human reasonableness. Significantly, the Chinese, who were generally, if vaguely, regarded as the most civilised of non-Europeans in the early seventeenth century, were seen to have a religion, Confucianism, which rested on natural reason.[49]

The concept of natural reason was taken for granted rather than spelled out at length in geographical works of the later seventeenth century. Both Robert Morden and Samuel Clarke saw glimmerings of natural light amid the incivility and corruption of Madagascar. "Nature hath taught them laws", wrote Clarke. "Nature abhorring Cruelty", said Morden, "instructs them to punish murther with Death, Adultery with publick Shame, Theft with Banishment . . ." The *Thesaurus Geographicus* saw a few redeeming qualities in the savagery of the Hottentots as "some remainders of Natural Light amongst them". And Richard Blome argued against the stereotype of unmitigated African savagery by declaring that Africans were not "so *faithless,* but that they have *Commerce* and *Society* among themselves . . ."[50]

These themes frequently recurred in the eighteenth century. In 1701 Francis Brokesby recommended Raleigh's *History* as essential reading for grammar schools and went on to outline a similar interpretation of the laws of nature as a basis of moral education. In 1732 an article in the *London Magazine* followed Raleigh and seventeenth century theologians in describing the law of nature as a "*Rule* for the human Actions besides the *written Word*". This law was imprinted in men's hearts and Christianity had only "re-established and perfected the *Law of Nature*". The difference in morality between nations, wrote another essayist in the same journal, "proves only that *Nations,* as well as *particular* Men, may not in every Instance, *see* the *Rule of Right,* or *seeing,* may *act* against it". For instance, the test of whether polygamy was immoral was the proportion of males and females. If this was roughly equal, "then it seems to be the *Design* of the Author of Nature, that one Man should have but *one Wife* at a Time".[51]

In 1769 Pierre Poivre offered a survey of the non-European world to show that backwardness in agriculture was a mark of blindness to natural reason. The wretched inhabitants of West Africa "never employ a thought in the cultivation of their lands", unless shown the way by Europeans. By contrast the Chinese had uniquely good agriculture among African and Asian nations because they were "subjected to the laws of reason alone".[52]

Despite these affirmations, eighteenth century theorists were far from unanimous in their attitudes to natural reason. The articles in the *London Magazine* in 1732 were provoked by a *Philosophical Dissertation on Death,* which argued that there were no absolute values of right and wrong, merely what custom ordained in different countries. This was an extreme view. But while most contemporaries retained belief in a universal morality, they were less certain that its tenets were self-evident truths. The anonymous critic in the *London Magazine* accused the *Philosophical Dissertation* of misusing the term "nature". Yet his own attempt at semantic precision was a reassertion of traditional definitions which were far from predominant in the eighteenth century. The biggest fault of the *Philosophical Dissertation,* he argued, was in interpreting "nature" in terms of physical impulse alone; "Our Author says *Nature* bids him, when Desire is *warm,* lie with any Woman he can come at; and when he wants Money, *Nature* bids him *rob, plunder,* or *murder* . . ." But "nothing has been made so bad an Use of as the word *Nature".* Physical impulses did not represent the "Voice of *Nature".* They were only a part of our nature

> and the *inferior part* too, which ought always to be under the Direction of the *superior* Part, *Reason* . . . nature is *perfect* and the Great and Good Authority of it has implanted a *Principle, Instinct, Light,* or *Guide* in every Creature on purpose to *direct* all its Motions so as to produce the *greatest Good* . . .[53]

The statement that "Nature is *perfect"* referred to a philosophical ideal, whereas to many contemporaries "a State of Nature" signified the actual condition of mankind at its most savage. In the same way, to define natural reason as instinct was to contradict the common contemporary use of "instinct" as the virtual antithesis of reason. As men became preoccupied with the dividing line between man and brute, "instinct" was increasingly used in its modern sense to denote certain capacities shared by all animate creatures. "Reason", on the other hand, was man's unique prerogative and increasingly equated with civilised education. The differences from the older view of natural reason were more than semantic. Savage man, in a state of nature, was guided only by his animal instincts. As Bishop John Ewer argued,

> This instinctive knowledge, common to him with the brute creation, he receives from nature, perfect and intire without discipline or study; and this is the only knowledge he so receives, of necessity and not of choice. All higher qualities, that adorn and distinguish men from beasts, are not implanted by nature, but to be acquired. Arts, sciences, morality and religion are all of this condition . . .

Man, concluded Ewer, was born not knowing these "higher qualities" but with the capacity of knowing them. Religion had never been understood "by mere strength of nature". Griffith Hughes was one who agreed with him. He saw "some shadow of Reason" in the ancient Egyptian worship of beetles and crocodiles, whose respectively destructive and dangerous propensities might thereby be assuaged. But he could see none in the West African custom of worshipping "a harmless black Snake" and concluded:

> Here we see the Effect of unassisted Reason; and that it cannot, to the Bulk of Mankind, under such Circumstances, be a sufficient Guide to a reasonable Service towards God.

More generally, many comments showed the ubiquity of the belief that men ruled by instinct alone were scarcely men at all. William Ten Rhyne revealed it in his strictures on Hottentot government: "as these barbarous Pagans live without Laws, so they only follow their Instincts without Controul . . ." John Hippisley argued that Gold Coast Negroes were devoid of emotional tenderness, except in their care of young babies: "In this . . . they seem actuated by instinct alone, and are (I might almost say) literally brutes".[54]

The censure universally bestowed on savages was, it cannot be over-emphasised, a product of an equally universal certainty that the dividing line between man and animal was clear cut. Even when they stressed the brutishness of mere instinct and the instinctive nature of mere savagery, theorists accepted this clear distinction implicitly. The savage might be almost devoid of reason, but he had the capacity to acquire reason in an incomparably greater degree than any animal. An anonymous essay of 1764 referred to certain human instincts which were purely animal, including self-preservation and procreation. But there were "other powers, of which Nature hath only planted the seeds in our minds, but hath left the rearing of them to human culture . . .":

> The two-legged animal that eats of nature's dainties what his taste or appetite craves . . . is, like a tree in the forest, purely of Nature's growth. But this same savage hath within him the seeds of the logician, the man of taste and breeding, the orator, the statesman . . .[55]

This potential was explicitly affirmed by numerous writers. Many presented savagery in the perspective of history, making comparisons between non-Europeans and the primitive ancestors of Europe or describing stages, ranging from a nomadic state of nature through various degrees of barbarism to civilisation.[56] Belief in progress towards civilisation was neither new nor unanimous in the eighteenth century. Similar beliefs and similar comparisons were expressed in the early seventeenth century, when progress was seen as a gradual reclamation of sinful mankind. The early colonisation of America was projected and accomplished amid rhetoric about the westward movement of the enlightening gospel.[57] But in the eighteenth century there were those who continued to take the gospel seriously and who yet regarded civilisation less exclusively in terms of Christianity. To such theorists savagery was neither the manifestation of a once universal blindness to natural reason nor the first stage in an inevitable, if uneven, progress towards civilisation: savagery was degeneration.

The barbarism of Africa, in particular, was very often regarded as degeneration, as men compared its contemporary condition with the high civilisation which had once prevailed in Egypt or Carthage. This was unfavourable to the Negro image, but not in a way consistent with the theory of Samuel Estwick, who argued that Negroes had degenerated to a point where they were incapable of improvement. The vast majority of geographical works remarked on Africa's cultural degeneration briefly and without analysis. For instance, J. R. Forster explained how American Indians and Africans had forgotten or lost most of the "ancient systems" and were "degenerated, debased, and wretched" because they had been unable to replace them "by new principles and ideas" from outside. Much the same message was conveyed to generations of youthful readers by William Guthrie's frequently reprinted *Geographical Grammar.*[58]

Far from speculating along the racist lines introduced by Estwick and Long, the vast majority of theorists found little difficulty in accepting one or both of two common hypotheses. The least controversial of these stressed isolation from the main sources of civilisation. Not only was this fundamental to the concept of degeneration expounded by Forster and others, but it was accepted by many who assumed that man was originally savage, including William Falconer, James Dunbar, and Adam Smith. Smith assumed the interior of Africa and much of Asia "in all ages of the world to have been, in the same barbarous and uncivilised state in which we find them at present". This was because remoteness and other geographical factors prevented communication with the more civilised world. Africa had no large sea inlets like the Baltic or Adriatic; and its great rivers were too far apart to produce any considerable inland navigation.[59]

This did not explain how civilisation had been acquired by the first people to begin the chain of communication. In the first half of the seventeenth century this question was seen exclusively in terms of the Old Testament. Civilisation was spreading westwards from the eastern Mediterranean because God had revealed Himself to the Jewish people there.[60] At later periods this explanation was inadequate as there was more general recognition that other peoples, such as the Egyptians, Greeks and Chinese, had been civilised earlier. In the exposition of alternative theories there was virtually no difference between the two basic attitudes to savagery: the same factors which were regarded by one group as retarding the development of civilisation were seen by the other as explaining its degeneration. Some regarded the formulation of general theories as impossible: the emergence or sustenance of civilisation depended on quite fortuitous local circumstances, such as the influence of an individual genius.[61] But many placed at least some emphasis on the environment and especially climate.

Since the Middle Ages writers had attributed the superiority of Europe over Africa to man's ability to withstand cold better than heat.[62] In the eighteenth century the continuing tendency to regard climate as a likely cause of the physical differences between races was part of an obsession with the environment which received its best known expression in Montesquieu's climatic explanation of the greater vigour of northern races.[63] Intellectually fashionable as they were, such ideas also served to provide a theoretical framework for normal ethnocentric processes, thanks to the intermediate climatic position of Europe and especially Britain.

Adam Ferguson felt that man had always achieved most in the temperate zone, since "under the extremes of heat or of cold, the active range of the human soul appears to be limited . . ." William Falconer concluded similarly that intermediate climates were "the most favourable to human nature". A contemporary essay solved the more trivial problem of why the English did not produce good dancers with a related conclusion. The warmer climates of France and Italy gave their dancers "light airy Dispositions" and more "spirited Temper and refin'd Genius . . ." On the other hand, the northern stiffness in the "Natural Motion of a true *Briton*" bestowed political and military strength, even if it meant that he would never achieve the "Capreols of the *French*, or the mimic gesticulations of the Italians". By the same process, Bernardin de Saint-Pierre explained the superiority of his native France over the tropics. Cold weather was more "wholesome" and an "inconvenience easily to be remedied, whereas the heat, is hardly to be endured, and can never be avoided . . ." It was no coincidence that Africa, America, and a large part of Asia remained in the grip of barbarity.[64]

Even Edward Long, despite his theory of innate Negro inferiority, denied the validity of the Duke of Montagu's educational experiments with Francis Williams, because of the influence of the climate, "which Montesquieu has learnedly examined . . ." It would have been much fairer for the Duke to have used a native African rather than a Negro born in Jamaica:

"The climate of Jamaica is temperate, and even cool, compared with many parts of Guiney; and the Creole Blacks have undeniably more acuteness and better understandings than the natives of Guiney". The same concept underlay the *Universal Modern History*'s expression of bewilderment at the advanced Negro society of Whidah: "One would be led to think that this happy little people have a soil, a climate, and a nature peculiar to themselves, and differing from those distant but a few miles from them".[65]

The most obvious effect on behaviour of a tropical climate was the laziness mentioned in virtually every work on Africa. John Wesley acknowledged the effect even while defending Negroes against the charge: they were "industrious to the highest degree, perhaps more so than any other natives of so warm a climate . . ." But there were different ways of explaining this effect. The simplest was to stress the discomfort and difficulty of activity in the heat. Another was to argue the direct effect of heat on the human body. J. R. Forster considered laziness inevitable for people whose "solids" were relaxed in hot climates.

A third explanation of the influence of warm climates was exemplified by William Robertson. The advancement of civilisation was a question of "acquired wants and appetites". The backwardness of many American tribes of Indians was to be attributed to a climate yielding "almost spontaneously what suffices them". Among those who applied this theory of challenge and response more generally were Dunbar, Falconer, Rousseau and John Hunter, the army physician. Hunter used the Samoyeds and the Negroes as examples of the ways in which a severe climate caused despair and an easy one laziness.[66]

Although climatic theories had a particular relevance to tropical Africa, they did not place Negroes in a uniquely unfavourable position among savages. In the first place many other races were seen to suffer similar climatic disabilities. One of the most thorough-going of Montesquieu's British disciples was William Falconer, who explained in detail the way heat facilitated such aspects of the savage condition as despotism, religious superstition, and moral depravity. Not only did Falconer make broad generalisations about the tropics but he failed to use Negroes as his most common illustrations. In arguing that heat caused indolence, timidity, and a lack of vigour necessary to combat despotism, he mentioned Africa along with Asia and the warmer latitudes of America. But in explaining how "almost all the religions of hot climates were connected with some sensible object" he made no mention of Negroes among many examples.[67]

In the second place, many found climatic theories ultimately unsatisfactory. John Millar was one who pointed out that nations in similar climates had produced quite different cultures, while the different manners of people in the same country at different periods provided even more satisfactory proof that "national character depends very little upon the immediate operation of the climate". He could offer no simple alternative to climate, arguing that the uneven progress of different nations towards civilisation depended on a complex interaction of historical and geographical forces.[68]

*   *   *   *

By the late eighteenth century a period of two hundred years had brought considerable changes in emphasis in explanations of non-European savagery. Where the early seventeenth century had seen little essential difference between savagery and heathenism later writers concentrated less on spiritual depravity than on environmental disadvantage. But wherever the emphasis lay, savagery was a definitively human condition susceptible of improvement as surely as it fell short of nobility. On the other hand, attitudes to particular races were much more than the application of theoretical principles. Attitudes to Africans, though influenced by the intellectual prejudices of geographers and the special pleading of propagandists, were shaped by the aspirations and frustrations of Europeans in Africa.

CHAPTER SIX

THE CULTURAL INFERIORITY OF WEST AFRICA

Much more than abstract theory was at work in depicting the Negro as an African with a culture to be condemned but a human potential to be upheld. Many of those who saw the Negro in Africa were aware of the intellectual conventions discussed in the last chapter, even though they referred to them less directly than John Atkins. But they were also practical men, predominantly traders whose reports were soured by commercial frustrations and tropical discomforts, yet occasionally illuminated by grudging admiration for the Africans with whom they dealt. The reports of observers were given wider currency by the editing of geographical popularisers and educators. Editing roles varied from an extreme which allowed reports to be reproduced verbatim to one which used them to illustrate a general theme—frequently of European superiority over the non-European world.

Observers and editors shared an ethnocentrism which insisted that Negro culture was inferior. This they displayed by a failure to view its elements in terms of Negro society as a whole. Instead, these elements were examined piecemeal and in relation to their counterparts in English society. Negro crafts, for instance, were compared with English crafts, with little consideration of their function or of the division of labour which produced them. Negro music and dancing were compared with western forms and rarely seen as an expression of specifically African traditions or aspirations.

Yet the image of West African cultural inferiority which emerged by mid-eighteenth century was one which made David Hume's oft-quoted hypothesis less ominous than it has seemed to historians. His supposition that Negroes were naturally inferior to whites rested on a belief that there were "no ingenious manufactures amongst them, no arts, no sciences".[1] This was a belief that was only partly corroborated by contemporary accounts of Africa. More important is the fact that the ubiquitous reports of cultural backwardness included numerous statements and implications of Negro potential.

*   *   *

Some of the influences at work on attitudes to Negro culture can by seen in the virtual absence of any tradition of Negro noble savagery. Noble savagery may have been a contradiction in terms by strictly theoretical criteria. But the major reasons why Negro noble savagery was almost exclusively confined to the imaginative literature surveyed by Wylie Sypher were practical rather than theoretical. Because notions about Negroes and their environment were long established their savagery could be rarely viewed with the admiration occasionally bestowed on more recently discovered peoples in the New World or the South Seas. Savage innocence was easier to accept among people remote from European knowledge and unaccounted for in Mosaic historical annals. To the many authorities who stressed the barbarity of a continent which had once nurtured great civilisations, African backwardness was characterised not by innocence, but by societies "everywhere degenerated into a brutish, ignorant, idle, treacherous, thievish, mistrustful, and superstitious people . . ."[2]

In those few cases where contemporaries saw the different social priorities of savages as a source of admiration rather than as a measure of cultural incompetence, the environment itself was of crucial importance. Edward Bancroft depicted among the Indians of Guiana a happiness which "may be envied by the wealthy of the most refined countries". The key to this was not merely the "simplicity of their wants" but the "abundance of means for their supply, and the ease with which they are acquired . . ." This rendered property superfluous:

> Each amicably participates the ample blessings of an extensive country, without rivalling his neighbour, or interrupting his happiness. This renders all government and all laws unnecessary, as in such a state there can be no temptations to dishonesty, fraud, injustice, or violence, nor indeed any desires which may not be gratified with innocence . . .[3]

As the previous chapter has shown, in some early accounts of the New World it was possible to find a combination of beneficent climate and social virtue similar to that extolled by Bancroft. But at the same time as some writers were reacting in these terms to the novelty of a new environment and an unsuspected branch of the human family, all authorities were continuing to depict Africa as it had been known for centuries, a sun-seared desert where human life was either impossible or a near-brutish struggle for survival. The *Geographia Universalis* of 1685 was typical of its contemporaries in juxtaposing accounts of Africa's "burning sand" and "insupportable heats" and dismissive generalisations about its people: "Some say, there's no Nation, but has some good and evil, but that the *Africans* have nothing that's good."[4]

When the image of burning sands changed fairly abruptly in the eighteenth century, with the publication of new accounts of the coastal regions, it was replaced by one of disease and mortality. As Europeans succumbed in their thousands to unknown tropical diseases, only one area was consistently described with a pleasure approaching lyricism. This was Whidah, the great international market of the Slave Coast. Thomas Phillips echoed the enthusiasm of Bosman and Barbot in accounting Whidah "the pleasantest country I have seen in *Guinea,* consisting of champaigns and small ascending hills beautify'd with always green shady groves of lime, wild orange and other trees, and irrigated with divers broad fresh rivers . . ." Later the *Universal Modern History* collated these and other views and concluded, "In a word, it is the true image of what the poets sing of the *Elysian* fields: and, to speak all its perfections, though the authority is undeniable, would appear to the reader as if we indulged a warm imagination at the expense of strict historical truth."[5]

But under Whidah's agreeable surface lay all the familiar West African inconveniences. Phillips went on to describe the "extraordinary and violent heat of the sun" and the sinister proximity of swamps emitting "noisome stinks" and "vast swarms of little flies called musketoes." Europeans who tarried there found themselves not in paradise but a graveyard, where survival depended on good luck and even sleep demanded a stiff dose of opium and a tireless slave with a fan. The manners of the Negroes of Whidah were as deceptive as their environment. From Bosman onwards, most works described graceful hospitality by people who were at the same time the "most artful thieves in the universe." Bosman's view that they exceeded all the Negroes he had known in both good and bad qualities was quoted or purloined by numerous editors. But Whidah stood widely condemned as anything but a haven of innocent savagery for more substantial reasons than the tendency to perpetuate a neat descriptive phrase. In Bosman's own time it was indelibly associated with the slave trade and a somewhat decadent, authoritarian ruling dynasty.

Later the name was inseparable from the massacres and allegations of human sacrifice and cannibalism which accompanied its conquest in 1727 by the forces of Dahomey. And reports of its decline—with weeds choking once fertile ground—emphasised that this had been a man-made, not a natural paradise.[6]

With no other area of West Africa offering even the superficial trappings of paradise, suggestions that there was anything admirable in the cultural backwardness of Negroes were rare indeed. In 1735 John Atkins contrasted the cruelty meted out to Negroes in the West Indies with the communal self-sufficiency of West Africa, where "the Woods, the Fruits, the Rivers, and Forests, with what they produce, is equally the property of all . . .'' The Astley *Collection* ascribed similar virtues to one particular Negro group in the region of Cape Monte. But both these authorities stopped well short of enthusiasm for Negro primitivism. It was only in contrast with the barbarities of New World slavery that Atkins found anything to admire in the "Nakedness, Poverty, and Ignorance of these Species of Men." And the Astley *Collection's* account showed that men who lived in "great Unity and Friendship" also lived briefly, thanks to a surfeit of sex and brandy.[7]

Significantly the only real glimpse of West African noble savagery was produced by Michel Adanson, a botanist sponsored by the French Academy of Sciences, who was the first European since Richard Jobson in the early seventeenth century to describe the region from a standpoint detached from the practical difficulties and economic motives of the slave trade. Anti-slavery writers were to make the most of Adanson's description of a Negro village in Senegal:

> Which way soever I turned my eyes on this pleasant spot, I beheld a perfect image of pure nature: an agreeable solitude, bounded on every side by a charming landskip; the rural situation of cottages in the midst of trees; the ease and indolence of the Negroes, reclined under the shade of their spreading foliage; the simplicity of their dress and manners; the whole revived in my mind, the idea of our first parents, and I seemed to contemplate the world in its primeval state.[8]

Yet not even Adanson could completely detach himself from the prejudices of his contemporaries. The Negroes of Senegal were not newly discovered primitives but people with a long-standing association with Europeans through the slave trade. Adanson noted that the "handsomest, largest, and most regular" town had been constructed under French guidance. Left to themselves the Negroes lived in badly sited clusters of primitive hovels. They did not bother to build roads even in areas where they had regular trade. "Can there," concluded Adanson, "be a stronger proof of the laziness and indolence of the Negroes?" Lengthy contact had wrought changes less tangible than European architectural influence. In the early seventeenth century Jobson had explained that Europeans meeting a native ruler did not uncover their heads, as the Negroes, who wore only fixed fetish ornaments, could not respond. But Adanson accepted his contemporaries' attitude which rejected any suggestion of European deference. On meeting the head man of the village of Sor—where he was moved to his rhapsodies on a "perfect image of pure nature"—he was careful to follow the French custom, "which is never to take off our hats to people of his complexion." The Negro leader knew that his own place lay on the extreme corner of the welcoming mat:

> This is a mark of respect they show the French, whom they look upon as great people; that is, as great lords, and far their superiors. Indeed they are not much in the wrong; and this kind of submission ought to be encouraged as much as possible . . .[9]

Although many writers referred, as Adanson did, to the inadequacies of Negro architecture,[10] and virtually all to laziness, the factor which most clearly established cultural inferiority was the lack of a written language and of the arts and sciences which depend on literacy. This was a deficiency which was always liable to prompt derisive comment. A common anecdote in late seventeenth century works told of a gift of books from the King of Portugal to the King of Congo, with an accompanying squad of professors to explain the mysteries of the printed word. The Negro king had had the books burned, "saying they would but puzzle the Brains of his Subjects, who stood in need of nothing but honest, reasonable, old-fashioned Thinking, and Common Sense".[11] Geographers and historians, attempting to give expanded descriptions of Africa, reported themselves defeated by the absence of written records and by natives "stupid, ignorant, and utterly strangers to geography."[12] Some eighteenth century works explained this ignorance in terms of the Negroes' own alleged traditions. At the time of creation, tradition was said to run, God had offered either gold or the "knowledge of the arts of reading and writing" to the white and black races. The blacks allowed to choose first, had opted for gold "and left the knowledge of letters to the whites."[13]

Far from being improved by increasing interracial contact, this image of illiterate ignorance was consolidated. Interspersed among seventeenth century geographical accounts of brutish African nations were references, chiefly culled from Leo Africanus, to Negro centres of learning. Richard Blome's *Cosmography* of 1683 devoted less space to the West African coast than to the empire of "Melly", which boasted "a famous *Colledge,* and many *Temples,* which are well furnished with Priests and Doctors, who read the Mohometan Law, and under whom the youth of this Kingdom, as also those of *Tombut,* and other parts of the Negroes are educated." Not only the great empire of Mali but its successor, the Songhay empire, had collapsed before the seventeenth century, yet a near-contemporary of Blome, Samuel Clarke, referred to Mali's impressive size and its "rich, civil and industrious" inhabitants. By mid-eighteenth century, however, Bowen's *Complete System of Geography* could report that this once cultured Negro empire had long since disappeared.[14]

Reports of Timbuktu—Tombuto—underwent similar modification. Leo's references to it as a centre of learning recurred in Ogilby's *Africa,* and as late as 1747 in Bowen's *Complete System.*[15] But by this time the city occupied a much more modest position in descriptions of Africa, which now reflected the European involvement in mercenary activity on the coast. Where Timbuktu was not ignored by geographers, it was its possible material, rather than cultural, riches which aroused enthusiasm. Gold, and the possibility of diverting its trans-Saharan traffic, was a recurrent preoccupation in accounts of the fabled city.[16] While some conceded that "the human understanding has made considerable progress in this country, considering the unenlightened condition of all the surrounding nations . . .", this was "only perceivable about the court, and has not yet extended itself visibly over the general manners of the people . . ."[17] In contrast to seventeenth century works, such as Petavius' *History,* which had referred without elaboration to "a great number of learned men", John Barbot declared that the college at Timbuktu shared the mediocrity of all Moslem educational institutions, where "all the extent of the students' learning consists in reading the Alcoran from one end to the other." At the end of this simple routine the typical Timbuktu graduate was "finely dress'd, mounted on horseback by his companions, and led about the town in triumph, with mighty praises and acclamations."[18]

The diminished space and respect accorded the learning of Timbuktu reflected the fact that in the eighteenth century Europeans were forming their opinions of Negro culture primarily through contact with the coast. Here the learning of Moslem areas was usually seen to be confined to a self-contained class of Marabouts, except among the Fulani who, as a later section of this chapter will show, were generally regarded as non-Negro. The Marabouts' ability to speak and write Arabic served to underline the ignorance of the mass of population. Yet the main practical function of their literacy was said to lie in the production of small scraps of paper, bearing excerpts from the Koran, which were carried by superstitious Negroes as talismans against disease or death in battle.[19]

Elsewhere there was even less to be said for Negro language. John Atkins, who was not alone in describing Negro amazement at European ability to communicate by writing, claimed that even spoken language was confined to the expression of simple daily needs. According to Fenning and Collyer's *Geography* Negro languages varied from area to area but were uniformly limited to a few words because "arts and sciences are entirely unknown to these people." With a vocabulary restricted to the "necessaries of life" they were unable to formulate any ideas "so as to enliven conversation, and furnish a constant fund of discourse." The *Universal Modern History* summed up this cultural sterility with typical scorn:

> . . . it would be as vain and absurd to seek for figs and dates growing in Greenland, as for arts and sciences flourishing among the *Africans*. If any of them have gained any tincture of either, it hath been from the Arabs that live amongst them . . . and even that so inconsiderable that it is scarcely to be discerned.[20]

Such sweeping condemnation partly reflected the fact that most areas did not even have a leavening of Islamic culture. But it also reflected the more important fact that Negro society was examined mainly through the medium of the slave trade. Bosman showed that illiteracy could be a practical inconvenience and irritation: "the *Negroes* can neither read not write, and consequently have no use of Letters; which renders it impossible for us to trace their Faults." Even oral transactions were not easy. The *Universal Modern History* referred to the "difficulty and tediousness" of trading with Negroes "whose language is unintelligible to *Europeans* and all the *European* languages still more so to them . . ." This mutual incomprehension produced slurs on Negro language and also reinforced a more general ethnocentric prejudice. John Lindsay explained how the "very uncouth language" of some Negroes led to communication by equally uncouth signs. He himself drew no unfavourable conclusions when Negroes tugged at his pockets. But other Englishmen, he reported, "forming different and disadvantagious opinions of their principles from their unpolish'd manners, have behaved to them with a cavalier roughness . . ." The Astley *Collection* summed up the usual reaction to such encounters: "it is hard to conceive what Patience is required to trade with most of these Brutes . . ."[21]

Language difficulty was merely one factor which led slave traders to dismiss native society with hostile generalisations. Hostility often reflected the fact that the natives held the initiative in trading relations. James Houstoun gave a catalogue of the tribulations of the Royal African Company's Gold Coast forts in the early eighteenth century and a contrasting description of the power wielded by "a very great Caboceer", John Conny. Others also referred to Conny and to equally powerful native Caboceers in other periods, such as John Cabez, some years earlier, and John Corrente some fifty years later. And in the mid-eighteenth century, also, John Hippisley described the domination of Gold Coast trade by the Fante, "a people exceedingly intelligent and tenacious of their rights."[22] Similarly there was a wealth of reports of the way trade at Whidah was completely under native control.[23]

One reason why the natives held the initiative was that the presence of separate or private traders and of competing European nations prevented the application of a consistent policy. Royal African Company spokesmen in books and a flood of pamphlets complained repeatedly that the activities of the separate traders left the company's agents liable to the "*Hardships* and *Impositions,* the barbarous Natives of Africa please to put upon them." Whether they referred to Negroes as "a very cunning, as well as deceitful people", or simply as "barbarous" or "naked", such writers were clearly not prone to present rounded appraisals of Negro life.[24]

Although the separate traders tended to condemn the company's agents for misusing the natives,[25] their own reports displayed similar prejudice. They were even less capable of balanced assessments of native society through the fleeting nature of transactions carried out, on the Windward Coast, at a considerable distance from shore. They were irritated at the universal demand for *dashees,* or bribes, as a preliminary to trade and at the need to indulge other native customs, such as the ritual insertion of a drop of sea-water in the eyes of the trading parties. Yet, as Atkins showed, nothing the Europeans did could guarantee success. In a detailed analysis of the most useful commodities of trade he was forced to admit that no amount of foresight by a captain could prepare for the caprice of Negroes "who make great demands one Voyage for a Commodity, that perhaps they might reject next . . ." And he was forced to conclude that "giving way to the ridiculous Humours and Gestures of the trading Negroes is no small artifice for Success." According to Salmon's *Universal Traveller,* on the other hand, trading at sea was the result neither of a difficult coastline nor of native initiative. Private traders were reluctant to go ashore "amongst the Natives, they being very barbarous and uncivilised."[26]

If the slave trade reinforced ethnocentrism, it was at least a flourishing commerce. Throughout the seventeenth and eighteenth centuries Europeans nursed other economic ambitions in Africa which produced more comprehensive frustration. The attitude which had led the eighteenth century to regard Timbuktu mainly as a possible source of material wealth provoked frequent denigration of coastal Negroes. From the earliest days of European contact it had been hoped that the natives' gold mines could be found and appropriated with the same success enjoyed by Spain in the New World.[27] In the eighteenth century such hopes faded. John Atkins reported that there were no mines near the coast. James Houstoun was equally pessimistic of European ability ever to penetrate the interior to discover the mines. And, fifty years later, the Abbé Raynal, referring to English and French projects to exploit the legendary gold mines of Bambuk, concluded that "far from having succeeded in their attempts at becoming masters of this country, they have not yet ascertained its existence."[28]

It was another Frenchman, the Sieur Compagnon, who had provided an account of the mines of Bambuk in the early eighteenth century.[29] But whether the mines were believed to exist or not made little difference to the Negro image. Those who came to doubt their existence saw themselves denied great potential wealth through natives too lazy to develop mines.[30] On the other hand, Compagnon and many others described hopelessly inept mining techniques. Unable to build ladders or pit-props, the Negroes merely scratched at the surface. At the most their mines were sunk to six or seven feet before they moved on, often abandoning a seam at its richest point. According to Labat, they had never even reached the main vein in any of their mines.[31]

In the coastal areas the methods of acquiring gold prompted even more scorn, although this often demonstrated not unusual European double standards. The Negroes were too lazy to dig mines and yet their methods of panning gold in the rivers were shown to be incredibly laborious. They displayed fiendish cunning in the way they extracted this gold, and in the way they could cheat Europeans with cheap alloys. And yet they were also alleged to be so stupid that they wasted enough gold by careless washing to yield a fortune to a European.[32]

Because it emphasised Negro involvement in the slave trade, a considerable amount of available contrary evidence about Negro skills was ignored by abolitionists. Barbot, for instance, had recognised the illiteracy of the merchants of Whidah but maintained that they were expert at account-keeping by memory, and able to perform commercial calculations as speedily as Europeans could with pen and ink. While Anthony Benezet had clearly read Barbot and made much of the reported physical beauties of Whidah, he did not reproduce these references to commercial ability. His argument was that Europeans should leave Africa alone or, instead of inducing corruption through the slave trade, they should "communicate to the ignorant Africans that superior knowledge which providence had favoured them with . . ."[33]

Although David Hume's claim that there were no arts and sciences among Negroes was widely corroborated, attention was not concentrated exclusively on these deficiencies. Despite the many broad generalisations about Negro ignorance, there was considerable published evidence to discredit Hume's references to a lack of "ingenious manufactures." This was especially true at the time he wrote in the 1750's when there was comparatively little interest in commercial schemes which were to lead men to judge Negro crafts primarily by European standards of productivity.

Ethnocentrism was invariably a factor but, where European pecuniary interests were not directly involved, a generally optimistic view of Negro craftsmanship prevailed. Both travellers and geographical editors offered numerous examples of mediocrity. Barbot described the clumsy workmanship of carpenters, weavers, and leatherworkers in Benin and concluded that "a boy who has serv'd a few months apprenticeship in *Europe,* would out-do them". Fenning and Collyer depicted comprehensive incompetence in the Congo. The region's vaunted iron-work (with the tradition of the inventor of iron as the founder of a royal dynasty) was primitive: weaving and pottery were rudimentary; and the houses were "no better than round huts." But far outnumbering such passages were admiring references to the skills of Negro craftsmen.[34]

Praise might sometimes be tempered by references to inferior tools, or by implications that laziness restricted output. But even in these cases there was general agreement that the craftsmen showed skills comparable to those of Europeans. This was true of the "great deal of art" of leatherworkers described by Jobson; and even more so of Senegalese potters praised by Barbot, who produced cooking utensils less liable to crack or break than those made in Europe.[35]

Although in the early seventeenth century Jobson had praised

Negro iron-workers, the *Universal Modern History* was convinced that their achievements were the result of European training. Even so, it departed from its usual hostility by declaring that the Gold Coast had "a great number of neat artisans, who work metals in a manner little inferior to the best *European* mechanics." John Atkins implied a similar point with rather different emphasis. The Negro goldsmith, who had "arrived to a good Skill in making Spoons, Buckles, Buttons", had done so "with very little instruction . . ." Bosman and Barbot even went so far as to doubt whether Europeans could equal these Gold Coast craftsmen, who specialised in decorative gold and silver hat-bands and a large range of metal utensils, including files "at least as well temper'd as we can make them in *Europe*."

Barbot condemned the blacksmiths of Senegal as lazy and inefficient.[36] But in contrast to the Gold Coast artisans, who worked their minor wonders with "sorry tools", the Senegalese had an "ingenious bellows." Thomas Salmon presented a similar picture of inefficiency and ingenuity. The natives had been taught by Europeans to use a hammer instead of a heavy stone in their forges and yet their bellows, which had three pipes and fanned a fire very quickly, was "said to be an invention of the Natives."[37]

Praise for Negro pottery, metalwork, and the like could be whole-hearted because' these crafts remained peripheral to European activities in West Africa. The same was not true of textiles. From an early date there was general agreement that Negro weavers produced good cloth. In the seventeenth century Ogilby referred to the fabrics produced in Timbuktu and Richard Blome to the "Cloths, Velvets, Damasks, Brocats etc" made under Portuguese guidance in the Congo. By the eighteenth century other areas were, according to Thomas Phillips and the Astley *Collection,* finding buyers in Europe and the New World. Late in the century Archibald Dalzel referred to the high prices Europeans on the West African coast were prepared to pay for "very pretty and durable cloths of cotton."[38]

Failure to expand production for a European market led to more hostility than in discussions of other native crafts. A minor incident reported in the early eighteenth century by James Houstoun foreshadowed later attitudes to textile production, even though it concerned a different kind of weaving. The Royal African Company's chief agent in Sierra Leone had organised a group of women slaves into making mats "to shew the Ingenuity of the Natives." Their efforts led to demands from the Company in England for fifty thousand such mats. "Whereas, to my certain Knowledge," said Houston, "it was with greatest difficulty he cou'd get so much Rattane, and as many hands to manage those few he sent for a sample".[39]

In mid-eighteenth century the *Universal Modern History* praised the visual qualities of Negro cloths and mats "curious enough to be sent into *Arabia, Persia,* and *India*." But because Negro weavers used a primitive loom without a shuttle they produced less in a month than an English weaver in a day. They had stubbornly ignored European encouragement "to fall into a more expeditious method by a proper improvement of their looms." Overall, they were to be despised for their "rude and tedious stupidity."[40]

European economic aspirations were eventually to stress agricultural schemes for West Africa. But long before the controversies surrounding such schemes emerged at the turn of the century the impression of agricultural incompetence had been established. Richard Jobson's report of a "most idle life, except two months of the year in their Seed-time and harvest" was echoed and confirmed by other seventeenth century works.[41] Francis Moore, a century later, referred to lazy natives who provided only for present needs in their agriculture. Although views varied as to how far the environment favoured the improvident, most agreed with Moore that Negroes would risk near-starvation rather than improve their methods and planning.[42] Jobson had shown some insight into the difficulty of year-long agricultural work with primitive implements. The Negroes had the advantage of predictable seasons but these were violent and made cultivation difficult. Since there was no rain for nine months in the Gambia region, the natives were compelled to work hard in the short period when the ground was soft enough to be dug and sown.[43] Most subsequent writers, however, merely remarked on the brief period of activity, without Jobson's emphasis on either the industry displayed in that period or the practical difficulties of labour at other times.

Natives who had failed to improve their methods after contact with Europeans were particularly condemned. Adanson offered details of the collapse of a potato-planting project in the Magdalen Islands to prove that Negroes "are negligent and idle to excess . . ." A French slave trade official had had potatoes planted "to engage the neighbouring Negroes . . . to continue and improve the culture of them . . ." But the natives merely removed the crop "without minding to plant the offsets again . . ." The *Universal Modern History* told of the "shameful indolence" of the natives of the Congo in failing to exploit the full agricultural potential of their lands, despite long contact with the Portuguese.

They had scorned Portuguese advice and revealed their stupidity by failing to domesticate animals, and by hunting and shooting instead of tilling the fields.[44]

While eighteenth century medical ignorance prevented proper appreciation of the difficulties of animal husbandry in many areas of Africa, ethnocentric bias was responsible for an attitude which regarded hunting as a frivolous sport. Part of the same attitude was the wide condemnation of the most obvious feature of Negro agriculture, its dependence on women. Many writers, discussing many areas, made the same point that women did all the work while the men indulged in idle pleasures.[45] This was, no doubt, a partially accurate reflection of the role of women in most Negro societies, just as there was substance in the portrayal of male enthusiasm for palm-wine and tobacco.[46] But the generalisation failed to take account of a division of labour which assigned to the men equally crucial roles in the family and community. Information about the importance of specifically male roles was available in the many accounts mentioning endemic warfare and in descriptions of the fishermen, boatmen, and tradesmen of the Gold Coast.[47] But such information was rarely separate from an ethnocentric moralising about the agricultural system.

As with many aspects of Negro society, the image of culpable agricultural incompetence was sustained more by secondary works than by reporters. Buried in Bosman's and Barbot's works was a good deal of information which might have been used to counter their own and others' generalisations about indolence. Barbot recognised that the indifferent husbandry among many groups would be widely attributed to their "slothful temper" but argued that

> it may as well be ascribed to the frequent wars among them. Whatsoever the reason may be, they are very often in want of corn, and sometimes come almost to a famine; which may proceed from other causes, since we see the same happens in the most fruitful countries of Europe, where people might perish, if not supplied from other places.

Bosman made the same point with less emphasis; and indirectly confirmed it by his account of how more stable areas of the Gold Coast, such as Axim and Acron, were able to export surpluses to their neighbours, because they were rarely at war.[48]

But such information was offered piecemeal, not as part of any attempt to correct a long established stereotype. It needed a dedicated antislavery writer like Benezet to find a few favourable passages about Negro agriculture amid the mass of hostile description.[49] Such passages could be conveniently ignored by other secondary writers, whether racialists like Long, or merely uncritical purveyors of the stereotype, like Charles Middleton or the editors of the *Universal Modern History*. The latter work was so committed to the proposition of Negro cultural inferiority that it put the worst construction on even potentially praiseworthy traits. Quoting Jobson's view that Europeans in tropical Africa would be healthier if they adopted the more frugal diet of Negroes, it insisted that native temperance "is not so much the result of virtue as laziness, which prevents their going in search of game . . ."[50] In short Negroes who frittered away their energies on the pleasures of hunting were matched in unworthiness by those who failed to hunt at all.

A different sort of superficiality operated in the commonest surveys of agricultural efficiency. No attention was paid to variations in climate or soil in those works which purported to show regional differences. Although particular writers might deal with individual areas with some care, works which surveyed the Atlantic seaboard as a whole relied on a series of regional stereotypes, which reflected the priorities of slave purchasers in the New World. In many works by West Indians, pamphlets by the English organisers of the slave trade and geographical collections, Negroes were said to vary in worthiness—which meant in effect usefulness—according to area of origin. Despite minor variations, a consistent scale emerged in which the Negroes of the Gold Coast were at the top, followed by those of Whidah and Senegal, with those from the Congo, and especially Angola, universally deemed the "worst" of all. Position on the scale depended on the ability to sustain plantation labour and in each case this ability was explained in terms of native agriculture. The Gold Coast natives were "best" because accustomed to hard work, the Angolans a "proverb for worthlessness" because in the New World they were liable to die when faced with wholly unfamiliar agrarian work.[51]

Despite references to these varying aptitudes, Negro agriculture was nearly always seen as primitive in technique and slovenly in execution. The objective Jobson's emphasis on the crudity of implements was confirmed by Morgan Godwyn in the 1680's. J. Hillier, resident on the Gold Coast in the late seventeenth century, explained that even the one tenth of available land under cultivation was quickly overgrown because the Negroes did not uproot but merely cut or burnt off the tops of shrubs. In the mid-eighteenth century the Astley *Collection*, in the process of praising the agriculture of the Cape Verde region, confirmed the worst generalisations of its contemporaries. Here, it reported, agriculture was in a flourishing state because the natives were free from laziness, "the epidemical Vice of the Negroes."[52]

A more significant exception to prove the same general rule was provided by the Fulani. To an extent these people—nomadic pastoralists in some areas, village dwellers in others—were less of an ethnological mystery in the eighteenth century than they are to modern scholars. Their different bone-structure and usually lighter complexions mark them out as distinct from other West Africans, yet their language is recognised as Negro, belonging to the "West Atlantic" group. The eighteenth century, innocent of such linguistic precision, widely considered them as a separate people, or perhaps a mixture produced by "alliances with the Moors." Eighteenth century accounts of their industrious habits, and of the enlightened equity of their government in areas where they were autonomous, leaned heavily on Francis Moore's *Travels*. But their pastoralism—unique in West Africa—had been noted since at least the early seventeenth century.[53]

Francis Moore also wrote favourably of the Fulani's most significant neighbours, the Mandingoes. Visiting their towns, he invariably met with a "most cordial" reception. But his conclusion that they were "more sociable, rational, and humane, than they had been represented by other travellers" indicated the ubiquity of less admiring reports. Labat had depicted them as lazy and ignorant. Necessity obliged them to cultivate some crops, "but this labour does not last above two months in the year; the other months are spent in idleness and sloth all the day, and at night in dancing under the shade." According to the *Universal Modern History,* which quoted Labat, this neglect of agriculture in favour of frivolous music was common among other Negro groups. Those in the Congo neglected any form of labour in favour of "dancing" and "leaping".[54]

Music and dancing were seen as more than distractions from agriculture by many writers. But although the importance which Negroes themselves attached to music was widely recognised, very few regarded their "addiction" with much favour. Because this was one of the few aspects of their culture which Negroes were able to transport into slavery, their enthusiasm was as well documented in works on the New World as in those on Africa. Jobson's early seventeenth century report from the Gambia that there was "no people on the earth more naturally affected to the sound of music than these people" was echoed by Raynal in the 1770's in his work on the West Indies:

Their organs are extremely sensible of the powers of music. Their ear is so true, that in their dances, the time of a song makes them spring up an hundred at once, striking the earth at the same instant . . . Music animates their courage and rouses them from their indolence . . .

Yet such reports could, at the extreme, make Negroes seem barely rational creatures. A mid-eighteenth century "Treatise on Dancing" confirmed that the "spirit" of dancing "prevails no where so much as in Africa." Gold Coast Negroes were "so passionately fond of it" that, at the first hint of a musical note, they were gripped with the irresistible urge to abandon every other activity:

> There are even well-attested stories of some Negroes flinging themselves at the feet of an European playing on a fiddle, entreating him to desist, unless he had a mind to tire them to death; it being impossible for them to cease dancing whilst he continued playing.[55]

Few commentators were free from ethnocentric bias as they discussed either the social role or the intrinsic qualities of Negro music. The Astley *Collection,* relying mainly on Barbot, revealed this ethnocentrism in contrary ways, as it discussed the Cape Monte region. On the one hand, it referred to a "School or College", in which Negro dancers were trained to sing "what they call the Belli Dong, the Praises of the Belli." On the other, it saw the result of this formalized education as "no other but a confused Repetition of leud, filthy Expressions, accompanied with immodest Gestures and Motions of the Body . . ." Michel Adanson was more appreciative of the physical prowess and technical ingenuity of Negro dancing, while sharing the same sentiments about its innate depravity.[56]

*   *   *

Although David Hume's views were scarcely consistent with the image of Negro culture in numerous seventeenth and eighteenth century works, it remains necessary to consider his hypothesis more specifically. James Walvin has claimed that from the 1760's pro-slavery propagandists depicted Negroes as an inferior species and that their arguments were given added weight by Hume's comments on African cultural sterility. Hume's views, contends Walvin, "achieved wide publicity", even though he chose to ignore contradictory evidence.[57]

The only part of this argument with which one can agree is the last. The contradictory evidence ignored by Hume included the many descriptions of "ingenious manufactures" published before his own work in 1753. Among these were such important observations as those by Bosman, Barbot, Phillips, Smith and Atkins, as well as all the relevant material in the huge Astley *Collection*. Some writers in this early period had referred quite explicitly to the Negro potential for education. Adanson found them remarkably knowledgeable about the stars for "such a rude and illiterate people." There was no question that, if they were provided with instruments and appropriate instruction, they would become excellent astronomers. Atkins was equally convinced of a more general potential. With more knowledge and instruction they could succeed in any field of human endeavour.[58]

As important as these predictions were reports of actual progress, albeit usually in modest attainments. It was commonly said that the Negroes of the Gold Coast were among the most ingenious and advanced of any; and in most works it was seen as no coincidence that this was also the area of most concentrated European influence. This theme, already present in Edmund Bohun's late seventeenth century geography, ran through the influential account of Barbot and that of Atkins, who reported that these people "from a long Acquaintance with *Europeans,* are much the best *Negroes* of the whole Continent." Similar claims about the Congo and Angola were occasionally advanced by travellers and given wider currency in secondary works, while visitors to the Gambia noted a fairly widespread native understanding of the principal European languages, a facility which contrasted with continuing European bewilderment at native dialects and which qualified the common slurs about linguistic inferiority. As a result of European contact the whole coastal area of West Africa was seen to stand out against a benighted interior. Atkins evolved an almost mathematical formula for measuring the incompetence of Negroes, as he labelled a consignment of slaves "stupid as is their Distance from the Converse of the Coast-Negroes . . ."[59]

The belief that Negroes were capable of improvement from the savage state was, of course, common to both pro- and anti-slave trade propaganda. From the 1730s anti-slavery writers made the point that only education separated the Negro from the European intellect.[60] The publication of Hume's hypothesis did not coincide with any new racist trend in pro-slavery writing. Indeed, far from adding strength to the pro-slavery case, Hume's views were ignored by propagandists for almost twenty years, as they continued to argue that the slave trade was a means of giving Negroes opportunities denied them in Africa by bloody despots. If Hume's views achieved the wide publicity claimed by Dr Walvin in these two decades after publication, this was solely through an extensive rebuttal by the Scottish philosopher, James Beattie, in his *Essay on Truth*.

The absence of sciences, argued Beattie, did not prove Negroes incapable of understanding them; and Europeans had scarcely sufficient experience of Negroes to pronounce on their collective potential. Here Beattie contrived to turn the most damaging Negro defect into an advantage: "These people write no histories; and all the reports of the travellers, that ever visited them, will not amount to anything like a proof of what is here affirmed." This lack of writing admittedly meant that Negroes had no sciences but they were known to have "many ingenious manufactures, and arts among them . . ." Despite the brutalizing effects of their servile status, Negroes "dispersed all over Europe, have often discovered symptoms of ingenuity . . ." They became craftsmen, musicians, and indeed anything their masters took the trouble to teach them. It was unreasonable to expect a Negro, constricted by slavery and a foreign language, to go beyond this and "so distinguish himself among Europeans, as to be talked of for a man of genius . . ."

Beattie concluded by minimizing the significance of the cultural inferiority of Africa and by attacking the ethnocentrism of his contemporaries. The invention of those arts and sciences which alone marked the superiority of European culture was not attributable to the higher capacity of a whole race. Inventions which were not sheer accidents, like gunpowder or the compass, were produced by a few individuals only. But other writers, he alleged, far from recognising these truths, adopted the principle that "every practice and sentiment is barbarous, which is not according to the uses of modern Europe . . ."[61]

While Hume's views were being attacked by Beattie and ignored by the defenders of slavery, the evidence for Negro potential was steadily accumulating in works on Africa. The 1750s and 1760s saw the publication of such important large-scale secondary works as Fenning and Collyer's *New System of Geography,* the *Universal Modern History,* and Gordon's *Geography Anatomized.* If these works varied in their attitudes to African achievement, they all gave publicity to old arguments about Negro ability. Gordon described Negroes as "a lively ingenious People, though unacquainted with arts and sciences." Even the most hostile, the *Universal Modern History,* concluded a long introductory indictment of Negro life with the rather lame qualification that these faults were true only of the interior, "those who live on the coasts and maritime parts, having been long since allured to a more active and laborious life, as well as civilized in their manners . . .''[62]

These two decades also saw the crystallization of hitherto vague economic aspirations into schemes which assumed that Negroes were capable of improvement. The English acquisition of French bases in Senegal was seen by some as an opportunity for developing gold mines and rescuing the natives from the twin evils of the slave trade and their own indolence. In 1759 John Lindsay put forward a detailed proposal to fulfil an English aspiration dating back to Elizabethan times. By a process of exploration and the establishment of small staging posts progressively further into the interior it should be possible eventually to divert some of the fabled gold of Timbuktu to the coast. This particular aim was to take advantage of existing mines, but an important subsidiary consideration was the development of new mines in intermediate areas much nearer the coast. Lindsay was convinced that if skilled men were sent to instruct the natives a lucrative industry could be established. And he emphasized that its potential lay not only in rich mineral deposits but in the Negro population, who had ''the ingenuity to do anything.''[63] Similarly a *Plan for Improving Trade at Senegal,* published in 1763, was predicated on the assumption that only social conditions made Negroes seem inferior.[64]

The gold potential referred to by Lindsay was also noted by Malachy Postlethwayt.[65] He looked for the development of much more than gold. Africa, with its enormous population, was potentially the greatest market in the world and a vast untapped source of labour. This labour, combined with the notable fertility of many areas, could make it an important producer of crops like coffee, tea, and spices. In the traditional home of many such crops, the East Indies, the Dutch had managed to civilize the natives sufficiently to make them valuable consumers of European products, as well as plantation workers. Negro potential was no less. The Portuguese had already shown the way by teaching Negroes to cultivate such fruits as figs, grapes, oranges, and lemons, which were unknown in other African areas. Postlethwayt had no truck with pessimistic theories of racial incapacity. Many Negroes were presently ''but a small remove above the brute creation.'' But African barbarism should be seen in the perspective of English and European history. By contact with other nations they could be raised to civilization as surely as the ancient inhabitants of England had been.[66]

It was thus against the background of numerous assertions of Negro potential that the West Indian racists finally made use of Hume's hypothesis. For them he was a usefully distinguished authority to be cited in support of the major theme of racial gradation. Whether his distinction was sufficient to popularise that theme is part of the story of the development of racial attitudes in the controversial atmosphere of the 1780s and 1790s—a story to be considered in the last two chapters of this book after further consideration of the images of West African life current in the mid-eighteenth century.

CHAPTER SEVEN

THE SINISTER SIDE OF
WEST AFRICAN LIFE

West African culture had more sinister connotations than the lethargic inefficiency which could be ridiculed as it was condemned. Human sacrifice, cannibalism, idolatry, witchcraft, and sexual debauchery would have figured prominently in most contemporary readers' mental picture of African barbarism. The slave traders reported much that balanced or contradicted these stereotypes. On some issues, notably sexual *mores,* this more favourable information was given considerable prominence in the descriptive and synthesizing literature. But on many others it required careful reading to see the redeeming details of Negro life amidst writing which consolidated the stereotypes.

Early eyewitness reports were published alongside ancient myths of a barely human Africa. Even when the record of contact was sufficient to obliterate these relics of an ignorant and credulous past, they were replaced by new descriptions of barbaric extremes. Reporters often obscured detailed information with vivid contrary generalizations. Propagandists invented new myths. And editors, through a desire to educate or entertain, accentuated these distortions with selective quotation or heavy-handed philosophy about the human condition. It is unlikely that many readers took the pains to mine the factual detail of African social *mores* from the mountain of commentary.

On the other hand, the Negro image was little different from that of the rest of the uncivilized world. It was on vague charges of "moral depravity" that the West Indian racists rested much of their case. Yet although the depravity of African religion and social customs was generally accepted, there were sound practical reasons, in addition to the intellectual imperatives discussed earlier, for regarding this depravity as an inevitable ingredient of savagery or barbarism. Significantly the racist case rested on minor or erroneous examples of Negro behaviour because no contemporary could ignore the fact that the most repellent activities—human sacrifice and cannibalism—were widely documented in numerous other non-European societies. At the same time the contemporary evidence which supported a stereotype of sexual depravity also made it clear that Negro sexuality was partly a function of European influence in Africa and domination in the New World.

Apart from the racists, few people advanced explanatory theories about Negro depravity. A few saw it in terms of African paganism, stressing blindness to natural reason, ignorance of Christianity, or the manipulations of native sorcerers. But for most paganism was merely one more facet of African barbarism rather than its underlying cause.

*   *   *

No aspect of the unfavourable Negro image had wider or deeper roots than the allegations of insatiable sexual appetite. The portrayal of lecherous Negroes in Elizabethan drama was a modern manifestation of a stereotype dating back to Classical works on Africa. Iulius Solinus Polyhistor's description of the Garamantes, who held their women in common, survived through the Middle Ages into the sixteenth century account of Robert Gainsh. Even in the second half of the seventeenth century the old label persisted. *The Golden Coast* (1665) included a verbatim transcription of Gainsh's account; and, while most other editions of the period apparently recognized that the Garamantes belonged to Roman times, they did not hesitate to associate Negroes with similar sexual anarchy. Richard Blome made a specific comparison with the Garamantes. Samuel Clarke, Pierre Duval, and Nicholas de Fer simply described Negroes living without wives or even names, and choosing as their children those with most resemblance to themselves.[1]

Many of the fuller, first-hand accounts of the early eighteenth century, which finally obliterated the old portrait, provided a picture of Negro marriage which was only slightly preferable. Polygamy was an almost insuperable obstacle for Capuchin missionaries in Portuguese Angola and Congo, whose accounts were included in the Churchill *Collection* of 1704. Armed with exceptionally broad powers of dispensation, they nevertheless found themselves frustrated by native refusals to be monogamous. Baptisms flowed in the usual Catholic profusion but marriage vows were rarely taken and speedily broken.[2]

If few other writers were actively involved in evangelism, it was still possible for them to condemn polygamy as the negation of Christian morality, or even, though wrongly, as solely the result of the pernicious influence of Islam.[3] Most, however, registered their disapproval by reporting its extravagant extremes. Seventeenth century reports that the King of Benin had hundreds of wives[4] were confirmed in worse detail in the eighteenth century. The King, it was said, inherited the wives of his subjects, often condemning them to public prostitution. Whidah, so favourably regarded in many ways, was distinguished by a king who had anything from one thousand to three thousand wives, according to the individual reporter, or perhaps the time of reporting. Bosman and Phillips reported that in slack periods of trade this king was liable to furnish a slave cargo among his own wives. His desire for fresh young women also caused a rapid turnover, so that, according to Bosman, the fate worse than death for a Whidah maiden was a royal marriage. Other reported extremes were child marriages in Ardra and incestuous ones in a number of widely scattered areas. Although these were scarcely typical of most societies, some secondary works, like the *Universal Modern History* and Burton's *English Acquisitions in Guinea,* contrived to suggest that such extremes were the inevitable ingredients of a depraved system.[5]

Other aspects of marriage were strongly disapproved. The system was seen as a means of ensuring the maximum idleness for men, with the status of women often compared to slavery.[6] And many discussions of marriage did little to correct earlier allegations of unbridled sexuality. The "oddly adjusted" system of inheritance through the children of a sister, which operated in a number of areas, was interpreted as suspicion about the wife's fidelity,[7] rather than as the function of more complex spiritual beliefs which modern authorities recognize.[8] While polygamy was seen, at best, as an inadequate system of control, other institutions and customs were condemned for actively facilitating sexual depravity. Children were initiated early and promiscuity was the norm among the unmarried.[9] For the men, indeed, there was organized public prostitution in Gold Coast and Slave Coast societies. Bosman and Barbot followed Ogilby in giving lengthy descriptions of the prostitutes' initiation and misery until their lives were cut short by venereal disease.[10]

It was on such aspects of Negro marriage and extra-marital sexual activity that Edward Long grounded a central part of his racialist case. The fact that Negroes were "libidinous and shameless as monkeys, or baboons" had given "probability" to the charge that Negro women had sexual intercourse with apes.[11] Yet although Long could find much evidence to support his charges of sexual depravity, it was only by a process of selection which perverted the major themes of reporters.

In making the most of the reports of polygamy, Long cited Bosman's account of a father with two hundred children at Whidah. Such extravagance, he claimed, contributed to the populousness of Africa which was a major reason for the slave trade. Yet both Bosman and Barbot, in describing the extremes of polygamy, were careful to show that they were indeed exceptional. The normal number of wives in most areas was fewer than ten. They saw the slave trade, which exported six times as many men as women, as an exacerbation rather than a result of polygamy, which was a means of catering for the vast superfluity of females. And they presented evidence that polygamy was an institution involving a wider range of functions than systematic lechery. On the Gold Coast there was a well-organized hierarchy of wives, headed by two with clearly-defined functions. The first wife, the 'mulier Grande', was in charge of the house and family; the second, or 'Bossum' wife was "consecrated to their deity", and in something of a privileged position over the rest, on whom devolved the routine, mainly agricultural tasks necessary for the support of the whole family.[12] Richard Jobson, whose work Long had certainly read, showed that similar systems worked efficiently in a different area: the women in the Gambia region were "excellent housewives" and there was little quarrelling among them. And over a long period a large number of reports had shown implicitly—though the specific conclusion was rarely drawn—that marriage was buttressed by strict sanctions against adultery. Although men were able to divorce their wives fairly easily, both men and women who broke the marriage contract were liable to punishments ranging from heavy fines to death or transportation as slaves.[13]

A more explicit obstacle to the conclusions drawn by Long was provided by William Smith's New Voyage to Guinea. In a lengthy passage on Negro marriage and sexual customs—purportedly the views of Charles Wheeler, ten years a Gold Coast factor of the Royal African Company—this work argued that European prejudice was the result of "a different Education." Both polygamy and public prostitution were effective checks on the sexual vices common in Europe: rape, incest, sodomy, and bestiality were unheard of among Gold Coast Negroes. Public prostitution—using segregated groups of female slaves—not only provided young men with sexual outlets but was less sordid than the soliciting common in Europe. Polygamy provided the opportunity for sensible taboos against intercourse with menstruous, pregnant, or nursing women.[14]

The major barrier to acceptance of Long's conclusions, however, lay not in this unusually dispassionate account but in the way the eighteenth century image of Negro sexuality was bound up with the European presence in West Africa. Any one who read the major accounts of the period could have been in no doubt that they were describing a process of social disintegration rather than pristine native customs. Two significant indications of this were the claims of the majority of writers that Negro women were more lascivious than the men, and that adultery was more severely punished in the interior than on the coast. Contemporaries sometimes explained the first factor in terms of female frustration arising out of the numerical imbalance of the sexes. The varying sanctions against adultery were seen sometimes as the result of a European restraining influence on coastal cruelty, sometimes as a native response to the lure of profits in the interior regions which were the slave trade's main catchment areas. There was probably some truth in these explanations. But there was ample evidence that the common factor in both allegations was the promiscuity of Europeans themselves. Scarcely any visited the interior and their reports of Negro immorality rested on observation of a coastal society in which indigenous customs had been modified by a long period of interracial contact.

Evidence for the natural "hotness" of Negro women rested almost entirely on the experiences of whites themselves. In the 1620s Richard Jobson reported that the natives were polygamous but that there was no "dalliance": "hardly any Englishman can say, he ever saw the Blackman kiss a woman." By the end of the seventeenth century the passion of Negro women for white men was accepted as commonplace in most secondary works. The Negro girls made it their "whole Business" to attract whites; were apt to fall "desperately in love with them"; and boasted of their "gallantries" with them.[15]

The Reverend John Lindsay attempted to modify this image. He maintained that native morality, including female chastity, remained intact in Senegal. Only a special class of prostitutes catered for Europeans. Englishmen attempting to force their attentions on other women were rebuffed with disdain and few could justly boast of having obtained "illicit favours." But the weight of contemporary opinion was strongly against Lindsay's claim. Charles Wheeler implied that on the Gold Coast interracial sexual liaisons may have been an extension of native custom.

Native grandees kept concubines as well as wives and customarily lent one of these to visiting grandees. Such offers were frequently made to Wheeler himself, "for it is a Compliment that is always paid an *European*." Similar offers in other areas were perhaps attributable to similar customs. But in the eighteenth century most reports suggested more mercenary arrangements. Oliver Goldsmith could draw on numerous reports for his generalization that among some Negro groups "nothing is desired so ardently as to prostitute their wives, or daughters, to strangers, for the most trifling advantages . . ."[16]

Barbot reported that Senegalese men would regularly prostitute their wives to visiting Europeans. The Astley *Collection* was able to cite other authorities for this depravity and for the prevalence of single girls soliciting Europeans in the streets, also in Senegal. But Barbot, Astley and others, such as Buffon, made it clear that this promiscuity had resulted from the European presence. Even now men were jealous of their wives, except in the economic transactions with Europeans. Adultery remained a serious offence when Europeans were not involved. Other reporters, such as William Smith and Francis Moore, showed the same social disintegration in other areas.[17]

Allegations about Negro prostitution were less common on the Gold Coast simply because European contact was much more intensive. Large numbers of mulattoes, generally deemed more vicious than Negroes, attested to the length of contact. But the more permanent nature of settlement meant that for most Europeans prostitution in the conventional sense was unnecessary, as native mistresses could easily be acquired. Bosman showed that, apart from gratifying sexual needs, such liaisons were tactically valuable for Europeans. In his period an English mulatto, Edward Barter, dominated trading activities in the Cape Coast Castle region. With eight Negro wives, and as many mistresses, he had a powerful network of contacts with the native population and wielded more power than the three resident English agents together. These men, however, were scarcely in a position to criticise his methods, as two of them had about six wives each.[18]

Some forty years later John Atkins provided a vivid picture of the way such marriages had produced an interracial society which blended and distorted customs of both Europe and Africa. A prominent official of the Royal African Company had a mulatto wife and four children with "fair, flaxen hair and complexion." The marriage was useful to him because of his wife's influential Negro relatives. But, apart from this, he was devoted to her. She attended chapel with him and he for his part showed some sympathy for "Negrish Customs", wearing precautionary fetishes on wrists and neck during such crises as the illnesses of his children. The success and apparent permanence of this particular union was probably exceptional. While this official was anxious to take his wife back to England with him, the usual custom was to discard such women at the end of a period of coastal residence and, indeed, to change them quite frequently at other times. As Thomas Phillips explained, "this is a pleasant way of marrying, for they can turn them off and take others at pleasure, which makes them very careful to humour their husbands in washing their linen, cleaning their chambers, &c. and the charge of keeping them is little or nothing."[19]

The corrupting influence of Europeans, implicit in so many accounts was explicitly stressed in the period before Edward Long published his theories. Barbot, in particular, produced a revealing insight into the social and psychological basis of anti-Negro assertions. The "horrid pictures of the manners and vices of the *Blacks*" were drawn by men driven from their own countries by necessitous or even desperate circumstances. Their condemnation of the natives was rationalization for the debauchery of their own lives. He found it almost incredible how many of the English on the Gold Coast shortened their lives by "lewdness with women, and excess of drinking . . ." Negro debauchery did exist but it was the result of European behaviour which "tended to harden them in their wickedness rather than turn them from it." He made it clear that the particularly sexual manifestations of this "wickedness" were a European innovation. The women of the coast were "more lascivious" than those of the interior because they were supplying European demand. Those kept as mistresses went out of their way to teach younger girls how to gratify the white man with sexual favours. Europeans, indeed, were "the occasion of that lewdness they seem to find fault with."[20]

Barbot's analysis was by no means as unusual as David Davis suggests in his contention that Negro sexual *mores* were a major obstacle to acceptance of the Negro as an equal being. If Philip Quaque's complaints of European exploitation of Negro women were published in the relatively specialized *Abstract of Proceedings of the S.P.G.*, they were merely echoes of similar accounts by such popular authors as Thomas Phillips and John Atkins. The latter described white traders in Sierra Leone, whose female servants were "obedient to any Prostitutions their masters command". He also attributed the heavy mortality on a particular slave trading voyage to the conduct of the crew "being ungovernable in their Actions and Appetites, pilfering from the

Negroes and debauching their Wives . . ." It was on the strength of such reports that the geographical editor, Thomas Salmon, echoed Barbot in condemning nominally Christian white traders who were as "abandoned Libertines as the Pagans" and guilty of "vicious Habits we censure them for."[21]

Criticisms of white responsibility for Negro sexual depravity were no less common in accounts of the New World situation, although here too it was possible for the superficial or biased reporter to ignore the social factors which governed the sex lives of the slaves. From as early as 1730 pro-slavery writers equated polygamy with sexual licence and presented it as justification of the failure to baptize significant numbers of West Indian slaves. They also made much of the conspicuous failure of Negroes to breed in slavery. While anti-slavery writers attributed this infertility usually to the rigours of slavery, the West Indians explained it in terms of promiscuity. Negro girls were said to employ a variety of methods of abortion in order to remain in continuous business as prostitutes. Long, who advanced this explanation, also referred with the same intention and effect to an almost universal "venereal taint" among Negroes.[22]

Yet despite such beliefs, the most obvious evidence of Negro sexuality in the New World was of interracial liaisons which could hardly be explained solely in terms of Negro depravity. Even Long himself, notwithstanding the importance he had laid on an allegedly racial trait, argued at length that in the West Indies Negro sexuality was bound up with white domination. In the course of a graphic warning that Jamaicans were in danger of becoming, like the Spanish American colonists, "a vicious, brutal, and degenerate breed of mongrels", the brunt of his attack fell on whites with "their infatuated attachments to black women . . ." Many of the women, despite lack of formal education, showed behaviour in public that was "remarkably decent." But the white men "of every rank, quality, and degree" lived quite openly with coloured mistresses. Instead of living in "pure and lawful bliss", they condemned a large proportion of white women to spinsterhood, while they revelled in the "goatish embraces" of their mistresses.[23]

In Edward Long's racialist system Negro sexuality had a double role. Not only was it in itself a brutish trait but it was also part of a wider behavioural pattern which proved that Negroes had no "plan or system of morality" and hence were incapable of progress to civility: "They have no moral sensations; no taste but for women; gormandizing, and drinking to excess . . ." This was a theme borrowed from Estwick, for whom innate moral depravity was the fundamental proof of the Negro's incapacity for civiliza-tion.[24] Once again the racialist case was implausible because it rested on selective use of contemporary reports of Negro society.

Several of Estwick's main illustrations were not in fact Negro customs. The cruelty to aged parents and the judicial system in which judges proceeded to club convicted criminals to death were Hottentot practices. They were scarcely valid evidence in an argument about Negroes and scarcely likely to be seen as such by the more careful readers of works on Africa. By the mid-eighteenth century distinctions between Hottentots and Negroes were stressed in every kind of travel literature.[25] Other aspects of his case were more consistent with certain reports about Negroes, though never with universally accepted traits. There was some evidence to support his claim that their "barbarity to their children debases their nature even below that of brutes", a claim which was borrowed verbatim by Long. John Hippisley had said that Negroes were loving towards their children in extreme infancy: "but once out of that helpless state, all tenderness and attachment are at an end." The Frenchman, Villault, reported that Negroes would let one another die "like Dogs, without Compassion or Relief, their Wives and Children being the first to forsake them . . ." And from the West Indies came similar reports. Negroes, wrote one pamphleteer in 1730, "hate one another, are void of the Seeds of Friendship . . ."[26] But it was significant that the racist case rested on such relatively minor aspects of Negro behaviour rather than on elements of African barbarism which betrayed extremes of sadism and emotional insensitivity. The more dramatic themes of cannibalism and human sacrifice were so widely documented that no one could claim they were uniquely racial tendencies.

Indeed one of the factors which encouraged belief in African cannibalism was its acknowledged prevalence in other parts of the world. In one eighteenth century example Negroes were themselves seen as the victims of cannibalism. A slave revolt in Guiana was suppressed by the employment of local Indians who, it was said, ate those they killed. Even Long himself concluded his arguments about Negro cannibalism with a footnote explaining that the existence of cannibals in New Zealand had been "un-questionably proved" by the discoveries of Banks and Solander. Human sacrifice, often associated with cannibalism in African reports, was also seen in terms of a world-wide savage depravity. Even William Snelgrave mentioned Mexican and other manifesta-tions before giving the most vivid of the African accounts until Archibald Dalzel's late eighteenth century work on Dahomey.[27]

If the ubiquity of these practices disarmed racialism, it did little to improve the image of Africa. Cannibalism, in particular, was so deplorable that no mitigating factors could be acknowledged comparable to the corrupting influence of Europeans, which modified the image of sexual depravity. Man-eating could not be excused by defenders of the Negro, only denied. John Atkins was one who attempted this with pertinacity and skill. But the weight of contemporary opinion was against him because of Africa's long association with legendary monsters, including Anthropophagi, and because the slave trade introduced new motives for emphasis on native cruelty.

By the seventeenth century only a handful of works on Africa used the legendary term 'Anthropophagi', although many assertions about "cruel man-eaters" and "wild and inhuman cannibals" in unvisited regions doubtless relied on uncritical use of the old authorities.[28] On the other hand, certain added details about African cannibalism both perpetuated and embellished the ancient accounts. The belief that in undefined areas African cannibals organized "shambles" of human flesh had a long antiquity. Several late seventeenth century works reiterated the charge without elaboration. And the *Thesaurus Geographicus* added a paraphrase of a passage in Ogilby's *Africa* that was at once gory and ludicrous:

> . . . they eat mans Flesh, and have publick Butcheries for it: The Father eats without any trouble or regret the flesh of his Son, and the Son of the Father, and so Brothers and Sisters eat one another, and as soon as their breath is out of their body they eat them . . .[29]

Some contemporary corroboration of the human shambles was provided by the seventeenth century Capuchin, Merolla, who referred to the "Pombo" or great market on the outskirts of São Salvador in Angola. Here the inhabitants had been accustomed to sell human flesh until the Portuguese had arrived and insisted that they would prefer live slaves. This was only an indirect report and in any case Merolla was an unreliable authority, plainly unable to forget legend. In the same work he referred to mermaids, unicorns and other monsters.[30] John Atkins required much more evidence to be convinced that the human shambles had ever existed. Probably, he thought, the origin of the legend had been the figurative use of the term "human flesh" as a synonym for live slaves. Alternatively the markets may have sold the carcases of apes, which were known to be eaten regularly in Africa and were often enjoyed by English sailors. Contemporary reports of European revulsion at the sight of skinned monkeys in Negro markets provided some indirect support for this latter conjecture.[31]

Yet despite this, and although Atkins was a popular authority, eighteenth century geographical surveys continued to describe the human shambles. The *Universal Modern History* referred to a system which made nonsense of the economics of the slave trade, inasmuch as "a dead slave shall sell for more at the public market than a live one." This description was used by Lord Monboddo, whose authority was in turn cited by Long.[32]

Another almost legendary element of African cannibalism, which continued into the eighteenth century with even greater force, was its identification with the Jagas. Often briefly mentioned in the old accounts as the organizers of the human shambles, the Jagas emerged in seventeenth and eighteenth century works as a great nation of "land-pirates", terrorising the more ordinarily savage inhabitants of the Congo and Angola. There was some substance to this shadowy horde. The Jagas were groups of mercenaries employed by the Portuguese from the late sixteenth century, as they expanded their area of settlement and influence in Angola. They may have been cannibals. But the picture which emerged owed little to any direct information. Edward Long described them as "savages barely human";

> . . . a barbarous race, hardened in idolatry, wallowers in human blood, cannibals, drunkards, practiced in lewdness, oppression, and fraud; proud and slothful, cursed with all the vices that can degrade human nature, possessing no one good quality, and in short more brutal and savage than the wild beasts of the forest.

Long's sources were secondary works which continued to paraphrase or embellish the sixteenth century account by Andrew Battell or the seventeenth century one by Ogilby without introducing any more modern corroboration. *The Universal Modern History,* in particular, in two sections of eight and twenty-nine pages, conveyed the impression that almost the whole of Africa south of the river Congo consisted of vast armies of wandering Jaga cannibals.[33]

In perpetuating these centuries-old accounts some writers may have been endeavouring to point up the civilizing influence of the European presence. This was a recurrent theme in the *Universal Modern History,* despite its hostility to the slave trade. But such motives were probably of secondary importance. Eighteenth century geographers, no less than their medieval and early modern counterparts, felt free—indeed almost under an obligation—to provide their readers with vivid entertainment where this did not clash directly with well reported facts. In 1768 the editors of the *Universal Magazine* introduced a series of essays on the Jagas with the following comment:

> Domestic Facts and Occurrences, as familiar, have not, most commonly, that Attraction for the Amusement of the Mind, as those that are foreign, because striking us with the Idea of some Singularity or Novelty; and this is the Reason, that we always take Pleasure in reviewing the Customs and Manners of other Nations, how barbarous soever.[34]

Such attitudes received some contemporary criticism, for example in a review of the Abbé Poyart's untranslated account of Loango and other areas adjacent to the Jagas' legendary haunts. According to the reviewer, the Abbé had shown that the worst aspects of Negro depravity were the result of European corruption or simply inventions by "mercenary writers, who disguise the truth, in order to please that numerous class of frivolous or libertine readers, who like to have their corrupt imaginations struck with descriptions of this nature . . ."[35] On the specific question of cannibalism Fenning and Collyer's *Geography,* in so many sections a plagiarized version of the *Universal Modern History,* was unusually critical. Reporters of cannibalism had "followed the method frequently observed in giving descriptions of countries they have never seen, by representing the natives as the most savage and barbarous, and particularly being fond of devouring all the white men whom they can get into their power." Repeatedly, it continued, the falsity of such allegations had been demonstrated by proper acquaintance: "the people of many countries who, when little known, were described as anthropophagi, or man-eaters, have been found to be friendly, benevolent and enemies to cruelty . . ."[36] Atkins reported the same process and concluded that the only Anthropophagi were mosquitoes and other voracious insects. He very much doubted whether there were cannibals anywhere in the world, "unless when provoked by Famine."

But Atkins also showed that the reports did not rest on invention alone. He saw fear and rationalization of cruelty and conquest as other significant factors. The experiences of sailors along the parts of the African coast without European forts had led to many such reports. Atkins himself was able to establish that the natives of Cape St. Mary, at the mouth of the Gambia, were not cannibals "as commonly reported among sailors; but a civilized People . . ." He explained similar accusations, levelled against people in the region of Cape Monte, as the result of a cumulative process of interracial mistrust. The natives were wary of European ships because of earlier kidnappings; if they did make contact, they tended to seek revenge for these injuries, "which has given rise to the Report of their being Savages and Cannibals."[37]

On the Ivory Coast the effects of similar unhappy encounters were reinforced by the appearance of the natives. Thomas Phillips was told by a fellow-sailor that these Negroes devoured prisoners of war, and their own relatives after death. Phillips was uncertain whether to believe this "but in truth their looks are very savage and voracious; and all their teeth, I observed, are pointed at the ends as sharp as bodkins, which looks very terrible." John Snoeck, who traded in the same area at much the same period, reacted in similar fashion. Trade was carried out at sea, the natives approaching in canoes and making off with speed, if their demands were not met or if the Dutch "speak warmly to them as to other *Negroes*." Snoeck had never seen "greater Savages". In particular their teeth, "with which they eat Human Flesh, when they can come at it, were as sharp as Awls; wherefore I should not advise any to set Foot on Land here, who is not fond of being buried in their Bellies."

William Smith was one who drew similar conclusions about these same Negroes before later writers, with greater acquaintance, denied the charges. By mid-eighteenth century the major geographical works numbered them among the most amiable of all Negroes, although "at the first view they appear rather frightful . . ." Even the *Universal Modern History* discarded its usual delight in cannibalism: "notwithstanding the prejudices conceived from their unhappy aspect", the natives of this coast were "the most rational, civilized, and polished people in all *Guiney*."[38]

On the other hand, the slave trade produced some evidence for cannibalism. It was reported, even by those opposed to slavery, that Negroes were terrified as they were forced on board slaving vessels because they imagined the whites were buying them to eat. Some, ignoring all the evidence of disease, mortality, and cruelty in the Middle Passage, saw this fear as the only reason for the frequency of revolts on slave ships. Others regarded it as proof that the Negroes were themselves cannibals. As John Snoeck argued, this "Jealousie would not probably enter their Thoughts, if they did not certainly know that there were Man-eaters in the World . . ." Atkins answered these arguments by pointing out that there was no record of any successful slave ship revolt ending in cannibalism, even though most slaves were from the allegedly cannibalistic interior.[39]

The biggest issue facing Atkins and other sceptics was created by the Dahomean conquest of Whidah in 1727. One account in particular, by William Snelgrave, came to dominate eighteenth century impressions of Negro cruelty. Snelgrave, a slave ship captain, arrived at Whidah some three weeks after it had been overrun. Amid scenes of desolation he found large numbers of human bones strewn haphazardly in the fields. Soon afterwards a visit to the camp of the conquering king of Dahomey, at Ardra, supplied him with more precise detail. He was told by an interpreter that four thousand Whidans had been sacrificed three weeks earlier "as an Acknowledgement for their Conquest."

These impressions were reinforced as Snelgrave was received by the King. He noticed human skulls lying nearby and at the same time saw a large number of prisoners from a neighbouring coastal state chosen by the king to be sacrificed to his fetish or "Guardian Angel". The horror of this scene was shortly after compounded for Snelgrave, when he was able to speak to a captive, the brother of the chief of Jakin, another nearby coastal state. The man's fright was understandable, as he had just seen so many people on their way to be sacrificed; but he was particularly upset, said Snelgrave, because "the People on the Sea-Coast abhor such Cruelty; but above all the eating their dead Bodies afterwards, as the *Dahomes* do." Later the people of Whidah were to explain to Snelgrave that it was this fear of cannibalism which had caused panic and very little resistance to the Dahomey advance.

For his part Snelgrave himself became convinced of Dahomey cannibalism after witnessing the sacrifice of some of the prisoners at the king's camp. Overnight the victims' bodies disappeared. Snelgrave's earlier frightened informant told him that the sacrificed bodies had been boiled and eaten. At first the Dahomey interpreter denied that this had happened and attributed the disappearance of the corpses to vultures. But eventually, after Snelgrave expressed doubt whether vultures would eat the bones as well, he was said to have admitted that the people had eaten them.

Snelgrave then went on to produce what he regarded as his most clinching evidence of cannibalism. At the same period human flesh had been sold publicly in the great market at the Dahomey camp. He had not actually seen this himself but had it on the authority of Robert More, a surgeon aboard an Italian ship and "a Person of great integrity." Snelgrave himself had no doubt "I should have seen the same had I gone into that Place, for there were many old and maimed Captives brought from *Tuffo* (besides those sacrificed) which no *Europeans* would have bought."[40]

Many other authors had asserted that Negroes often ate those

who were killed in their wars.[41] But Snelgrave was the first to give
the old allegation an air of authenticity and an extra note of horror,
by reporting at first hand the massacre of prisoners destined to be
eaten. Yet Snelgrave's evidence for cannibalism was far from
convincing, if this aspect of his story was scrutinized apart from the
directly observed murders and corpses which lent it plausibility.
Eventually Thomas Salmon concluded that Snelgrave was the only
one among many writers of the period to allege cannibalism in this
instance, although in all other aspects there was agreement about
the overthrow of Whidah. Some of these authors, continued
Salmon, "give us very substantial Reasons to believe that the
Charge is not well grounded; particularly Mr *Atkins* . . ." Atkins
had concentrated on the obvious weaknesses in Snelgrave's story.
It was a second-hand account which rested crucially on the
unknown linguistic ability of the Negro interpreter who had
changed his story under pressure from Snelgrave. Above all he
objected to the use of More to confirm the story about the market.
These criticisms were summarized in the Astley *Collection,* which
had also given an abstract of Snelgrave, and which then proceeded
to throw its editorial weight in favour of Atkins. Instead of relying
on More, "we may add that he might have known this by only
going to the Market, where he believed Man's Flesh was sold; or
else by going, or sending, to see what became of the sacrificed
Bodies set-apart to be eaten . . ."[42]

The doubts which continued to surround allegations of
cannibalism only slightly qualified the image of Negro depravity.
Human sacrifice, which Snelgrave had described so vividly at
first-hand, was a practice often closely associated with the reports
of cannibalism, and one which was documented with far greater
plausibility. Only a dedicated anti-slavery writer like Anthony
Benezet could claim that there was no evidence that slaves taken
to the New World might "otherwise have been sacrificed to the
implacable revenge of their conquerors."[43] Even if Snelgrave had
been dismissed as a liar—which no one chose to do—there were
other Europeans who could vindicate his account of the massacres
which followed the expansion of Dahomey. The most significant
English corroboration was provided by Bullfinch Lambe, a factor
at Ardra, who was taken prisoner and carried inland to Dahomey.
He remained there two years because the king was reluctant to
release a white man who was both a novelty and a potential source
of help in Dahomey's plans to develop the slave trade on its own
account. He eventually secured his release only on the pretext of
returning with other whites who would help to put these plans into
effect.

Lambe reported, in a famous letter despatched before his release, that the king's palace was surrounded with human skulls "as thick as they can lie on the Walls by one another, and are such as he has killed in War." But his experiences at the time of his capture provided even more telling proof of this penchant. He was led out to what he was convinced was to be his own sacrifice. With a drum beating a sinister dead march, hundreds of Negroes gathered around him "jumping and roaring enough to rend the Skies." Many of them held swords and knives, "which they flourished about me, as if ready for execution." Eventually his fears were put at rest; but the less valuable local inhabitants were not so lucky. Throughout Ardra "there was scarce any Stirring for Bodies without Heads; and had it rained Blood, it could not have lain thicker on the Ground."[44]

Although the Dahomean bloodshed was no doubt real and considerable, the defenders of slavery did their best to exaggerate the extent of such massacres. According to Griffith Hughes, Africa, before the slave trade, had been embroiled in unending warfare. The greatest mercy to the conquered was sudden death. As a result the trees along the sea-coast in inhabited areas were permanently festooned "with the Limbs and Heads of their Vanquished Enemies." Edward Long did not deny that there were deaths in the Middle Passage but considered it "better that a few should perish by such casualties, than that all should die by the hand of an executioner." He argued that polygamy caused a huge excess of population, which could be checked either by the slave trade or by native warfare and cruelty. Echoing Barbot, who had referred to the civilizing influence of Europeans on the coastal Negroes, as well as to the indirect effects of their trade, Long reported that there was still reason to believe that human sacrifice continued in the interior, "though much fewer are butchered than formerly."[45]

Here Long was striking a balance between the extremes of the pro-slavery case. Many chose to refer to the worst aspects of Negro society in the past tense: thanks to Europeans Negroes were now no longer slaughtered, eaten, and otherwise abused by their own people. As John Hippisley pointed out, Negro warfare was "infinitely less bloody" than in Europe. Hardly any prisoners were now put to death but almost all were sold and taken to the coast.[46] On the other hand, others chose to ignore the fact that the slave trade had long been flourishing and portrayed it as a continuing rescue operation, rather than an effective civilizing influence within Africa.[47]

These contrary views could be advanced with confidence

because so little was known about the interior. John Millar was a non-partisan whose opinions combined elements of both views. But they rested more on deductions from the customs of other savages than on African evidence. American Indians nearly always killed their prisoners of war because it was hard to support them as slaves. In contrast the slave trade gave Negroes economic reasons just as strong for sparing their prisoners. "At the same time," he added, "it cannot be doubted that, as encounters of those barbarians have upon this account, become less bloody, their wars have been rendered more frequent."

The fate of prisoners of war was, however, only one aspect of human sacrifice. Although the Dahomean massacres provided the most dramatic evidence, sacrifices were more often seen as a product of African religion, a ritualistic slaughter of compatriots rather than enemies. John Seller's late seventeenth century *Geography* claimed that some Negroes sacrificed their children to the devil. If this was a rare charge, confirmed in the eighteenth century only by the credulous Capuchin, Merolla, other seventeenth century allegations were more durable. Ogilby's references to the sacrifice of wives and slaves at royal funerals in several areas were confirmed by most eighteenth century visitors to Africa. Some implied that because of the European presence the practice was less frequent than earlier or mainly confined to the interior.[48] But others presented strong evidence that such murders still took place in coastal regions regularly visited by Europeans.

Again Snelgrave provided some of the most quoted anecdotes. In 1704, visiting Old Calabar, he saw the body of a child hanging from a tree. The king was sick, he learned, and the child had been sacrificed to secure his recovery. In 1713 he went ashore in the same area with an armed party and was able to insist on the release of a child tied to a stake and about to be sacrificed to the gods. Subsequently a touching reunion was effected with the child's mother who happened to be among a batch of slaves recently boarded on his own ship.[49]

If Snelgrave had a suspiciously happy knack of finding or thwarting sacrifices, he was not alone in claiming to be a witness of such practices. The Frenchman, Marchais, reported the funeral of a village chief on the Windward Coast, culminating in the live burial of the wife of the corpse.[50] The most vivid description was also the most convincing because its author, William Bosman, despite a frank contempt for Negroes, was unusually scrupulous in describing only what he had seen himself. Significantly he made no contribution at all to the rumours of cannibalism; but he did provide a much borrowed description of a royal funeral. He found it especially deplorable that old and infirm slaves were sold on these occasions for the specific purpose of sacrifice. Even more barbarous was the lingering agony of their fate: "what with Hacking, Piercing, Tormenting, so they endure a Thousand Deaths."

Although the evidence for ritualistic human sacrifice was convincing, the same processes which had stimulated belief in cannibalism were also at work in exaggerating its extent in the eighteenth century. The way in which Bosman's account was borrowed and distorted by the English version of Barbot is a good illustration of the eighteenth century tendency to generalize and exaggerate. After commenting on the protracted deaths of sacrificial victims Bosman had provided a specific example of brutality which he had witnessed himself. One victim's pain was prolonged even further by his delivery to a six year old child, who had struggled for an hour to remove the head with a cutlass. In the Barbot account this incident was generalized into a customary practice. After using Bosman's account of "hacking and tormenting" verbatim, this went on to say that a proportion of victims were normally handed over to six year old children, who would take an hour to remove the heads.[51]

Inevitably such accounts were used to the full by pro-slavery writers. Snelgrave became a favourite authority, with Edward Long, for instance, citing the Old Calabar incidents as evidence of a vast slaughter. Elsewhere, perhaps conscious that Snelgrave's account was slender evidence of genocide, Long referred to "a vast number of human victims at the obsequies of their kings and relations . . ." Adding personal gloss to old rumours and modern reports, he claimed that there had been public markets at which slaves were sold especially for sacrifice. They had been offerings to the gods, slaves for dead kings, and part of the general proceedings "at all great feasts." Another West Indian, Samuel Martin, supplied a New World anecdote to support the African evidence for human sacrifice. A Negro girl had fled from the plantation when her mistress died, "through fear of being burnt."[52]

While many—especially pro-slavery writers—saw ritual human sacrifice in terms of a general Negro propensity to cruelty, others saw it as merely the most shocking manifestation of African heathenism. And a considerable number argued, in the intellectually orthodox terms outlined in a previous chapter, that African blindness to religious truth was the root cause of the Negro's savage depravity. Some of these—such as Thomas Secker in a S.P.G. sermon—simply made crude equations between "the grossest Idolatry and the most savage Dispositions." Some emphasized the inevitable heathenism of a continent not yet penetrated by Christianity. Middleton's *Geography,* for instance, depicted Africa as "regions of ignorance and barbarity . . . nations tainted with the most horrid and cruel superstitions . . ." and contrasted it with Europe, "where the gospel light prevents errors, checks criminal offences, meliorates each propensity to evil, and humanizes the rational soul . . ." Others saw the manifold vices of Africa not in terms of blameless ignorance of Christianity but as the product of superstition, blinding man to natural reason: as Thomas Salmon put it, "their Superstitions do not restrain them, but rather encourage them in the practice of those Vices." On the other hand, some avoided these intellectual generalizations and attributed depravity to manipulation by unscrupulous religious and political leaders. A Capuchin missionary referred to "abundance of Sorcerers and Inchanters . . . who are the ruin of those People . . ."[53]

If, overall, such general causal explanations were unusual, they did reflect very widely held beliefs about the essential depravity of African religion. Such beliefs reflected, in their turn, the superficiality and distortion of most European reporting. The modern editors of Bosman's work take the Dutchman to task for regarding the Negro "fetish" as a god. In describing fetishism, they argue, Bosman was writing about witchcraft rather than the central beliefs of West African religion. Bosman's misconception was not unusual, although by no means universal. While Richard Blome's late seventeenth century survey referred similarly to Negro offerings to their "Fetisse or God", Vincent Le Blanc's similar work, published twenty years earlier, described Wolof idols "which nevertheless fixe not their faith . . ." In the same period Ogilby referred to Negro belief in a supreme deity and in the spirits of departed ancestors. In the eighteenth century many observers and all the large scale geographical surveys asserted that Negroes believed in a supreme deity; and several reiterated Ogilby's references to ancestor spirits or discovered the belief independently.[54] With many works referring also to varied traditions of the creation,[55] to belief in an after-life,[56] to native veneration of elements of the natural world,[57] and to the practice of magical arts,[58] virtually all the main elements of traditional West African religion were reported in the eighteenth century.

But this information was available only piecemeal. No single individual listed the full range of beliefs and practices and no one saw how they fitted into the coherent system outlined by modern authorities. Geoffrey Parrinder describes this system as a pyramid, with God at the apex, ancestors and nature gods at the sides, and lower magical powers forming the base, while man is the centre "subject to influences from every side." In contrast, most seventeenth and eighteenth century writers concentrated on one aspect, usually the conspicuous idolatry or sorcery. Where attempts were made to form a general view the best that could be said was that African religion was a mixture of "good sense and absurdity."[59]

There were many reasons why eighteenth century Europeans were unable to unravel the complexities of beliefs which have taxed the skills of modern scholars. Few had adequate linguistic ability. Thomas Thompson, the solitary eighteenth century European missionary on the Gold Coast, found his evangelism thwarted by the language barrier. His attempt to learn the local language was largely unsuccessful but in any case, he claimed, it was quite exceptional: none of the English on the coast even tried to learn the language.

Even without this handicap, Thompson would have been unlikely to see native religion on its own terms. He made more enquiries about native beliefs than most contemporaries but inevitably judged them by the tenets of Christianity. He regarded the Cape Coast version of a Sabbath—on which special offerings were made to the main idol—as the result of European influence. And he saw as mere pretence the Negroes' claim that, in apparently worshipping a rock, they were in fact worshipping "a being or *Fetisa* which inhabits there."[60]

Although Thompson's missionary role was unique, his ethnocentrism was shared in some degree by all. Even half-educated slave traders were armed with the conviction that only monotheism was intellectually respectable and that in idolatry and witchcraft lay the superstition which was a negation of true religion. To a man like Thomas Phillips African religion could be dismissed without further analysis as "delusion and obstinacy . . . in superstitious paganism." Barbot argued that it was "hard to give a good account" of native beliefs because most Negroes were "gross superstitious pagans, living after the wildest manner, in woods and forests, preying on travellers, and making deities, according to their own extravagant fancies, of the similitudes of many ridiculous and absurd productions of nature, or of their own imagination." And Bosman reflected the Protestant bias of many Dutch and English observers by equating Negro idolatry with the cruder forms of Catholicism.[61] In the same way, numerous allegations of devil-worship were a product of Christian preconceptions rather than accurate observation.[62] Moreover, those who, with a little more insight, saw African religion as more than idolatry, expressed the Christian's censure of men who acknowledged a deity and yet lavished their devotion on creatures and objects.[63]

If many slave traders were only too glad to ridicule every aspect of Negro society, their over-simplified emphasis on the visible aspects of religion was shared by defenders of the Negro. Granville Sharp referred to the "most barbarous ignorance" of African idolatry; and Morgan Godwyn admitted that "nothing is more barbarous" than "their placing confidence in certain Figures and ugly Representations . . ." John Atkins so successfully divested himself of the common contemporary prejudices that his response to reports of ritual human sacrifice was the matter-of-fact observation that "it looks as though there were some dark Notions of a future state among them . . ." And he argued that for Negroes to worship woods, lakes, or pieces of metal was "not that unaccountable and ridiculous Folly some would have it." yet Atkins showed as much ethnocentrism and less insight than many of his more hostile contemporaries. He believed that "it is impossible to expect in such a state of Nature as theirs, naked of Education and Science, that they should be able to form any refined Notions of a Deity . . ." He saw Negro worship solely as idolatry. And where Negrophobes like the editors of the *Universal Modern History* accepted native belief in a deity, he believed that Negroes were merely learning the notion of a God from Europeans.[64]

Even without their constricted intellectual perspectives it was inevitable that the baser visible aspects of Negro religion should make more impact on Europeans than the wider system of beliefs in which they operated. Reports revealed many instances of frustration, impatience, and ridicule as visitors to West Africa stumbled into conflict with native observances and taboos. They found to their dismay that potentially gold-bearing areas were proscribed as sacred. In Whidah Barbot discovered that to insult the venerated local snake was a useful way of ending tedious discussions "when we are weary of the *Blacks.*" Also in Whidah, Phillips thrust a piece of wood into the mouth of an idol and fired a musket ball into its eye to disprove the native claim that it could speak. While not all Europeans were so openly contemptuous, similar clashes were common. It was said that a group of seventeenth century English traders had been massacred in Whidah for unwittingly killing a snake. And even the uniquely academic Michel Adanson reported at least three occasions when he provoked native ire by inadvertently slaughtering sacred creatures.[65]

The sorcery often associated with fetishism was equally obtrusive. Witchcraft was one of the standard crimes which supplied slave traders with their human cargoes. Its use in various forms of trial by ordeal was both a frequently observed ingredient of native judicial procedures and a practice occasionally invoked in interracial disputes. Moreover, in other forms it was not only encountered by slave traders in Africa but seen to be a central facet of slave societies in the West Indies.[66] The extent to which Europeans believed in the occult powers of Negro magicians varied considerably. Ogilby referred to Negro "Sorcerers, Southsayers and Witches", who were "deeply skill'd in *Necromantick Arts.*" Some could work "strange effects with Herbs, Powders, Characters, and Figures . . ." and others "in the absence of any person . . . can fetch out his bloud, and bring him by that means into a Malady." Barbot regarded such claims as mere pretence and others saw them as a means of exploiting gullible native masses.[67]

*   *   *

The image of Negro religion was a typical composite of truth and distortion. The realities of African barbarism were measured against European moral precepts even by those whose own behaviour flouted them. Promiscuous slave traders and tyrannical slave owners were not consciously hypocritical in condemning Negro sexuality, cruelty, or sorcery. Neither by motivation nor training were they equipped to evaluate African customs by African standards. But the image of savage depravity was also accentuated by wilful distortion. Pro-slavery writers constructed an almost entirely imaginary picture of a continent in the grip of the most extreme cruelty. Underlying most of this cruelty was an equally distorted picture of arbitrary government.

CHAPTER EIGHT

ANARCHY AND DESPOTISM

Condemnation of African government was both pervasive and inconsistent. In the early seventeenth century it was regarded as loose or non-existent. By the eighteenth century the image had reached the opposite extreme of unmitigated despotism. The damaging implications of these differences lie in the way the ideals of government changed in the opposite direction over the same period. If the eighteenth century would not have condoned reports of anarchy, it would have found them more palatable than they seemed in the early seventeenth century, with its emphasis on civil order and strong government.

To a small extent this changing climate of opinion was itself a formative influence, rather than merely a standard against which to measure disfavour, as some writers highlighted English ideals of liberty against a background of African despotism. But much more important obstacles to a balanced assessment of Negro government were the ethnocentrism of reporters, the selective methodology of editors, and above all, the motivations of propagandists. David Davis has suggested that abolitionists were reluctant to refer to the well-documented power of native potentates because, while this information attested to "a high level of cultural development", it also proved that "Negroes played a larger part in the slave trade than abolitionists wished to believe."[1] But from very early indeed anti-slavery writing had emphasized this native role in the slave trade. Indeed this emphasis—combined with an attack on the corrupting effects of the trade, to which Davis gives due weight—was a major factor in perpetuating an image of bloody despotism.

*   *   *

For most of the seventeenth century reports about Negro government rested mainly on the dismissive generalizations of geographers who never set foot in Africa. There were few accounts published by English slave traders, whose activities were in any case too restricted for more than fleeting impressions of the organization of native society. The approach of Robert Gainsh, one of the earliest of all English visitors to Africa, is revealing. He told of tribes with considerable business organization and acumen: "They are very wary people in their bargaining, and will not lose one spark of golde of any value. They use weights and measures and are very circumspect in occupying the same." Yet in the same account he happily fell back on the generalization that they were without a God, religion, laws, or commonwealth. This, like his description of Blemmines, Satyrs, and other monsters, was a stereotype derived, perhaps via some medieval encyclopedist, from such classical authorities as Solinus or Pliny. The same terse references to anarchy were produced by Samuel Purchas. And as late as 1665 the anonymous *Golden Coast* incorporated an almost verbatim transcript of Gainsh in its account of a West African region now the focus of organized English slave trading activity.[2]

Negro Africa of course embraced many systems of government. But it was not until the mid-eighteenth century that descriptions of near-anarchy rested on the observations of contemporaries. The Astley *Collection* represented the Serer, inhabiting the Cape Verde region, as a rulerless, godless people, governed by no laws except those of nature. True to the period, it was inclined to regard this as a virtue, praising their industry, honesty, and hospitality. But it made it clear that this was a tiny minority so far from the West African norm "that you cannot affront other Negroes more than to give them that Appelation."[3] And by this period many other works had accepted that Negro government, far from being informal or non-existent, was tyrannous in the extreme.

Even while some seventeenth century writers were perpetuating the old labels of anarchy, others presented a contrary picture of autocratic government. This was mainly because the same over-simplifying methodology had produced a distorted version of Léo Africanus' survey of the kingdoms of the western Sudan. Leo had presented a balanced picture of such remote empires as Mali, Timbuktu, and Gao, even if he had displayed little awareness of their historical evolution and their fluctuating fortunes in his own day.[4] While some geographers used Leo's references to the cultural life of Timbuktu and Mali,[5] all showed most interest in his portrayal of despotic monarchy. Their treatment of the great Songhai empire of Gao well illustrates the process. Such writers as

Blome, Clarke, Le Blanc, and de Fer, all omitted most of Leo's references to the flourishing commerce of the Empire, as they concentrated their attention on a monarch who demanded grovelling obeisance from subjects liable to be sold as slaves at the slightest offence. Leo had given some evidence of regal power, with a description of vast retinues of concubines, eunuchs, and slaves. But in depicting the king as arbiter of all public controversies, he had added a qualification ignored by the later popularizers: "albeit the king be in this function the most dilligent, and performeth all things thereto appertayning, yet hath he about him his counsellors and other officers, as namely his secretaries, treasurers, factors and auditors."[6]

Towards the end of the century the image of all-powerful monarchy was extended by much the same process to those areas of Africa more directly under the scrutiny of Europeans. Before any of the slave traders had published their accounts John Ogilby reproduced many scathing generalizations. He described the power of the king of Quoia near Cape Monte as "absolute and unlimited". This monarch allowed counsellors sometimes to give opinions, "yet they signifie nothing, for he follows his own single resolved determinations". The Gold Coast kings were shown to be equally absolute in their own small territories, despite the existence of a hierarchy of Caboceroes and other administrators. True to the methodology of the period, Robert Burton combined these observations by applying the description of Quoia quoted above to Dixcove on the Gold Coast.[7]

But from the late seventeenth century new pressures were at work, as destructive of the truth as the glib generalizations of geographers. From this period reports of African government were never completely free from the polemical distortions of slave trade controversy. At the turn of the century the first pamphlet debate, between the Royal African Company and the separate traders, produced conflicting accounts which reflected the interests of the authors rather than the realities of Africa. One of the central issues—over the wisdom of conducting trade through forts—depended crucially on interpretations of the character of native government. Company spokesmen proclaimed the need for forts to provide political stability in the midst of barbarity:

> As the Settlements are numerous, and under divers Petty Kings, they are seldom free from Differences amongst one or more of their Neighbours, Friends to other Europeans; Also they are illiterate People, and have not (or are they govern'd by) any Religion, Laws or Courts of Justice, or any civiliz'd Rules of Discipline.[8]

Quasi-diplomatic relations through the commanders of forts were necessary, argued other company advocates, not because Negro government was in any way comparable with European, but because "there was never yet any substantial Commerce in the World carried on, but by means of mutual Alliances and Confederations made with the Natives, how Barbarous soever . . ."[9]

The separate traders countered the frequent company references to native barbarity and treachery[10] with arguments about the corrupting influence of the European presence which foreshadowed many similar allegations in the abolitionist debate.[11] Where Negro government was allowed to flourish uncontaminated, they went on, it presented an orderly appearance which would do credit to Europe. Ignoring the claims of one company pamphlet that "the defenceless *Out-Factories* at Whidah" had several times been over-run by the forces of the "potent Inland Nation" of Dahomey,[12] the separate traders declared that forts were an irrelevance, since native government offered all necessary security except to those bent on swindling and extortion. Whidah, wrote one such pamphleteer, was "a Neutral Port for all Nations, as free as *Genoa* and *Leghorn* . . ." It lay eight miles inland and "at that Distance from the Influence of either *French* or *English* Settlements, who carry their Cargoes up to this Town over Land, putting themselves and Goods under Protection of the Natives."[13] All foreign traders at Whidah, argued another, flourished without friction "under Protection of the King".[14] Not only were such pamphlets, on both sides of the debate, numerous and repetitive but their basic arguments were incorporated in less specialized works in the eighteenth century.[15]

Geographers, however, gained little detailed information from these sources about the character of native government. Few pamphlets, even from the private traders, contained any details about the internal organization of Negro states. But from the same period some of this information was available elsewhere as such participants in the slave trade as Bosman, Barbot, Phillips, Houstoun, and Atkins published their accounts of West Africa.

Bosman divided Gold Coast society into five ranks, ranging from the kings through Caboceroes and those claiming inherited or trading wealth to the common people and slaves. He showed that considerable administrative and judicial powers were entrusted to the Caboceroes or "civil Fathers", who were required to take an oath of fairness towards both European traders and those within their own nation. A near-contemporary, the Frenchman, Le Maire, outlined a similar hierarchy with similar functions in Senegal, as did Barbot some years later. The kings, said Barbot, were assisted in the administration of justice by "several officers, who have also their subalterns in every part of the land, and in every town of any note, an *Alcaide,* or a *Geraffo.*"[16]

Even Whidah—in this period regarded as the most powerful Negro state—was shown by Thomas Phillips to be something less than a centralized autocracy. Despite elaborate ceremonies of kneeling and grovelling, obligatory for European and African alike in the royal presence, much of the administration was in the hands of "cappasheirs". Further north on the Windward Coast the same writer was taken by one king to see the "council-hall, where they meet to hear all causes, dispense justice, and debate their state affairs . . ."[17]

There were many reasons why such information had little effect in checking the growth of unfavourable opinion about Negro government. In the first place even those who retailed it gave it a place of little prominence in works which were consistently derogatory towards Negroes. It would have needed a reader of unusually independent mind to separate the proffered facts about government and society from the pervasive accompanying ethnocentrism. Bosman, whose account was perhaps the fullest, albeit of a restricted area, introduced the relevant chapter with a comprehensive slur:

> The *Negroes* are all without exception, Crafty, Villanous and Fraudulent, and very seldom to be trusted; being sure to let slip no opportunity of cheating an *European,* nor indeed one another. A Man of Integrity is as rare among them as a White Falcon . . .[18]

Few writers could resist the temptation to ridicule the unreal appearance of Negro potentates. John Atkins, for instance, presented mocking accounts of several kings on the Windward Coast, who imitated European ways with inept sartorial affectations. One of them, sporting wig, hat, and breeches, made "a fifty times more ridiculous and scaramouch Figure, than any of his naked Dependants . . ." His conclusion that the man assumed the "Title of King, without knowing the meaning . . ." had an unconscious irony, for Atkins, like many contemporaries, made no attempt to distinguish between traditional rulers and "kings" who were merely successful slave trade entrepreneurs.[19] Bosman was one of the few to note the changes in the power structure which had developed out of European activities in this period.[20]

At the same time, those who purveyed the fuller information contrived to undermine any favourable message by qualifications and generalizations. Phillips revealed the slave traders' hostility to the restrictive powers of the Whidah "cappasheirs": Europeans were powerless to resist their ingenious sharp practices. Moreover he made their limitations on monarchical power appear of little benefit to the native population: not only were they themselves corrupt but the king retained certain autocratic powers, notably on the disposal of a vast harem, which put his state clearly beyond the pale of civilized behaviour.[21]

A consistent theme in the reports of this period echoed Ogilby's portrayal of monarchical power obscured but in no way restrained by the presence of cohorts of counsellors. Barbot and Le Maire showed the judicial hierarchies in Senegal to be an irrelevant charade in a land of arbitrary and bloody government. Succession to the monarchy might, said Barbot, variously depend on heredity, election, or naked violence. But "by whatsoever title these kings get the crown, the moment of their inauguration they assume a haughty carriage towards their subjects, what quality soever, and do tyrannize over them at discretion, so absolute is their authority . . ." Not even members of the "highest rank" were safe from an arbitrary power liable to order summary executions almost at whim. Le Maire showed the same propensities in operation lower down the scale. Itinerant justices went through the motions of hearing people's complaints but ended up by doing "Justice out of hand".[22]

Le Maire was one of many at this period who drew attention to the common practice of trial by ordeal, a system which was at best a source of ethnocentric ridicule and at worst seen as a device for trumped up verdicts. The method he described—of the accused's licking a red hot iron three times—was presented as bizarre rather than as a tool of injustice. A much more commonly described form of ordeal was the drinking of "red water", which, it was claimed, poisoned the guilty and left the innocent unscathed. Phillips described the practice with some scorn but relative detachment in view of the fact that he himself was almost forced to submit to it on one occasion. But Atkins claimed that it was common for judges to vary the toxic content of the potion in order to obtain the verdict they desired.[23]

The geographical popularizers perhaps had an even more important role than the observers in projecting an image of corrupt despotism in the mid-eighteenth century. Most secondary works of this period gave more space to Africa than their seventeenth century counterparts and at their best they gave a fair summary of the views of reporters. The Astley *Collection,* in particular, summarized the observations of virtually every commentator on Negro government. If its overall picture was unfavourable, this was only because it reflected the biases of its sources.[24] For instance, while it quoted all the strictures of Barbot and Le Maire on the excesses of monarchical power, it also gave full weight to their depiction of social and administrative hierarchies and the functioning of a judicial machine.[25]

Many other editors, however, while devoting almost as much space to the question, were far less objective and scholarly. Whereas the Astley editor always cited his authorities and carefully balanced contrary opinions, commenting on obvious discrepancies, some others were content to rely on one or two reporters, showing little regard to their contemporary relevance. The *Universal Modern History* and Charles Middleton, for example, both leaned virtually exclusively on Bosman as the authority for their accounts of Whidah.[26] This was to ignore the well publicised invasion by the forces of Dahomey, which had completely altered the situation which had been described by Bosman. Superficiality can have been the only reason for this particular distortion, for Dahomey provided an example of despotic power which far surpassed even the accounts of early eighteenth century Whidah. Other secondary works took the obvious opportunity to make the most of Snelgrave's and Lambe's early account of the Dahomean invasion.[27]

Yet, in addition to being superficial, the secondary works also contributed a measure of didactic distortion to the image of African government. In a rare moment of analysis Thomas Salmon argued that the republican sentiments of such Dutch writers as Bosman had been partly responsible for the unflattering portrayal of monarchy on the Gold Coast. "The Hatred and Contempt they have for all Kings" had led them to give royal designation to petty figures, some of whom the Dutch could number among their own servants. The true kings, Salmon averred, were "Sovereign Princes, whose Dominions are very extensive, rich, powerful, and arbitrary; Monarchs limited by no Laws, or any other Restraints . . ."[28] Whether his criticism of the Dutch was accurate or not, there is no doubt that his own kind of sweeping generalization about African despotism was often itself the result of English political idealism.

The main concern of at least some eighteenth century editors was not to describe the details of non-European societies so much as to dramatize the contemporary ideals of limited royal authority and individual liberty, by contrasting the political achievements of Europe, and especially Britain, with a crudely over-simplified version of the barbarism of the outside world. For Fenning and Collyer their survey of the world's uncivilized fringes was a "useful entertainment":

How great are the intellectual advantages arising from the contemplation of the different Religions, Manners, and Customs of our fellow-Creatures! How adapted is this pleasing study, not only to gratify the most unbounded curiosity, but to enlarge the mind, to banish prejudices, and to make us set a just estimate on our real characters and advantages! By examining the History of the human Heart, and the uncultivated Mind, in various regions, where the absurdest Prejudices usurp the place of Reason; and Cruelty, Vice, Folly, and Tyranny are sanctified by the vulnerable name of Religion; we shall see how much we owe to Education, to the Embellishments of Science, and to the purity of our Holy Religion—how much we are indebted to Providence for many peculiar blessings—how much to Heaven and our brave Forefathers, for the System of Religion and Civil Liberty handed down to us![29]

Charles Middleton concluded his account of Africa by expressing relief at emerging

from savage countries, where despotism reigns triumphant, and tyranny shows its most ghastly features, to polish'd states; where, if despotism dares appear, it is obliged to put on a placid countenance; and arbitrary power is under such limitations, as to be compelled to wear the most kindly smiles.[30]

Some years earlier an article printed in both the *London Magazine* and the *Gentleman's Magazine,* had used a distorted summary of part of Francis Moore's *Travels* to argue that the iniquities of African despotism were of universal significance. The writer was not concerned to balance the accounts of two rapacious and dissolute Negro kings with the favourable information Moore provided about other monarchs. This would have undermined his central theme that

ridiculous as this Account of the *Negro Kings* may seem, if we examine it closely, and compare it with the History of *other arbitrary Princes,* both ancient and modern, we shall find the difference to consist in little more than the Degrees of Power, which they possess, and the Prevalence of particular Customs or Appetites.

"In short", he concluded, "the *African Monarch* imitates his Royal Brethren of *Europe,* in most Particulars; for he gets as much as he can by *fair Means,* and then as much more as he is able by *Force* or *Fraud.*"[31]

It was no coincidence that all these authorities just quoted were firmly opposed to the slave trade, which was seen to infringe the basic liberties of mankind as surely as despotic monarchy. The article in the *Gentleman's Magazine* appeared in the late 1730s at a time when that journal was in the vanguard of the anti-slavery campaign in Britain. Fenning and Collyer's *Geography* contained a long section, identical to one in the *Universal Modern History,* attacking in great detail *"the barbarous Manner in which the Slaves are transported by the Portuguese from the Congo and the neighbouring Kingdoms to America.'*[32] And Middleton used a long, unacknowledged extract from the Abbé Raynal which explicitly equated the European slave trade with despotic power:

> The subject of an absolute prince is the same as the slave in a state repugnant to nature. Every thing that contributes to keep a man in such a state is an attempt against his person. Every power which fixes him to the tyranny of one man, is the power of his enemies; and all those who are about him are the authors or abettors of this violence.[33]

The Scottish philosopher, George Wallace, placed his anti-slavery argument on the same theoretical plane. He argued that the end of government was the welfare of mankind. Royal power did not include the right to make subjects miserable. Negro kings had no power to dispose of their people and if the slave trade was to be justified then "every crime, even the most atrocious, may be justified."[34] But although this concept was basic to the period, such theoretical arguments were exceptional. Anti-slavery writers helped to paint the picture of bloody despotism not mainly in abstractions about natural rights but more by the reiteration of specific allegations about the practical circumstances of the trade.

The notion that slaves were sold at the whim of despotic rulers, already current in geographical works of the seventeenth century, was accepted from the beginning of anti-slave trade agitation. In 1709 an anonymous tract, in the form of a speech purportedly made by a Negro at Guadeloupe, launched an impassioned attack on the arbitrary nature of African government. The source of "all our woes and miseries", the slave was made to say, was a society in which the only sanction was naked force. Slaves were either seized by the superior force of a neighbouring state or condemned within their own state by "the Will of some Great Man, to be sold by way of banishment for some suppos'd Crime."[35]

Anti-slavery writers were not monolithic in motives or priorities. But the idea of despotism was central to each of the main schools of thought. To the predominant humanitarian impulse it was clearly anathema that Negroes themselves should voluntarily participate in the trade, no matter what European encouragement was ultimately the root cause. As J. H. Wynne argued in a tirade against the inhumanity of the trade: "Should those regions which now supply America with that species of commodity . . . ever come to be inhabited by a wise, civilized, and well policed people,

this commerce would, no doubt, from that area be at an end . . ."[36]
A mid-century "Description of the River Senegal" was
representative of an economic motive for abolition. Without the
slave trade much more lucrative commerce in gold and gum could
be initiated. But this would only be achieved if despotic rulers
yielded to a freer system of government which would encourage
instead of stifling native enterprise.[37]

Naturally, along with abolitionist slurs on native society went
claims that the slave trade itself was largely responsible for
arbitrary acts of violence. To meet European demand kings or
native slave dealers stole people from neighbouring countries or,
in the absence of adequate supplies of these "prisoners" of war,
they pillaged their own populations. Eventually these arguments
were to become almost automatic insertions in every abolitionist
tract. But long before this happened in the 1780s, the point had
been advanced by John Woolman and Anthony Benezet.[38] More
important, a stereotype about the predatory activities of Negro
kings had been established in the literature on Africa over a much
longer period. Many years before the slave trade was a major issue
this theme had been presented by geographical editors like Blome
and Le Blanc in the seventeenth century and Paschoud and de Fer
in the early eighteenth. Later eighteenth century works, like the
Universal Modern History, were consciously motivated by
opposition to the trade. But they were able to draw on the reports
of such observers as Barbot, Le Maire, and Atkins, who wrote in a
period when slave traders had no need to be wary of the use to
which their reports might be put by opposing propagandists.[39]

Moreover, when the trade did come under attack, the first
impulse of its defenders was to rationalize it as a rescue operation.
When the Bishop of London castigated the West Indian colonies
for neglecting the spiritual welfare of slaves, an anonymous reply
in 1730 stressed among many obstacles, including language
difficulties, the background of savagery from which slaves were
recruited. Although some were criminals and others prisoners of
war, many were sold as ordinary marketable commodities by their
rulers or by native kidnappers.[40] In the same period a pro-slavery
writer in the Gentleman's Magazine addressed himself to
rebellious slaves in Jamaica, stressing the beneficence of
merchants, who "first redeemed you from native Slavery to savage
Tyrants of your own Complexion, and planted you here in easy
Servitude." Another argued that "the first Authors of this Trade
are the Gentry that rule in Africa, and sell them to the Traders
from England . . ." A writer in the London Magazine made
similar points: Negroes in the West Indies were as well off as the

poor of European countries, and certainly more fortunate than their brothers in Africa who lived under the slavery of arbitrary monarchs.[41]

Although most popular at this period in the 1730s and 1740s, such arguments were neither new nor quickly dropped by West Indian defenders of slavery. Richard Ligon in 1673 claimed that slaves were sold by powerful rulers; and exactly a century later the fifth edition of Samuel Martin's *Essay on Plantership* was making the same point: "all the kingdoms of Africa are slaves, from the highest to the lowest, to the arbitrary power of lawless tyrants, who have the lives and properties of their subjects absolutely at their disposal."[42]

Even though so many factors were conspiring to establish a stereotype of tyranny, there was in one important respect clear evidence to refute generalizations as sweeping as Martin's. The position of slaves within African society was clearly seen to be different from that of slaves sold to Europeans. Unlike some of the details of administrative organization overshadowed by accompanying hostile qualifications, this evidence emerged with some force long before the abolition debate made it a key issue of official inquiry. While modern authorities may doubt the accuracy of analyses which separate indigenous West African slavery from the influence of the slave trade,[43] contemporary observers confidently made distinctions and even offered revealing comparisons.

Early impressions of Negro domestic slavery were somewhat distorted by semantic confusion. Some claims that whole populations were slaves to their rulers stemmed from the stereotype about despotism and were exactly comparable to the common eighteenth century equation of slavery with political repression. Indeed, the term continued to be used in this sense throughout the period and not all abolitionists, for instance, echoed Thomas Cooper's definition that "they are not slaves to their prince in the same sense as they become so to the European purchasers". Other generalizations reflected inadequate understanding of purely nominal native designations; for example, in Benin, where every man was said to be the slave of the king. Barbot provided insight by explaining that in Benin every male child was presented to the king "as of right belonging to him; and therefore all males of the country are call'd the king's slaves . . ." In spite of this, said David Van Nyendael, in an appendix to Bosman's work, the men were all free and their title of slave was considered an honour.[44]

But through most of the eighteenth century, while the term

"slavery" continued to be ambiguous, it was generally accepted as descriptive of an African class broadly comparable to New World slavery, in as much as their status was permanent and hereditary through the mother. A wide range of writing, including first hand reports, geographical surveys, economic tracts, and pro- and anti-slavery opinion established, with very little dissent, that such domestic slavery was very common, perhaps universal, in areas of Africa where the slave trade flourished.[45] Long before the debate over the slave trade was a major formative factor on opinion, primary and secondary works had described with some precision the nature of this institution. As early as 1695 the *Thesaurus Geographicus* made a clear distinction between the "Slaves of the Country" and those who were captured in war. In the next century many works related that the main reason for enslavement was voluntary submission in times of famine: whole families would barter their freedom for food.[46]

This in itself implied a relatively benevolent institution; and although these descriptions might confirm native improvidence, the specialized knowledge of reporters was allowed to establish a relatively favourable impression. The sympathetic descriptions of Francis Moore, for instance, were widely repeated by such geographies as the Astley *Collection,* the *Universal Modern History,* Middleton's *New and Complete System,* and Salmon's *Universal Traveller.* Moore had described the treatment of the numerous domestic slaves among the Mandingoes as being so favourable that it was hard to tell master from slave. Although such slaves were sometimes sold to Europeans in other parts of Africa, this was never done by the Mandingoes. Here the slaves even enjoyed the right to decide judicial cases involving one of their number. A similar situation was described on the Gold Coast by John Hippisley, in other respects a hostile reporter of Negro society. Claiming that "the slaves of a family are considered as no unrespectable part of it", he reported that they were sold only for "very great crimes" and even then only after consultation with their fellow-slaves. A unilateral decision to sell by a master would simply lead to the rest of his slaves absconding. The only demand made of such slaves was that they should "acknowledge subservience from time to time" and offer occasional presents to their masters.

In a passage consciously in contrast with explanations of the infertility of West Indian slaves, Hippisley pointed out that the Gold Coast slaves were never afraid to have children because their "masters and mistresses have almost the same fondness for the children of their slaves as for their own, and are equally careful in the bringing them up . . .'' Like Barbot and Bosman some fifty years earlier, Hippisley also reported that some domestic slaves achieved such wealth and influence that they became substantial slave owners themselves.[47]

While most West Indians followed Samuel Martin in ignoring domestic slavery as they castigated Negro government, Edward Long himself gave it more attention than he perhaps intended. Like Martin he proclaimed that an African owner had "absolute dominion over his slaves, their bodies, life and goods, as the kings have over those of their vassals." Under this "vilest species of bondage" slaves were mere beasts of burden. Yet only a few pages away Long reproduced, without acknowledgement, most of Hippisley's description. This inconsistency did not spring from a desire to present two sides of a question. It was simply that Hippisley had introduced his account with a remark about the Negro character too scurrilous for Long to resist.

Addressing himself to the problem of why Africa was not depopulated by the slave trade, Hippisley argued that slavery within Africa did not hinder propagation as it would in the civilized world, "where liberty is highly prized." A sensitive, educated man or woman would "refuse to give being to wretches doomed to inherit the misery their parents feel . . ." He had then gone on to modify this slur with his explanation of the unique benevolence of African slavery. Long used these arguments almost verbatim, not merely the references to Negro insensitivity but also Hippisley's outline of the institutional superiority of African slavery. And he even used Hippisley's assertions about the power and wealth achieved by some slaves.

Usually Long was more careful than this. Elsewhere he claimed that African owners bred slaves "like cattle" for sale to Europeans. He may have acquired this notion from the *Universal Modern History,* which had mentioned such a practice by a Portuguese mulatto in the Gambia region. But Long depicted as general practice what the *Universal Modern History* had shown to be an isolated case. For other areas it had accepted the reports of the slave traders that such domestic slaves were rarely sold and then only after trial for crimes.[48]

Part IV

Racial Attitudes in an Era of Controversy: 1780–1807

CHAPTER NINE

THE CHAINS OF SLAVERY AND THE CHAIN OF BEING

For twenty years from the 1780s the abolition debate brought long-established images of the Negro into new focus. The combatants turned to the record of British race relations and attitudes with new interest, citing authorities as far back as Leo Africanus and sponsoring new editions of African travel literature. But the era of debate offered far more than regurgitation of old attitudes. Now for the first time propaganda outweighed the detailed descriptive record of geography and travel. Now reporters as well as editors were influenced by the same polemical considerations, making every portrayal of the Negro much more completely than hitherto a response to issues of controversy.

In general that controversy was not marked by urgent preoccupation with the most radical theories of racial inferiority. Such theories gained some ground, most completely in Charles White's development of the concept of racial gradation. White did not have the ulterior motives of a West Indian apologist. He did draw on some new theories emanating from academic circles. But he was not representative of a new trend. The early stages of abolition pressure revived interest in the theories of Edward Long. But the unfolding controversy circumscribed such theoretical racism because the debate over the slave trade never developed into a debate over the nature of the Negro. It did, however, develop into a debate over the institution of slavery. Controversy prompted official inquiry and in the voluminous reports and pamphlets documenting the Negro's exploitation in the West Indies was all the evidence to counter arguments of immutable racial difference. In the era of debate it was, in short, the practical racism of slavery rather than the racism of ideology which dominated attitudes.

*   *   *

While it can never be proved exactly what people are thinking on the basis of what they are reading, there is no question but that racialist views gained publicity in the late eighteenth century because of polemical issues rather than a general uncertainty about the human status of Negroes. Estwick and Long both wrote at a time when the main social issue concerning Negroes was their legal status in Britain. No sooner did their views appear than this issue died down as a matter of public controversy and it was another fourteen or fifteen years before their theories received urgent discussion. In the late 1780s, with abolitionism reaching its peak, these theories suddenly precipitated both opposition and emulation.

In 1788 a third edition of Estwick's pamphlet was published and his theories were promptly attacked in an abolitionist tract and in a letter to the *Morning Chronicle* by Thomas Cooper.[1] But it was Long's theories, with their colourful references to Negroes and apes, which held the stage. In the atmosphere of debate distorted versions inevitably appeared. An anonymous Jamaican planter attacked the prejudices of his own society by declaring that Long had argued that Negroes were no better than orang-outangs,[2] a subtle but crucial distinction from Long's actual views. Peter Peckard attacked pro-slavery claims that Negroes were a "spurious brood arising from some impure mixture". In 1788, the same year that Peckard reported these oral discussions, this idea found literary exposition. John Kemeys, another West Indian, in a lengthy footnote to a pro-slavery argument, claimed that it was "not a question with some naturalists that many of the negroes imported from Africa partake of the brute creation". He referred to a cargo of Negroes recently arrived in Jamaica

> whose hands had little or no balls to the thumbs, whose nails were more of the claw kind than otherwise, and their want of intellectual faculties was very apparent. Every planter knows that there are negroes, who will for ever remain almost as much uninformed as when they were first bought, that they cannot be humanized as others are, that they will remain, with respect to their understanding, but a few degrees removed from the ouran-outang from which many negroes may be supposed, without any very improbable conjecture, to be the offspring. It is an undoubted fact that those brutes will copulate with the females of the human species . . .

Kemeys was clearly influenced by Long, whom he cited frequently and from whom he borrowed most of his illustrations of Negro-ape liaisons.[3] The fact that his central argument was inconsistent with Long's hierarchy of mutually infertile species points up the extent to which polemics could override intellectual orthodoxies.

Kemeys, like every other racist of the period, provoked swift counter-attack from abolitionists. An anonymous article ridiculed his theories as destructive of the "harmony of the animal system". If ape-Negro copulation produced offspring, these must be infertile. If not, the new animal could mix with another of different species, producing another hybrid and so on *ad infinitum*. "Thus might this intercourse proceed, till the whole order of animals would be in the utmost confusion."[4] By such arguments—so precisely consistent with Long's own theory—the defenders of the Negro could rout racialist slurs which separated Long's extravagant illustrations from their theoretical framework. As a result the concept of racial gradation was kept before the public, in print at least, more by rebuttal than by assertion. Some abolitionists—including a group of ten London Negroes in a letter to the *Diary*—simply poured scorn on the "Orang Outang" philosophers. Others, notably Thomas Clarkson, presented detailed arguments, stressing the anatomical superficiality of racial difference and the orthodox definition of species.[5]

Such intellectual victories could not alone kill racialism now that the question of the Negro's place in nature had urgent social and economic connotations. There is some evidence that Long's theories were being discussed without finding their way into print. William Dickson referred to the vogue of the "orang-outang system" before going on to attack "that silly scepticism respecting the moral and intellectual faculties of the Africans . . ." Peter Peckard seemed unaware of Long's or any other written formulation, when he referred to the currency of racialist theories in pro-slavery circles. He thought such people might be too ashamed to publish their opinions; "but this I know, that too many are both earnest and artful in this unworthy work; having not only been present at debates of this sort, but been a witness also to their unhappy effect: in which ideas of imaginary policy have been of a power superior to the Precepts of Religion, and the Dictates of Humanity." In 1795 Thomas Gisborne referred to the extreme arguments about Negro inferiority advanced a few years earlier. Even now, he wrote, similar "shameless" assertions were occasionally heard, even though they were "equally unphilosophical and unchristian".[6]

Nevertheless by the only measurable criterion—recorded opinion—theoretical racialism remained a minority attitude. The reasons for this lie only partly in the numerical preponderance of abolitionist over pro-slavery publications. James Walvin, in arguing a very strong racial prejudice in Britain, claims that in the late eighteenth century there was some modification of the dominant image of Negroes as a "sub-human" species.[7] But it is more plausible to argue that the abolitionist debate brought into the open a weight of opinion in favour of the Negro's human integrity which had long existed. The new element in the late eighteenth century was not that people began to insist on the Negro's human status but that a small minority began to argue to the contrary. Such people were well aware that their claims were new and unpopular. One newspaper letter-writer, calling himself 'Civis', introduced his theory of gradation as an argument "on that side of the question, which has scarce found a single defender . . ." By the time the protracted controversy aroused by his letter ended—after being waged in the *Morning Chronicle* throughout 1788—only one more defender of racialism had appeared, while eight correspondents had rejected at length and several times over his claim that Negroes were a species of animal between man and monkey.[8]

Although it is possible that this predominance was produced by editorial bias, there is good reason to see it as an accurate reflection of opinion in the period. The reasons for this are to be found by analysing pro-slavery arguments rather than by stressing the impact of the humanitarian movement, as Walvin does. Very few pro-slavery writers indeed used racialist arguments. Most had clearly read Long but few, at least publicly, accepted his racialism. One abolitionist, in a letter to the *London Chronicle*, referred to the kind of theory advanced by Long but concluded, "I do not stoop to consider them, or to combat this argument, as it is not generally insisted on by the abettors of slavery".[9] Many defended slavery solely in terms of economic expediency or on legalistic grounds about the rights of property.[10] Many more reiterated long-standing arguments which saw slavery as a device for civilizing savages. One correspondent was clearly influenced by Long in reporting that on arrival in the West Indies Negroes appeared very low "in the scale of beings, I could never discover that they had any other ideas than such as are common to brutes . . ." But, he added, kind treatment under slavery wrought great improvements in their abilities.[11] A pamphleteer regarded African Negroes as "apparently useless in the great scale of human society . . ." The only way to promote their civilization was to introduce them to activity in the more beneficial climate of the West Indies. Far from from depicting slaves as well-trained near-apes, this writer wished to dignify their status. The outcry against slavery would evaporate, he declared, if the emotive word "slave" was dropped and Negroes were described as "ASSISTANT PLANTERS".[12]

Such implicit recognition of Negro potential showed that Long's influence was superficial. More important were a significant number of explicit rejections of racialism by pro-slavery writers. James Tobin in 1785 produced a detailed point-by-point answer to James Ramsay's famous anti-slavery tract. But his only response to Ramsay's extensive rebuttal of Long was that such controversies were "not of much consequence". It "has never been pretended", claimed Tobin, that Negroes "were, or are, in any way *inferior* to their masters, except in strength, policy, or good fortune". Others addressed themselves more directly to theories which did "pretend" inferiority. William Beckford denied that Negroes were a "different species" or that they lacked "ideas of moral rectitude". An anonymous West Indian reproduced Long's survey of African cultural sterility but concluded that he was "not convinced of the truth" of racialist theories. Another foresaw economic disaster if the slave trade was stopped but added "I would by no means be thought of so callous a heart, nor so void of a fellow-feeling of humanity, to suppose those black people are scarce human beings, as a celebrated author has quoted upon the occasion . . ."[13]

Such views were no doubt based to a great extent on the dominant intellectual orthodoxies of the period, reinforced by the West Indian's first-hand knowledge of the Negro's human capabilities. Some of their rejections of racialism consisted of simple assertions of the unity of mankind. "I do not attempt to prove the African inferior in his nature to the European", wrote one in an open letter to William Wilberforce; "they fundamentally are equal to us . . ." Others presented detailed arguments indistinguishable from those of abolitionists like Thomas Clarkson. A "strong advocate for the interests of the islands" reproduced the standard scientific and theological rebuttals of racial gradation:

> God created man, that he might beget his own image and likeness, that is his own species, now this cannot happen between men and monkies, or other parts of the Brute Creation, whereas in sexual intercourse between the White and the Negroe, the propagation of the species is as complete as between Whites themselves, and in time they become as white.[14]

But West Indian hostility to Long was not entirely disinterested. Planters might dismiss his racialism because, for instance, they knew only too well that mulattoes were fertile: but equally important was the way in which their own role in creating a mulatto population had been severely censured by Long. Moreover, Long's criticisms of slave owners went far beyond their tendency to revel in the "goatish embraces" of mulatto mistresses. He produced criticisms of the slave system so fundamental that his work, for all its racialism, came to be used far more by abolitionists than by pro-slavery writers.

Long's strictures on the large-scale importation of Negroes into Jamaica were motivated by fears of rebellion but were seized on by abolitionists as support for their campaign against the slave trade. They used him as a principal authority for their argument that there should be no need for the slave trade to sustain the numbers of Negroes in the West Indies.[15] While abolitionism concentrated on the slave trade, it was widely seen as a threat to slavery itself. Here again Long provided ammunition, with his criticisms of planters' managerial shortcomings and especially of the agricultural inefficiency of slavery. Among the published letters citing such criticisms was one which claimed that Arthur Young in his *Annals of Agriculture*, had conclusively demonstrated that slave labour was inefficient "from Long's data in his *History of Jamaica*".[16]

Because Long's work as a whole was so useful to abolitionists racialist theories remained largely anonymous. This may even have been a minor additional factor in restraining their acceptance, since no one at the height of the abolitionist debate was prepared publicly to mention their location. In 1784 James Ramsay specifically took issue with the "author of the *History of Jamaica*."[17] Thereafter there was almost a conspiracy of silence, as abolitionists dismissed his theories without mentioning Long, and yet cited him almost reverentially as "the celebrated historian of Jamaica" and his work as the "West India gospel".[18] Wilberforce, for example, in Parliament frequently cited Long as the great authority on slavery but referred only in anonymous terms to reprehensible theories of racial inferiority, which he could not have failed to read in Long's *History*.[19] In the parliamentary debates Long's work was cited overwhelmingly more times than any other and yet no one referred to his racialism. To the same effect only Kemeys among the minority of pro-slavery racialists referred directly to a man whose work as a whole was so ill-suited to their polemical purposes.

Suggestions that the Negro was fundamentally different from whites did not have to be argued in terms of the Chain of Being. Both the tropical labour argument and the hypothesis of David Hume were potentially no less damaging. Much of the evidence which helped to offset these influences in the late eighteenth century was part of the changing image of West Africa examined in the next chapter. But in addition to this largely implicit evidence both theories attracted direct attention in the era of debate, yet only in ways which confirmed that the nature of the Negro was not a fundamental issue.

After Long and Estwick had cited him, there was only one further significant endorsement of Hume among hundreds of pro-slavery pamphlets and articles. This was by the correspondent, 'Civis', whose letter to the *Morning Chronicle* contained the explicit acknowledgement that racialist defences of slavery were extremely unusual.[20]

The publicity accorded Hume's hypothesis came chiefly through abolitionist denunciation but even this was relatively slight. James Beattie was not closely identified with abolitionism but his rebuttal of Hume was used by such abolitionists as Sharp, Clarkson, and William Dickson. Sharp, whose main concern was always with the inhumanity and illegality of the slave trade, made his only significant defence of Negro racial capacity with a series of long quotations from Beattie. On the other hand, Clarkson, who went very deeply into questions of racial difference, was content to deal with Hume in a footnote referring his readers to Beattie's work.[21]

The relative insignificance of Hume's influence can be seen in the cursory way the issue of individual talented Negroes was discussed in Britain. Hume had made a short, oblique reference to Francis Williams, arguing that a Negro displaying apparent literary skills was comparable to a parrot imitating human speech. Later the pseudonymous 'Civis' made a similar disparagement of Gustavus Vassa (Equiano), whose talent he compared—in an allusion to the major contemporary attraction at Astley's Amphitheatre—to that of a "learned pig". But 'Civis' assumed that Hume's reference was to Ignatius Sancho. Significantly, only one other writer, apart from Edward Long, developed the attack on Williams. An anonymous pamphleteer, writing in 1789, claimed that Williams was the son of a freed Negro and a woman slave owned by the father. After his father's death, Williams had eventually sold his own mother "to the best bidder." This anecdote was not apparently designed to echo Long's racialism, for it referred favourably to Williams' career in England, where he "prosecuted his studies with great applause, finished his education at one of the Inns of Court, was called to the bar . . ." Rather it served to question the expediency, in a slave society, of "indulging" Negroes with an education, instead of giving them "only a moderate share of useful information . . ."[22]

The denigration of Williams was challenged by a handful of abolitionists but most simply ignored the issue. This relative lack of discussion partly reflected the fact that it was some fifty years since Williams had been in England. But, more important, it reflected the irrelevance of Hume's and even Long's racialism to the main issues of the abolition debate. Abolitionists, it is true, briefly referred to other talented Negroes. But these references were much less a response to the stimulus of racialist writing within Britain than a casual regurgitation of aspects of contemporary American abolitionist writing.

One defender of slavery argued that the British were apt to form too high an opinion of Negro capacities because "we see only the very best of them, chosen out of many thousands for their abilities and character, and educated as the common people of any country."[23] Yet British abolitionists virtually ignored such individuals, as they proclaimed their faith in Negro potential. Some mentioned Ignatius Sancho but almost invariably his literary talents were bracketed with those of the American Negro poetess, Phillis Wheatley.[24] The success of Anthony Benezet's Negro school in Philadelphia received far more publicity than the education of Negroes in Britain.[25] No propagandist, for example, mentioned the regular influx of young West Africans who were taught the rudiments of English language and behaviour in Liverpool. And if Philip Quaque received modest publicity in the monthly press,[26] he too was ignored by abolitionists. One pamphleteer, indeed, who referred to Benezet's school, had clearly never heard of Quaque, for, in suggesting the despatch of Negro missionaries to West Africa, he remarked: "I do not know that Missionaries have ever attempted to proselyte the inhabitants of Africa . . ."[27]

Similarly, in referring to unusual Negro genius, British writers ignored the presence of the musical prodigy Bridgetower, preferring examples taken from the works of the American, Benjamin Rush. Rush's report of Thomas Fuller, a Negro mathematics prodigy, received publicity in the monthly press and in abolitionist propaganda. There were also borrowings from Rush's account of the less spectacular abilities of James Derham, an American Negro physician.[28]

The second-hand, perfunctory nature of these descriptions of individual Negroes showed that, while abolitionists wished to combat racialism, it was not one of their major problems. In the same way, while they fairly consistently argued that the apparent inferiority of Negroes was due to the effects of slavery, they did so briefly and without emphasis.[29] They made equally terse references to the existence within West Indian slave society of a skilled class of Negro tradesmen, who worked as sugar distillers, carpenters, or mechanics.[30] William Dickson quoted newspaper advertisements for such tradesmen, which must have been familiar to all West Indian spokesmen.[31] Indeed for over half a century this small class of skilled slaves had been mentioned in pro-slavery and non-polemical works.[32] But in the era of debate it was the official investigations into slavery, rather than the urgent defences of abolitionists, which added substance to these brief references.[33]

The same investigations added substance also to the long-standing claim that only the Negro could work in the tropics. As officialdom probed the necessity for slavery there was some new emphasis in the replies from the West Indies on the protection afforded by black skins against the heat of the sun.[34] But this innovation remained an isolated example of reference to a distinctively racial trait; and the bulk of replies continued to be generalized assertions no different from the claims of the past 150 years. As these claims were repeated in the polemical literature there was some greater polarization, with many more abolitionists than previously claiming that ability to work in the tropics depended on acclimatization rather than race. These claims usually referred to the way Barbados had been originally cleared by white pioneers: other white West Indians could do the same, if they were not "debauched with ease and luxury."[35]

Yet even now such abolitionist claims were relatively unusual. The stereotype about aptitude for tropical labour continued to be advanced with very little challenge. This was not because of deeply held doubts about the Negro's place in nature but because the debate was principally concerned with other issues. The central issue was, of course, the necessity as well as the morality of the slave trade. This in turn focussed attention on West Indian slavery. Abolitionists had little need to devote space to countering the argument about tropical labour when they examined a system which used up Negroes in prodigious quantities. The evidence which negated intellectual racism was, in short, largely implicit and understated. It was incidental to a massive indictment of practical racism, the slave system of the West Indies. The indictment included by now standard catalogues of plantocratic cruelty and neglect.[36] It also included renewed emphasis on the Negro's response to slavery: rebellion, suicide, and melancholy leading to sickness and even death.[37]

Occasionally this response was presented as explicit argument against racist theory. If, said Thomas Clarkson, Negroes had been an inferior species, "they would have wanted many of those qualities which they have, and which brutes have not: they would have wanted that *spirit of liberty*, that sense of *ignominy and shame*, which so frequently drives them to the horrid extremity of finishing their own existence.''[38] But such arguments were largely unnecessary. Negro resistance or demoralization was mainly cited to mock pro-slavery claims stressing the essential benevolence of the institution. These claims rang rather hollow for a number of reasons, not least because the defenders of slavery made admissions which undermined their common theme that Negro slaves were no worse treated than the peasantry of England. In denying the worst allegations of cruelty they nonetheless argued the need for special standards of rigour in dealing with savages. And they explained the Negro response to slavery in terms of savage perversity, cruelty, or even ingratitude. The usual argument was that all the more extreme responses were the work of newly arrived Negroes. The civilizing role of slavery, so often proclaimed in references to Africa, was revealed as little more than a system of breaking this savage spirit. Hector McNeill frankly compared the process to the breaking of horses, even while acknowledging that Negroes were men: "The sentiment of Liberty, though inherent in the human mind, in almost all countries and ages, may certainly by a combination of circumstances, be eradicated from it . . ." In the words of another pamphleteer, those who emerged from this process were contented enough: "They have a system of their own; their minds are conformed to that system; they look not, they know not beyond it; and being capable of certain perceptions of pleasure and of pain, they are affected by them according to the turns of a life little eventful indeed . . ."[40]

The irony in an argument that slavery was benevolent, because slaves had had some of their human aspirations systematically smashed, did not escape the more perceptive pro-slavery writers. Increasingly there was grudging admission that the cruelties of slavery did exist, though much exaggerated by abolitionists. But they were an unfortunate necessity because the slave trade was so vital to the British Empire. Bryan Edwards typified this attitude. It was "frankly and candidly" necessary to admit that the rigours of slavery were among many factors preventing it from sustaining itself by natural increase. But it was "out of our power" to alter this factor. He himself had publicly attacked plantocratic cruelties he had witnessed as a youth. He disliked slavery and had once favoured abolition of the slave trade but was now convinced that it was a necessary evil. Abolitionists who gave second-hand distorted accounts of cruel punishments should also consider the alternative to strict racial controls in societies heavily dependent on Negro slavery. Rape and murder perpetrated by rebellious slaves were far more shocking than the rigours of slavery.[41]

Abolitionists did frequently cite old authorities, particularly Hans Sloane with his lists of sadistic punishments. But the abolitionist ranks also included men with first-hand experience of the West Indies, such as James Ramsay, who were able to cite more recent arguments for which there was no ready answer. From the recent, but less controversial, past they could quote claims by Samuel Martin to corroborate arguments that slavery could be self-supporting if it were less rigorous. And while most abolitionists dwelt in some detail on the rigours, others made equally telling comment more economically, by arguing that the statistics of continuing slave importations were proof enough of the exploitation of human life.[42]

*   *   *

It was symptomatic of the nature of the debate that theoretical racism made its significant advances outside the polemical battleground. With pro-slavery spokesmen putting their emphasis so firmly on economic expediency and on denials that slavery was inhumane, it was left to others to develop the concept of gradation. Foremost among these—in enthusiasm rather than intellectual stature—was Charles White. The fact that he was a self-proclaimed opponent of the slave trade can be used as evidence for some increasing academic enthusiasm for radical theories about race.[43] Even now, however, such theories reflected minority attitudes. Their unsoundness was recognized in the period and White did not overcome the theoretical problems which had confronted Long. Equally important it was the debate over slavery which decisively isolated his theories. A mass of new evidence about the Negro, much of it unearthed by the official investigators, showed once again that the key issues were the inhumanity of slavery rather than the racial peculiarities of Negro slaves.

White, a Manchester physician, was much influenced by Long. The calibre of his argument is typified by the emphasis he gave to Long's claim that Negroes were infested by black, instead of white, lice. This fact—"which seems to have escaped the observation of other naturalists"—strongly suggested that Negroes were a distinct species, since elsewhere in nature other species tended to nourish different parasites.[44] But White also introduced more modern—and apparently less partisan—allegations about the Negro's nature. He included, in an appendix, substantial translated passages from H.T. Soemmering's derogatory *Essay on the Comparative Anatomy of the Negro and European*, hitherto only available in the original German edition of 1785. More important, he acknowledged as his chief inspiration the eminent surgeon, John Hunter, whose museum contained skulls which could be arranged in a regular gradation, descending from the European, through the Asiatic, the American, and the African, to the monkey. Hunter had outlined these possibilities in a lecture attended by White:[45] but he did not publish them. Both he and White, however, were influenced by a substantial written exposition of a similar theme by Petrus Camper, a Dutch anatomist, who introduced, in his concept of "facial angles", a theory directly linking apes and Negroes.

The facial angle lay at the intersection on the profile of imaginary lines drawn from lips to forehead and from the ear to the base of the nose. Clearly this angle is very narrow indeed in animals such as dogs, somewhat wider in apes, and wider still in men. The sinister aspect of the concept was that Camper argued a racial gradation, in which the widest angle was found among Europeans, and especially in the heroic sculpture of Classical Greece, and the narrowest among Negroes. His contention that this did not represent a hierarchy of intellect or merit was overshadowed by reiterated emphasis on "the striking resemblance between the race of Monkies and of Blacks".[46]

This may have contributed to unrecorded popular belief in Negro inferiority. But judged by the standards of Camper's own academic milieu, his theory was already clearly destined for a minor place on the fringe of intellectual history. Partly this was because his explanation of the causes of racial difference was inconsistent with his basic theme. To argue a completely symmetrical racial gradation it was almost essential to believe that races were originally different rather than accidental varieties. Charles White, in developing Camper's concept, was to follow Edward Long to the logical extreme of claiming that races were separate species. But Camper was insistent that the whole of mankind had descended from one pair and that racial differences could be explained in terms of the popular eighteenth century environmental theories. He did not attempt to explain how a complex interaction of climatic, dietary and social influences could have produced his orderly hierarchy of racial types.[47]

Camper's theory was also methodologically unsound. Even his English translator, T. Cogan, pointed out that the attempt to "shew that national differences may be reduced to rules" was a form of natural history

> which requires the joint labours of physiologists to surmount all the
> difficulties attending it. It is alone by forming a very large collection

of the craniums of different people, that a discrimination can be made between what is general, from what is merely accidental; what is personal and to be ascribed to the diversities observable in individuals, from that which is national and characteristic of a particular people.

In a footnote Cogan added that J. F. Blumenbach had published two *Decades* on skull formations which differed from Camper: "As each has formed his opinion from the specimens in his possession, those differences manifest the difficulties hinted above, and prove that further investigations alone will enable us to distinguish between accidental forms and *national* marks."[48]

Blumenbach's work itself represented a less circumspect criticism of Camper. At first he had been impressed by the Dutchman's claim that the European appearance of many pictures of Negroes betrayed the ignorance of artists, who merely "copied from Europeans whose faces had been blackened for that purpose". but after he had the opportunity of seeing Negroes and procuring "a great many anatomical preparations from Negro bodies", he became convinced that there was as much difference between individual Negroes, "particularly in the lineaments of the face, as between many real negroes and other varieties of the human species."[49]

Not only was Blumenbach translated into English but he was already in the eighteenth century acclaimed as the leading authority on the subject. For instance, an article in the *Monthly Review*, while sceptical about some of his definitions of the differences between man and brute, summarized his criticisms of Camper and proclaimed that "of all the living authors of Europe, Dr. BLUMENBACH has perhaps bestowed most time in reading and reflecting, as also in making internal and external observations, on the varieties of the human species."[50]

This pre-eminence was an important counter-balance to the theories of Charles White. For, as well as rejecting racial gradation, Blumenbach stated explicitly that "the negroes, in regard to their mental faculties and capacity, are not inferior to the rest of the human race."[51] This was a far more intellectually consistent conclusion than the similar protestations by Camper and Hunter. On the other hand, although White's exposition of Negro inferiority fitted logically into the framework outlined by those two exponents of gradation, it embraced too many unfashionable theories to inspire intellectual conviction.

White's rejection of Camper's insistence on monogenesis may have been more consistent with their common theoretical framework but it was based on an equally shaky methodology. On the basis of a tiny investigation he formulated general conclusions about a much wider range of racial characteristics than skull formations. After examining fewer than a half dozen Negroes in Liverpool, he suggested that Camper's belief in environmentally induced varieties would have been shaken had he known that "the lower arm of the African was considerably longer than that of the European . . .".[52]

Moreover, in developing the contrary view that races were species, White shared the intellectual isolation of Edward Long. As well as substantially accepting Long's claims about the infertility of mulattoes,[53] he developed the argument to its logical extreme by claiming that many other apparent varieties lower down the Chain of Being were also in reality species. In doing so he had to ignore a treatise entitled "Observations tending to show that the Wolf, Jackal, Dog, are all of the Same Species",[54] which was published by the same John Hunter who had been his major inspiration. Far from accepting that these diverse animals were of the same species, White found it impossible to believe that all the different breeds of dog could have descended from one original pair:

> I should rather suppose that the different kinds of dogs, which, from time immemorial, have preserved their distinctive qualities, are in reality separate species of animals; and that all others are only varieties, or mongrels, produced by the intermixture of species, and which, like the mule, in one, two, or more generations in the mongrel line, lose their prolific quality, and consequently become extinct.[55]

Despite this bold confrontation of awkward phenomena, White's thesis was not free from internal inconsistencies. He gave some prominence to reports from China that a certain species of ape was believed to be "originally a mixture with the human kind",[56] even though this conflicted with his central theme summed up in a proud concluding generalization:

> The opinion here maintained, so far from degrading, tends much more to dignify the human race than the opposite one. For if, according to the latter, we admit that such great varieties can be produced in the same species as we find to exist in man, it would be easy to maintain the probability that several species of *simiae* are but varieties of the species Man . . . But the opinion advanced above effectually precludes any such consequences, as it places each species upon its own proper basis, and debars them from intermixing with other species, unless nearly resembling themselves, and even that in a limited manner.[57]

In the same way, White was not averse to selective quotation from other exponents of gradation. Introducing his thesis, he quoted extensively from Richard Watson's outline of the Chain of Being but ignored his explanations of racial difference:

The *genus* to which man belongs (Watson had written) includes a great many subordinate *species:* or, to speak in a manner more conformable to nature, and more consonant to the account we have of its origin, the human species, from the diversities of climate and of food, from changes introduced by disease, and from other causes which are unknown to us, hath been launched out into a great many varieties . . .[58]

Equally selective was the use White made of another treatise by Petrus Camper, which had—paradoxically, in view of his "facial angle" theory—done most to discredit the longest-standing assumption about the physical similarity of man and ape. He had rejected Edward Tyson's eighty-year-old claim that there was no essential difference between the organs of speech of man and "orang-outang". Camper had attempted to minimize the most damaging implications of his outline of racial gradation by referring to this earlier "physiological dissertation", in order to argue that "the whole generation of apes, from the largest to the smallest, are quadrupeds, not formed to walk erect; and that from the very construction of the larynx, they are incapable of speech." According to White, Camper's dissection had exploded a belief in apes' "great inferiority to man" by showing a physical rather than mental reason for their lack of speech.[59]

As with Edward Long, textual criticism gives an incomplete picture of the contemporary credibility of White's theories. On the one hand, it is plausible to assume that his ideas had a popular impact despite their intellectual defects. But on the other hand, readers of every class of literature had opportunities to measure such theories against detailed reports about Negroes in both Africa and the New World. White went further than Long, not only in carrying the concept of racial gradation to its logical limits, but also in basing his arguments on a mass of disputable claims about the physical nature of Negroes. These claims were not put directly to the test by scientific circles, which remained largely apathetic about race questions in general and White's theory in particular. But, in probing the fundamental questions about slavery and the slave trade, contemporaries were in the process of giving the lie to most of White's specific allegations even as he published them.

White argued in great detail that Negroes differed from whites in their susceptibility to disease just as much as any other distinct animal species in nature's hierarchy. He commented on the heavy death rate from tetanus among new-born Negroes, attributing it to a racial sensitivity to cold only one degree less than that which had prevented any "orang-outang" from surviving a European winter. A unique disease among adult Negroes was dirt-eating. On the other hand, he argued, Negroes were immune from fevers, especially yellow fever, which caused great European mortality.[60]

Had he been writing prior to 1780 his views might have seemed more credible. Yellow fever, in some travel accounts, was occasionally seen to follow a racial pattern, leaving Negroes unscathed while ravaging whites; and some of his other allegations might have carried weight in the absence of strong contrary evidence. Although infant mortality had received some discussion—notably by Buffon[61]—there had been comparatively little attention paid to tetanus or to dirt-eating, which is now known to be a symptom of infestation by hook-worm.[62] Moreover until the last two decades of the century the question of Negro disease was dealt with only obliquely. In medical works even the most emphatic statements about Negroes were only passing references. In travel reports and geographical surveys allusions to Negro disease or immunity were always subordinate to the larger themes of European mortality or the terrors of the tropical environment. As a result, although the great majority of writers either assumed or mentioned briefly the essential homogeneity of Negro and European constitutions, this message was not conveyed with any great force to their readers.

But in 1799 White was producing his claims about unique racial disease against a background of contrary assertion. As abolitionists focussed on the failure of West Indian slavery to sustain itself by natural increase, their opponents chose to justify their continuing dependence on the slave trade in terms of Negro culpability. Their allegations of maternal ignorance and indifference, and of deliberate and involuntary abortions in the pursuit of sexual pleasure, amounted to a considerable indictment of the Negro's moral character.[63] And it meant that far more attention was paid by polemicists to the Negro's social than his racial image, as abolitionists mounted counter-attacks accusing slave owners of inducing and condoning immorality.[64]

But while the question of racial disease was never the subject of debate, it was brought very explicitly into the open in this period of controversy. In an attempt to discover the reasons for the failure of slavery to sustain itself naturally, the Privy Council and Parliamentary investigators questioned colonial authorities and medical and other expert witnesses in a way which gave ample scope for racialist explanations to emerge but which also suggested that such explanations were not envisaged: "Are the *Negro* slaves subject to any peculiar diseases to which *white* inhabitants or free *Negroes* are not subject?" In proportions of three to one those questioned answered with a flat negative. But even the positive replies amounted to, at most, a highly qualified assertion of Negro peculiarity.

The only disease which emerged with any consistency as peculiar to Negroes was yaws. Yet even here racialism was muted. While the official replies from Jamaica, Grenada, and St. Vincent—together with those from three doctors—mentioned yaws without any explanation, just as many others reported that it was occasionally contracted by whites. The reply from Dominica revealed how colonial apologists of slavery felt threatened by the question and yet responded in terms of the Negro's social and moral deficiencies rather than his racial peculiarity. While yaws was peculiar to Negroes, there were one or two instances of whites contracting it through "impure contact". Other apparent differences, the reply concluded, were due to the laziness and negligence of Negroes, not to hard usage by slave owners.[65]

Much the same pattern of social explanations emerged in references to dirt-eating. Although some respondents mentioned this as "peculiar" to Negroes, they went on to describe it as a "depravity of appetite" occasioned by hard usage, grief, lack of proper food, or, on the pro-slavery side, as a form of rebellion.[66] Similarly, the official reply from St. Vincent referred to the quality of Negro food in explaining the prevalence of worms among children.[67]

The official investigators also included a question about infant mortality, which even pro-slavery writers conceded to be abnormally high among West Indian slaves. The question, "do Negro children suffer from peculiar diseases?", prompted much propagandist emphasis on social factors. Pro-slavery people stressed lack of maternal affection, "libidinous pursuits",[68] and incompetent midwifery, while abolitionists referred to poor living conditions and inadequate medical care.[69] One disease—tetanus—emerged as the major cause of this mortality, with many authorities declaring that it claimed the lives of between one third and one quarter of all Negro babies in the first nine days after birth. But although one or two islands replied to the question about peculiarity with a brief affirmative reference to infant tetanus, the more detailed replies provided no foundation for White's racialist claims. The authorities in Jamaica, for instance, included three detailed appendices of medical opinion which totally ruled out any such interpretation of the simple reference to tetanus in their reply to the questionnaire. The arguments of the three medical practitioners concerned—John Chisholme, Adam Anderson and John Quier—concentrated on such social factors as living conditions and on medical hypotheses, of which the most favoured was infection of the navel due to insanitary bandaging by Negro midwives.[70]

Other opinions were different but no more conducive to racialism. Samuel Athill, a doctor in Antigua, argued that a major cause of tetanus was exposure to cold and damp, caused by the "nocturnal rambles" of Negro mothers.[71] The evidence of George Baillie implied that tetanus was a West Indian rather than racial disease. He claimed that in 25 years as a planter in South Carolina and Georgia he had never seen tetanus in Negro babies.[72]

Although the detailed picture of Negro disease was contained in reports and answers to questionnaires presumably read by few, its broad outlines were given wider publicity in the polemical literature of the period. James Adair, for instance, included in a pro-slavery tract his own answers to the official inquiries. He based his negative response to the question about peculiar diseases on analysis of the social roles of different Negro groups. Variations due to the circumstances of labour were illustrated by reference to considerable differences in patterns of health between field and domestic slaves. The possible racial implications of his statement that infant tetanus was equally prevalent among slaves and free Negroes, while non-existent among whites, was offset by his rider that "from the superintending care of the mistresses of some plantations the disease is become less frequent."[73]

An anonymous planter published a pamphlet commenting on the material submitted by the Jamaican Assembly in response to the British inquiries. His detailed criticisms of the medical opinions of Chisholme, Anderson, and Quier served to emphasize still more the social reasons for Negro disease. Accepting Chisholme's argument that irritation of the navel was responsible for infant tetanus, he rejected the doctor's reservations about the feasibility of prevention. Before admitting that maternal carelessness was the cause, West Indians should consider the carelessness of doctors who claimed to be in charge of huge numbers of Negroes on widely scattered plantations.[74]

Apart from these direct comments, the official inquiries also stimulated considerable parallel publication on the salient questions. While the commonest allegations in newspapers and pamphlets were of planters' cruelty or Negroes' irresponsibility, there were a number of specific references to disease quite typical of the trend already outlined. In 1788 the *Public Advertiser* printed a physician's social explanations of tetanus and dirt-eating and the *Morning Chronicle* a detailed criticism of medical care on West Indian plantations. Another published letter attributed

infant tetanus to incompetent Negro midwifery but a range of
other diseases to the inadequate diet imposed by the slave
system.[75]

This period of quickened interest in the lot of West Indian slaves
produced only one statement which substantially anticipated
White's arguments. Alone among pro-slavery writers Hector
McNeill justified slave mortality by referring to the "various and
dreadful disorders peculiar to the AFRICAN." But even McNeill
was equivocal. He cited as peculiar diseases yaws, dirt-eating, and
especially, infant tetanus, but then argued that this last disease was
much   less   prevalent   with   an   experienced   midwife   in
attendance.[76]

The only aspect of Negro disease which had not been clarified by
the inquiries into slavery and the slave trade, at the time White
published his work, was the immunity to yellow fever which
seemed implied by the experiences of many in West Africa. But a
combination of other circumstances had produced a prolific output
of medical publications on the subject, which had discounted the
implications of racial immunity. An epidemic in New York in 1795
killed some seven hundred people and there were recurrent
outbreaks in Philadelphia through the decade. And as the
upheavals of the French Revolution produced considerable
movements of people in the Caribbean, outbreaks of yellow fever
wrought great mortality among emigrants from the French islands
and "unseasoned" British troops newly arrived in the West Indies.
Although Europeans were the greatest sufferers, at least seven
medical works, stimulated by these American and Caribbean
epidemics, commented explicitly on the lack of immunity among
Negroes similarly removed to new environments, while none
proved any grounds for White's assertion of racial immunity.[77]

In the same way White's reference to racial immunity to other
fevers was even less plausible in the 1790s than it would have been
earlier. Medical and other writers continued to explain
susceptibility in terms of inappropriate diet and alcoholic
indulgence[78] and added new references to "nature cures" to
accounts of Negroes' sounder regimen which dated at least from
the time of John Atkins in the 1730s.[79] Abolitionist interest in the
economic development of Africa as an alternative to the slave
trade led to some propagandist rejections of the image of a "White
Man's Grave".[80] And if this propaganda was belied by the
mortality attending the first attempts at colonization in Sierra
Leone, the same disasters brought out more strongly than ever
that immunities to fever were acquired rather than racial. A
newspaper article in 1789 reported white mortality with the

comment that "European constitutions were never designed to live and settle in Africa . . ." but added that almost as many black settlers had perished, "as it was found that none but those who were born in Africa could stand the inclemencies of the clime and weather."[81]

*   *   *

Even in the era of debate the category of sources on which much of this book has been based—the often mediocre bulk of gentlemanly libraries—acts as a useful barometer of opinion. It helps to clarify the important arguments and beliefs among so much that was specialist, ephemeral, and polemical.

In this period the concept of gradation was much in evidence in the versions of natural history put forward in works of education, entertainment, and reference. But this scrutiny did not focus particularly on Africa. The anthropoids of the East Indies were at least as important a source of scientific confusion. Partly this was the result of a vagueness which lumped together numerous different species under the name "orang-outang": naturalists as far back as Tyson and as recent as Camper regarded their studies as relevant to either Africa or Asia, while popular surveys of natural history listed the two continents as equally important homes of anthropoids.[82] Moreover some of the most radical assessments of the orang-outang's place in nature derived solely from the East Indies. John Payne's *Universal Geography* depicted the orang of Borneo as the link between man and brute. Richard Watson, in a rare example of tacit support for Lord Monboddo, casually numbered the "Orang-outang of the woods of Java" among the human race. In an article in the *Philosophical Magazine* in 1798 F. B. von Wurmb showed how the "wild-man" syndrome rested mainly on evidence from the East Indies: this had led even Linnaeus temporarily to place the Javanese orang-outang—or "night-man"—between man and ape.[83]

These tendencies to practical application of the Chain of Being were specifically attempts to promote apes rather than demote men. Even then they were far from dominant. Monboddo, their most thorough exponent, became an object of ridicule. Conversational jibes by such as Samuel Johnson were matched by the heavy irony of reviewers in the monthly journals. His name became so inextricably associated with a despised theory that even his obituaries concentrated almost exclusively on the "absurd whim and conceit" of his "orang-outang system".[84]

It was significant that it was Petrus Camper's scientific attack on the claims of anatomical similarity between man and ape—rather than his "facial angle"—which received attention in the periodical press and in published monographs.[85] For if the Chain of Being made only a limited impact on popular versions of natural history and geography, the concept of racial gradation made even less. Its only significant treatment was in John Walker's *Elements of Geography and Natural and Civil History.* In discussing the classification of natural history, Walker used the term "imperceptible gradations" in an opposite way to the racists—to refer to a confused jumble of characteristics which defied orderly arrangement. He went on to dismiss racial gradation as an "absurd position" advocated only by those who were actively oppressing the Negro.

If Walker's book succeeded in reaching its prospective audience, it could stand alone as summary of British racial attitudes at the turn of the century. According to the Preface of the third edition of 1800, it was designed for use of the "public in general", of "free Schools, Academies, and Universities", and "especially for Mothers who superintend children's education and for the female sex in general."[86] More certain than its readership is the representative nature of its arguments. Walker's opposition to the slave trade was typical of most geographical editors of his period. Books too short to reproduce, as his did, long sections of standard abolition propaganda, still found space to pass judgements in their African sections, while elsewhere merely describing the non-European world. The relevant passage in J. Ouisseau's *Practical Geography* exemplifies the tone of the smaller school text books: "The chief trade of Guinea, Congo, and Nigritia, can hardly be named by *Men* without a blush, or rather without horror. It is a traffic of tears and human blood, which is called *Slave-Trade.*"[87]

Yet despite the quickened humanitarian conscience, the years of debate over the "Negro question" did nothing to undermine traditional assumptions of white superiority in a cultural and aesthetic sense. James Gordon's survey of geography and "modern history" included a standard diatribe against the "relentless and unfeeling avarice of Europeans" in the slave trade. But it had no doubts but that Europeans were quite simply the most beautiful people in the world. "The Saxons of Germany and the English are particularly remarkable for whiteness of complexion, and are probably not surpassed in this respect by any people." Gordon's contention that females from these fortunate regions "furnish finer models to the painter" was echoed by Walker's claim that it was from Europeans that "sculptors seem to have derived all that they term sublime and beautiful."

Such attitudes sounded not a little like the preamble to Camper's "facial angle" theory, placing Negroes and Classical sculpture at opposite poles of human beauty. And though the geographical popularizers showed no interest in Camper's theory, their exposition of a centuries-old theme did show at least a superficial influence of the newer vogue for gradation. Negroes, wrote Gordon, with their "peculiar deformity of face" seemed "in direct opposition to the northern Europeans with snowy skins, long pendent hair of a flaxen hue, and fine regular features." According to Walker, skin colour varied from Europe to India "by slow and imperceptible degrees". Yet even in the countenance of the "black Asiatic" there seemed "a beautiful symmetry, or a certain neatness and delicacy of feature, which does not appear to us, either in the flat noses or thick lips of the inhabitants of the torrid zones of Negroland and Guinea, or in the broad faces and high cheeks of the Laplanders and little Tartars of the bleak and frozen zone."[88]

It was not merely abolitionist sympathy which restrained such authors from any more thorough-going endorsement of racial gradation. The intellectual barriers were also strongly in evidence, most particularly the environmental theories which explained both racial and cultural difference. Indeed the extravagant aesthetic prejudice displayed by both Walker and Gordon was incorporated in elaborations of the environmental theme. Walker was so completely committed to the kind of environmentalism displayed by Buffon that he divided mankind into three groups at once racial and cultural. While "Tartars" showed the physical effects of cold, and "Negroes" those of heat, the third category was neither "Europeans" nor "whites" but simply "Citizens", whose physical attributes stemmed from the fact that they were a "polished people".[89]

If Walker's simple formula was unusually terse—or naive—it was much more typical of the trend in contemporary attitudes to race and culture than the theories which set the Negro permanently below other human beings. On the other hand, the assumptions of cultural superiority embodied in his formula could reflect more than traditional views about the inferiority of Africa. One striking characteristic of the geographical *genre* was how little it revealed of the contemporary attention focussed on the West Indian slave system. More than ever, in this category of publication, the Negro image was African rather than New World plantation slave. And in the era of debate the image of Africa had changed considerably.

CHAPTER TEN

OLD AND NEW IMAGES OF AFRICA

The changes in the image of West African society and culture in the three decades before abolition of the slave trade cannot be summed up as either more or less favourable. There was more information available but it was seen and even compiled under the distorting influence of propaganda. Propaganda was not entirely new; but it had never previously put eyewitness reporters of Africa so much on their guard. This defensive stance meant that there was a crucial division between slave traders and West Indian defenders of slavery. In contrast to the continuing West Indian emphasis on blood and despotism, the slave traders revealed much more about the variety and complexity of Negro systems of government and jurisprudence. But the overall effects of this trend were limited. Much of the more detailed information was presented only to the official committees investigating the slave trade. Its favourable implications were more widely publicized only when it suited the purposes of abolition propaganda, as in the case of domestic slavery within Africa. In general, the abolitionists avoided such information. They saw the slave trade as the prime cause of most African deficiencies but they were prepared to condemn Negroes as well as Europeans for running it. Because of this major preoccupation; because of particular tactical aims; and because they were men of their time, sharing ethnocentric assumptions displayed in every medium of publication, the abolitionists were far more concerned with upholding the Negro's character and potential than praising his culture.

There were factors other than the debate over the slave trade encouraging reappraisals of the Negro. The early struggles of the Sierra Leone venture introduced more polemics. And the activities of the Association for Promoting the Discovery of the Interior Parts of Africa yielded their first tangible results with the

publication of Mungo Park's *Travels* in 1799. But new
perspectives, and even new information, were largely subordinate
to the central issue of the times.

*   *   *

On the pro-slavery side the tendency to use reporting as
propaganda was most obvious with Archibald Dalzel and Robert
Norris[1] on Dahomey but it was also evident more unevenly in John
Matthews' account of Sierra Leone. On the other side, Alexander
Falconbridge and John Newton were the notable examples of slave
traders turned abolitionist spokesmen. From both extremes the
polemical pressures combined to intensify ethnocentric impatience
with Black Africa, for even abolitionists were more concerned with
changing than preserving Negro culture.

Thomas Clarkson was exceptional among abolitionists in the
way he praised Negro artistic and craft skills in print and illustrated
the same point by carrying samples on his tours of Britain.[2]
But even he was countering allegations of Negro stupidity
with evidence of potential rather than with enthusiasm
for an established culture. The trend was more marked
elsewhere. In these years at the turn of the century the early
tendency to judge African craftsmanship, and particularly
textiles, in terms of European ideas of commercial viability
was enormously strengthened. In a country in the early
stages of industrial revolution it is perhaps not surprising
that the long-term admiration for the finished products of
Negro craftsmanship should be increasingly overshadowed
by impatience at uneconomic methods of production.
There were more immediate reasons for the tendency. Sierra
Leone Company propaganda had obvious reasons for stressing
the potential of Negro textiles. And abolitionists turned the
old, rather vague aspirations of the Postlethwayt era into a
more urgent search for economic aiternatives to the slave
trade. No less convinced than their predecessors about the
evil effects of the slave trade, they were much less inclined to
prescribe a European withdrawal to allow Negroes to enjoy an
uncontaminated primitive life. Negroes were potential producers
and consumers worthy of being incorporated in a wider British
pattern of trade.[3]

These attitudes do not mean that the humanitarian
characteristics of abolitionism were disguise for essentially
economic motives. They merely illustrate the continuing virility of
ethnocentric assumptions about cultural difference. There could

be no more practical expression of compassion for the Negro than to help him to become more British than African.

This desire, however, provoked inevitable opposition. William Fox, in presenting an abolitionist *Summary of the Evidence produced before a Committee of the House of Commons relating to the slave trade,* was able to draw on favourable reports of native textile production from men with experience of Africa.[4] But increasingly such reports came from those detached from, or hostile to the slave trade. While John Newton and a number of others stressed the quality of native cloths and dyes,[5] a large number of slave traders presented directly contrary evidence. They claimed both that production was intrinsically crude and inferior and that native laziness would prevent any worthwhile commercial exploitation.[6] The evidence of John Matthews indicated the pressures at work. Questioned by the official investigators he denied that Negro textiles offered any hope of commercial development. Yet in his *Voyage to Sierra Leone,* published in the same period, he had written of one group who were "very ingenious in fabricating cotton cloths, which they sell to their more southern neighbours."[7]

Each group of protagonists failed conspicuously to discuss craftsmanship in terms of a society fundamentally different from European forms. It was left to a geographical editor, John Leyden, to point out in 1799, albeit only implicitly, that ingenious native workmanship was the product of a society lacking the technology and the essential division of labour for large-scale commercial production:

> When we consider the imperfection of their tools, and their ignorance of machinery; when we also recollect that the same individual spins, weaves, sews, hunts, fishes, and forms his baskets, fishing-tackle and instruments of agriculture, the neatness of their manufacture in iron, gold, fillagree-work, cotton-matting, and basket-work, may excite our admiration.

As an opponent of the slave trade and an admirer of such visionaries as C. B. Wadstrom, Leyden was prepared to support the fundamental alteration of native society which commercial schemes demanded. Yet, in this last year of the eighteenth century, he could report little success. Wadstrom had been so struck with the potential of Negro cotton spinning that he had gone to Manchester to acquire such knowledge "as might qualify him for instructing the natives of Africa." But his efforts, including his *Essay on Colonization, particularly applied to the western coast of Africa,* had achieved little practical result.[8]

Many aspects of African culture had little connection with

economic potential. James Ramsay and John Luffman were 150 years ahead of their time in seeing such potential in the presentation of Negro music to a London society gripped by a "continued rage for Italian singers." In most works music and dancing continued to be seen by the Negro's friends as evidence of cultural inferiority and even depravity. For George Gregory, sympathetic to abolition, these were almost definitive signs of barbarity: "in all ages the vulgar have been more affected with sound than with sense; and dancing is one of the first diversions of barbarous people."[9] Most attitudes were, however, simply polemical. Pro-slavery pamphleteers cited the music of West Indian Negroes as evidence of contentment: as James Adair put it, their dancing and singing were so cheerful "there is no reason to suppose they consider bondage as a great evil." Similar claims by slave traders about the spontaneity of Negro festivity aboard slaving vessels[10] were countered by numerous abolitionists, who argued that dancing was a compulsory form of exercise into which slaves were coerced by the whip.[11] While other abolitionists cited musical proficiency as evidence of Negroes' human capacities,[12] some opponents found that emphasis on a physical and sensuous proficiency underlined the poverty of Negro achievement in more intellectual pursuits. To Archibald Dalzel it was less proficiency than a ludicrous racial trait which impelled bound sacrificial victims in Dahomey to beat time to the ceremonial music preceding their own slaughter.[13]

Dalzel's account was mainly concerned with aspects of Negro culture far more repugnant than music. He offered both explicit and implicit support for the controversial picture of Negro bloodshed presented half a century before by William Snelgrave. He declared that Snelgrave's work had "irresistible evidences of truth", and ridiculed such critics as John Atkins. And he went on to present an even more comprehensive account of Dahomean annihilation of prisoners of war and other captives, which included descriptions of particular massacres and of piles of human skulls decorating houses and royal palaces.[14]

Dalzel's work illustrated both the polemical preoccupations now influencing reporters and a shift in the emphasis of pro-slavery propaganda. Less and less was the slave trade presented as a civilizing mission within Africa. It was almost exclusively seen as a continuing rescue operation from violent death. Dalzel reproduced a long speech allegedly by the king of Dahomey which, in answering one common anti-slavery argument, undermined the older pro-slavery claims that the slave trade had a civilizing effect. The king claimed that the trade had in no way encouraged him to wage war; if circumstances warranted, he would always be prepared to murder rather than sell prisoners of war. Whether or not such sentiments were invented by Europeans, Bryan Edwards was correct in claiming that there were many reports that slaves rejected by European traders were butchered on the spot.[15]

In general the abolitionist response made no concessions. It did not admit that human sacrifice might occur in some Negro societies and not in others. It did not draw from such favourite authorities as Bosman and Barbot conclusions that sacrifice was sometimes associated with ritual. It merely provided its own generalizations to obscure the realities of regional and cultural variety. While virtually all abolitionists blamed endemic warfare on the slave trade,[16] a few denied categorically that prisoners of war had ever been sacrificed. Ottobah Cugoano referred to the general custom of absorbing them into the community as domestic slaves. And Alexander Falconbridge mentioned the specific case of a lull in the slave trade during the American War of Independence which had led, not to increased bloodshed in Africa, but to corresponding quietness. Negro traders at Bonny had complained to him that, with only one ship arriving in three years, "they were obliged to dig the ground and plant yams."[17]

Much of the debate over the slave trade developed into an argument about—and eventually an inquiry into—the nature of enslavement in Africa. It was in this field that the opportunities were greatest for reassessment favourable to the Negro, as slave traders sought to legitimize their activities as an orderly commerce conducted with responsible trading partners. But this opportunity was not seized by abolitionists. Their obsession with the horrors of the slave trade blinded their perception of African realities.

The claim that Negroes sold their children and other relatives into slavery is a good illustration of the trends. This allegation could be used as part of the denigration of Negro character, an illustration of the alleged lack of social affection which had long been intermittently reported.[18] Abolitionists were quick to defend the Negro. But their method was either to deny the allegations flatly or to argue that such transactions were so rare as to be unworthy of consideration as a character trait.[19] They failed to search for reasons inherent in the mechanics of the slave trade to explain a charge which had been made constantly since the seventeenth century in non-polemical works.[20] When probable explanations emerged in the investigations into the slave trade, they were an incidental result of descriptions of trading procedures. Abolitionists failed to draw conclusions from reports that Negro traders presented their children as security for payments advanced by Europeans. These "pawns" were held until the Negro traders returned from inland markets with slaves. Occasionally, it was said, the Negroes had been unable to redeem their children, who were then carried away as slaves.[21]

Subject to the same pressures were the fundamental question of how Africa was ruled and ancillary ones about judicial processes, civil liberties, and social institutions in general. The old humanitarian intolerance with Africans, as well as Europeans, who flouted natural rights, continued. Clarkson's attitude was typical. Even if slaves were criminals in their own countries, they could not justly be transferred to European jurisdiction: "The state alone is considered to have been injured, and as *injuries cannot possibly be transferred,* the state alone can justly receive the advantages of his (the slave's) labour." A Negro king who sold his subjects was therefore "usurping a power, which no ruler or rulers of a state can possess, and which the great Creator of the universe never yet gave to any order whatever of created beings."[22]

If the argument here was coldly legalistic, elsewhere Clarkson and others focussed contemptuously on the moral depravity of African rulers. Noting that warfare in Africa was now waged for the sole purpose of sustaining the slave trade, Clarkson asked rhetorically, "But if the African kings could be capable of such injustice, what vices are there, that their consciences would restrain, or what enormities, that we might not expect to be committed?"[23] Thomas Day dismissed attempts to justify the trade with a scornful generalization: "A wretch, devoid of compassion and understanding, who calls himself a King of some part of Africa . . . seizes his innocent subjects, or engages in an unnecessary war to furnish himself with prisoners . . ."[24]

As in this case, abolitionist intolerance towards African society was nearly always subordinate to attack on the slave trade itself. The depredations of Negro despots, as they waged war or pillaged their own populations, were publicized in virtually every medium of abolition publication as part of a denunciation of the corrupting influence of Europeans in Africa.[25] For this very reason there was in this later period a belated attempt by the Europeans involved to present a more favourable view of Negro society. The many slave traders who gave evidence before the official inquiries into the trade denied that native rulers had the power arbitrarily to dispose of their subjects. Some, like Harry Gandy, who had made two slaving voyages to Sierra Leone, claimed that nearly all slaves came from far in the interior.[26] Many others put the emphasis more positively on coastal governments which were claimed to be the antithesis of despotism. In some cases this new emphasis was not entirely favourable, producing an impression of mutually hostile, internally divided petty states.[27] Thomas Eldrid, an American trading to Senegal, even argued that if there were occasional instances of kidnapping, this was not because of tyranny but because government was too weak to prevent it.[28] But generally the slave traders contrived to describe restricted monarchies in terms of institutional assets rather than impotence.

Captain Heatley outlined a pattern of varying government in the Gambia region, consisting mainly of monarchies "with Powers variously limited."[29] John Matthews described the very limited powers of governors of small independent states in Sierra Leone, while James Penny claimed that the area to the north comprised many small states, none of them despotic: councils of elders decided on all civil and military affairs. According to Richard Miles, there was only one despotic government on the Gold Coast, at Cape Appollonia. Elsewhere there were petty states with monarchical powers limited by councils of elders, who decided the succession.[30]

For many reasons these more favourable accounts could have had small effect on public opinion. In the first place they contained many internal inconsistencies and qualifications. For men with first-hand knowledge of two or more widely separated areas it was difficult to match the comfortable generalizations of abolitionists. Robert Norris, for instance, while echoing other reports about the limitations on monarchical power on the Gold Coast, was forced to remark that on the Windward Coast the pattern varied from extreme despotism to less oppressive monarchies and republics. Similarly Archibald Dalzel and William Devaynes, after describing the functions of Caboceroes and councils on the Gold Coast, could only depict the kingdom of Dahomey as the most oppressive tyranny on earth. More damaging than these admissions of regional variation were inconsistent accounts of the same areas. Usually these were the result of different reporters' varying awareness of the polemical implications of their evidence. Thus while Robert Norris was concerned to counter allegations about the corrupting influence of Europeans in his account of the Gold Coast, Devaynes virtually corroborated the same abolitionist case. According to Norris there had been substantial improvement in native civil rights in areas long in contact with Europeans. According to Devaynes, the enjoyment of civil rights dated back to long before the advent of Europeans and in general the worst blacks were those most concerned with the European settlements. More generally, the favourable information was frequently purveyed by men who, in the same official inquiries, were at pains to depict their activities as a means of saving Negroes from human sacrifice and other barbarous fates hardly consistent with a picture of equitable government.[31]

The impact of the slave traders' case was also reduced by the fact that the same inquiries brought forth a probably heavier volume of evidence in support of the abolitionists' claims. Some of this came from reformed slave traders recruited by the industrious Clarkson.[32] And some was provided by travellers whose knowledge of Africa had been gained outside the slave trade, mainly Army and Royal Navy officers but including the Swedish naturalists, Wadstrom and Sparrman.[33]

Not only did Wadstrom and many others repair the slave traders' omissions about the "pillage" in Senegambia and other forms of kidnapping but there were many flat contradictions of the claims that monarchy was limited in most areas. In contrast with Heatley's description of limitations on royal power in the Gambia, Thomas Poplett, an army officer, and John Hills and Sir George Yonge, both of the Royal Navy, all saw the same region as subject to the most severe despotism. Poplett agreed with the slave traders that the area boasted councils of elders but these were of no importance and their advice liable to be ignored by the kings.[35]

The belated attempt to play down injustice and tyranny was also at odds with the arguments of West Indian defenders of slavery. While the slave traders increasingly tried to present themselves publicly as participants in a legitimate commerce conducted with responsible governments, the old West Indian arguments were far from dead. In 1788 an anonymous *Essay on the Slave Trade* dwelt on the barbarous incivility of Negro government, while the *Gentleman's Magazine*, now firmly in the pro-slavery camp, described an Africa of small communities each under the control of a ruthless despot. And Hector McNeill, defending the planters of Jamaica, reproduced the old contrast between New World comforts and the bloody despotism of Africa. He described kidnapping and the "pillage" as evidence of the depravity of the Negro character. Typically, Edward Long had attempted to have the best of both arguments: the trade saved Negroes from all the usual catalogue of autocratic abuses; and yet, he had claimed elsewhere in the same work, 99 per cent of all slaves were convicted felons precisely comparable to those deported by the British government.[36]

Bryan Edwards was far more honest about this particular debating point, which affected the image of native government no less crucially than the arguments about kidnapping and the "pillage". Whereas most West Indians were probably unwitting opponents of the arguments of the British slave traders, Edwards deliberately accepted most of the contentions of their arch-enemy, Wilberforce, about the African background of the trade. He conceded that Africa was "a Field of warfare and desolation; a wilderness, in which the inhabitants are wolves towards each other." In particular, the claim that most slaves were properly convicted criminals was "mockery and insult." The only pro-slavery argument about Africa that he would accept was that unilateral abolition would damage Britain economically with no advantage for the Negroes, who would be sold to other European nations in the same numbers.[37]

With such dubious allies the slave traders were fighting a losing battle in arguing that the African coast comprised orderly native societies with equitable systems of justice. Some of the witnesses before the official inquiries offered careful descriptions of the judicial machine in various countries. According to Eldrid and Penny, trials in Senegal and Sierra Leone were conducted before juries of head-men. The kings pronounced sentence in Senegal but strictly subject to the advice of these juries. Dalzel and Miles described a similar process on the Gold Coast.[38] And a great many witnesses, dealing with numerous areas, claimed that Negro trials were fairly conducted.[39]

But once again the combination of internal inconsistency and abolitionist counter-attack overshadowed these claims. Because the ideal slave trade rationalization praised native institutions while denigrating native character the slave traders' accounts furnished some less favourable incidental information about the nature of offences deemed appropriate to sentences of slavery. Some of the witnesses were on their guard about these matters. Witchcraft was claimed by a few to be a covert native activity beyond the ken of most Europeans and outside the framework of orthodox jurisprudence.[40] In arguing its irrelevance to European activities Heatley also used it to disarm the long-standing criticisms about trial by ordeal. The "red water" was administered only to those suspected of witchcraft, whereas those sold as slaves underwent a normal criminal trial.[41] But others contradicted this by admitting that some of their purchased slaves had been convicted of witchcraft.[42] And others showed that the harsh penalty of slavery was exacted for such moral misdemeanours as adultery and gambling, as well as for unspecified degrees of theft.[43]

Some of the hostile witnesses argued that such offences lent themselves to trumped up charges. Thomas Trotter,[44] a Royal Navy surgeon, and John Simpson,[45] a lieutenant in the marines, argued that adultery charges were especially suspect. Thomas Deane, a captain engaged in non-slave trading activities in Africa, explained that women frequently acted as enticers to gain adultery convictions and that witchcraft allegations were often used similarly as an excuse to obtain slaves.[46] But the main abolition case was concerned less with the nature of imputed crimes than with alleged corruption of the judicial machine. Whatever the outward form of litigation the slave trade had led to a general perversion of justice. Many witnesses echoed the claim of the Reverend Isham Baggs, a former Navy chaplain recruited by Clarkson, that native codes of law were now "wholly subservient to the slave trade" and that trials were invariably rigged to secure convictions.[47]

Like the charges of kidnapping this abolitionist point was well established long before this period of intensive debate late in the century. As well as early propagandists like Benezet, most of the secondary geographical works of the mid-eighteenth century had argued that since the coming of Europeans all penalties had been changed to slavery and that the same pressures had led to a general corruption of judicial systems. The same works gave a wealth of information about the role of women as enticers in adultery cases, about trial by ordeal, the sentencing of whole families for the crimes of one individual, and similar practices equally remote from contemporary ideas of justice.[48] Nothing more clearly indicates the existence of unfavourable stereotypes than the questions about judicial matters which the committees of inquiry eventually chose to ask. Many of the more favourable assertions came in the form of negative answers to questions about the prevalence of summary justice, witchcraft trials, and the influence of European demand on procedures and sentences.

Viewed objectively, the picture offered by the slave traders of societies with formal political and social institutions cannot be dismissed as entirely propagandist. Although carefully selective, it also reflected a much greater familiarity with Africa than was enjoyed by all but a few abolitionists or by the navy and army officers who gave evidence before the committees. Significantly the better informed abolitionists offered corroboration of at least some parts of the picture.

John Newton, the ex-slave trader, provided written and verbal accounts of the Windward Coast very different from the usual dismissive abolitionist generalizations. He rejected completely the image of despotic monarchy. Kings were weak and the real power lay with the many members of the *Purrows,* committees of elders which provided strong but equitable government. On the whole a fair system of justice prevailed and all local slaves were indeed properly convicted criminals, although much the greater part came from the distant interior. Newton, under questioning, was not even certain that the demands of the slave trade had encouraged warfare in Africa, although he did confirm that some slaves were kidnapped. Similar points were made by Equiano, either from greater personal knowledge or a desire to uphold the character of his fellow-Africans. He himself hailed from an Ibo district under the suzerainty of the King of Benin. But no tyranny was involved in this political arrangement and his locality was equitably ruled by councils of elders who provided a machinery for the settlement of disputes within the community.[49]

Even Thomas Clarkson, lacking Newton's or Equiano's first hand knowledge but undertaking far more research than other abolitionists, produced a fairly detailed description of the social hierarchy and administrative and judicial systems in the area contiguous to Fort St Louis and Gorée. He described government sophisticated enough to embrace a system of provincial deputies and subordinate officials, as well as a series of offices created especially for conducting relations with Europeans on the coast. Law and order were effectively enforced by a combination of these officials and the military; and the whole machinery was sustained by regularly collected taxes, mainly in kind. But he concluded by observing that none of this in any way tempered the despotism of a monarch who could pillage his own subjects at will in order to meet European demand for slaves.[50]

To present Negro society in more favourable terms it needed a synchronization of this more specialized knowledge, on the one hand, and the demands of both abolitionist and pro-slavery propaganda on the other. This synchronization was brought to bear on only one aspect of African society, the indigenous institution of slavery. As a previous chapter has shown, distinctions between slavery in Africa and the West Indies were well established before the abolition debate, not least in John Hippisley's account published in 1764. Now, in the testimony of such traders as Richard Miles, Dalzel, Devaynes, and Matthews, confirmation that these slaves were rarely sold to Europeans, and then only after due judicial process, helped to confirm that they were participants in a legitimate commerce, rather than receivers of stolen human property. The only modification by others with knowledge of Africa came from those, like John Hills, who wished to present evidence of the corrupting influence of the slave trade. In common with other observers, Hills said that domestic slaves were well treated: but he maintained that the desire for brandy led native owners to condemn them for European sale on the slightest pretext.[51]

On the whole, however, the reports of African slavery presented such striking contrasts with the West Indian institution that abolitionists for once united with the slave traders in projecting a favourable image. Clarkson described in some detail the work required of an African slave. Domestic duties included the collection of wood and water by the men, cotton spinning and the pounding of millet by the women. The men cultivated crops from five to eleven a.m. only, which demanded no more that the "ordinary exercise which men should take." This was in glaring contrast to the work demanded in the West Indian plantations. Cugoano was able to add the authenticity of first hand knowledge to a similar comparison: "So far as I can remember, some of the Africans in my country keep slaves, which they take in war, or for debt: but those which they keep are well fed, and good care taken of them, and treated well . . ."[52]

Inevitably West Indian voices were raised in protest against such favourable descriptions of the African institution. Mostly their arguments were vague general statements, such as that by an opponent of James Ramsay: "As for Africa it teems with slaves reduced to the most irksome subjection."[53] But on this one issue the combination of abolitionist propaganda and eyewitness reporting overwhelmed the West Indian case. Even at its most hostile, reporting produced a view of African slavery markedly in contrast with the West Indies. Nothing more clearly demonstrated the decisive dichotomy within the pro-slavery ranks than John Matthews' unusually hostile description of domestic slavery, which made a distinction between the treatment of the house slave and the field labourer in Sierra Leone. While the former "is in some respects considered as a branch of the family, assumes his master's name, and calls him father", the latter "is as it were fixed to the soil, and held in no higher estimation than any other animal that contributes to its cultivation." Yet both categories found their situation in Africa quite tolerable, whereas if sold to Europeans they exhibited symptoms of stunned shock.[54]

*   *   *

The era at the turn of the century was dominated by propagandist views of Africa as never before. But it also yielded in Mungo Park's *Travels* a perspective on African government and society uniquely detached from the slave trade controversy. Although Park was on record as opposing the trade, his work was the first important product of a new interest in Africa as a field of geographical and scientific inquiry. As such it provided corroboration for elements of both pro- and anti-slave trade propaganda. Government was shown to be more stable and more institutionally complex than the crude abolitionist generalizations about tyranny. But on the other hand the corrupting influence of the slave trade, in such practices as the "pillage", was thoroughly confirmed.[55]

Park's reports on other aspects of Negro culture were fascinating to the specialist but they did little to modify general images of black barbarity. One specialist, J. D. Carlyle, Professor of Arabic at Cambridge, wrote that it was well known that Arabic was understood to a degree wherever Islam flourished: "but it is only from the recent discoveries of the Sierra Leone Company, and still more from those of Messrs. Park and Brown, that we have become acquainted with the *degree* to which this language prevails in the interior parts of Africa." These discoveries made it clear that many Negroes carried to the West Indies as slaves "must be capable of understanding the Scriptures in Arabic."[56] Yet at virtually the same moment a reviewer of Park's *Travels* was confirming traditional conclusions about Negro ignorance:

> The author found, on the borders of the desert and on the banks of the Niger, what has been found in all countries, a mixture of good and evil: he saw no people exempted from the influence. of passion, and solely guided by a predominating reason . . . The inhabitants of Africa, possessing few arts, could have few of the conveniences of life; and without books, they must be without any stories of imagery, principles of science, and comprehension of knowledge. Their wants were to be found few, yet their means scarcely adequate to supply them; and their vices and virtues were gross, simple and circumscribed in their operation . . . we must exclaim with Kafra the slave-driver, "Black men are nothing."[57]

Exciting though they may have been to a Professor of Arabic, revelations about Islamic culture in black Africa were unlikely to impress a general reading public brought up on such text book slurs as John Richardson's account of Negro enthusiasm for the tenets of the "famous Imposter Mahomet."[58] Certainly they did not impress Richardson's fellow schoolmasters and the country parsons who together formed the nucleus of those purveying précis of available geographical knowledge to a popular audience. For all their sympathy with the abolitionist cause, the editors continued to keep alive images of a bloody and barbarous Africa and of an indigenous population stupid, lazy, and oppressed. According to one much reprinted schools' text book of the period, the human "shambles" of the Congo still existed: moreover one hundred men per day were killed for the "king's table", not because they were criminals but because "human flesh is looked upon as a delicious dish."[59]

The perpetuation of such images, at a time when so much more was being revealed about Africa in the official investigations, reflected the old tendencies to mix entertainment and information. John Leyden's contemporary survey, for instance, a far more substantial work than the school texts, included up-to-date information on African exploration; detailed abolitionist arguments; a discussion of African colonization schemes; and an account of the man-eating Jagas or Central Africa based on Andrew Battell's sixteenth century experiences.[60]

The days of the slave trade might be numbered but the associations between blackness and cultural inferiority were as firmly entrenched as ever. Virtually all published geographical editors shared—even if they rarely expressed it so neatly—John Walker's assumption that the antonym of "Negro" was "Citizen". John Free's public lectures, "compiled for the Use of his Younger Pupils", were typical of the cultural condescension which the educated classes imbibed from an early age. While Africa "appears to produce only Barbarians and Monsters", said Free, Europe had produced all the world's great men; and European men in general "have not the clownish, proud and uncultivated Nature, which one meets with in the inhabitants of other parts of the World. They are fair, well-proportioned, agreeable, and nothing which disgusts the Sight, as other People have."[61]

In the same period a newspaper review of a Drury Lane production of *Othello* voiced only one criticism: "is it necessary the Moor should be as *black* as a native of Guiney?" The rest of the article—and a letter to the same paper a few days later—made it clear that it was inconceivable that the cultivated and socially elevated Othello could be anything as low as a Negro. Indeed it appeared that his Moorish clothes in this production were something of a shock to audience and critics accustomed to seeing him garbed as a Venetian nobleman.[62]

The period produced a revealing minor controversy about the racial identity of the Ancient Egyptians. Lord Monboddo, for one, had referred to them as "black, woolly-haired men . . . but with features very different from those of the Negroes." The French traveller, Volney, went further and argued that they had indeed been Negroes. This opinion was given full publicity by James Anderson in a vigorous anti-slavery polemic which was, however, in itself an indication of the strength of unfavourable physical stereotypes. Noting that "the same original race of people still exists in Egypt", he went on to admit that they were now "as rude and as barbarous, and as ignorant as their brother negroes . . ." The incredulous response of Daniel Webb to Volney's assertion was equally revealing: "Negroes! O ye Muses, can ye pardon the profanation? . . . I have this moment in my fancy, a picture of Plato taking his lecture in philosophy under a Negro Professor". Webb conceded that Greeks of Plato's era did not have prejudice against black complexion: "nor should we, after the first surprise, did we not connect it with the image, and, with that, the character of the Negro."[63]

CONCLUSION

"Am I not a man and a brother?", asked the kneeling, manacled Negro symbol of the British abolition movement. If old assumptions about the slave trade as a furtive, unpublicized activity were true, then the responses to this question—and hence racial attitudes themselves—would have been no more than debating points. But the responses were not clear cut: there was as much consensus as disagreement among pro- and anti-slave trade writers; and few contemporaries could honestly have answered the question with either a simple affirmative or negative.

The long period of the Atlantic slave trade marked a most important stage in the developing history of racial attitudes. It was important not only because of New World slavery and the foundations laid there for subsequent racial bitterness. It also established a knowledge of, and prejudice against, black Africa both more detailed and more widely circulated than has been previously realized. Vast areas of Africa remained unknown. The known coastal fringe was described with various degrees of distortion. Europeans were describing an Africa already transformed by their own presence. But these descriptions were so widely disseminated that they must stand as the most important ingredient of British attitudes to the Negro by the late eighteenth century.

The vicarious African experience was certainly more significant than domestic British race relations. Many people in Britain had seen Negroes but for few was this more than a fleeting, isolated experience. Only once—and then very briefly and locally—did any part of Britain experience a "Negro problem." Black immigrants were generally no more than reminders of the major stories of interracial contact unfolding overseas. While a majority remained in servile roles long established in the New World, those who received most publicity were individuals receiving privileged treatment as "princes" or more humble representatives of the African end of the slave trade.

The African experience was also a more significant component of British racial attitudes than the New World slave systems. This was partly because the abolitionist target was the slave trade rather than slavery. But even when abolitionism was seen as a threat to West Indian slavery, the pro-slavery response rested as much on derogatory assertions about Africa as on positive claims about the slave system. The same emphasis emerged from the mass of travel and geographical writing which was non-polemical or only partly so. Not only were there more works specifically about Africa than about the New World but within every class of writing the logic of argument placed more emphasis on African barbarism than on plantation slavery. Relationships with Africans were central to the experience of slave traders; there was little in their writings which was not in some way a comment on native manners. By contrast those who wrote about the New World were commenting on far more than the Negro. Slavery may have been fundamental to the society described by West Indian residents and their visitors but the fundamental functioning of a uniform system of coercive labour required less explanation than often complex and difficult relations in Africa. The Negro could largely be taken for granted by West Indians whose major preoccupations were with the role of sugar colonies within the British mercantile system. Even the most notable racist, Edward Long, devoted more space to these broader aspects of Jamaica's history and economic role than to the Negro. And it was characteristic that Long's most extreme disciple, John Kemeys, offered his own racialist hypothesis in a footnote to an argument about sugar duties. Moreover, both men rested their theories of inferiority far more on African than New World evidence; Long saw Creole Negroes as undeniably more accomplished than Africans; Kemeys saw the slave trade as a means of humanizing part-brute Africans. In their emphasis—though not in their specific arguments—the two men were typical of West Indians. Where the Negro's role in slavery was analysed, it was in terms of stereotypes about African tribes or in even broader comparisons between Creole and African Negroes. And where details of a West Indian Negro culture emerged—as in descriptions of witchcraft, polygamy, or music—these were presented as extensions of corrupt African practices.

The secondary geographical works—which were probably the major influence in disseminating information about the Negro—reflected the bias of their sources. Whether they were large-scale summaries of first-hand reports—such as the Astley *Collection*—or compact surveys aimed at youthful readers, such works found far more to say about the Negro's cultural condition in Africa than about his degradation in the New World.

Despite attitudes varying between the extremes of sympathy and hostility towards the Negro, the image of black Africa was unfavourable. The slave traders, who had the most intimate knowledge of African societies, frequently rationalized the uncertainties of the trading relationship in mutually contradictory charges about native incompetence and sharp practice. The detailed information which many of them provided came in the context of mistrust and ethnocentric contempt. It was only when the abolition attack reached its peak that the essential orderliness of native society and government received more emphasis from the slave traders than cruelty and dishonesty. But this new attitude—presented mainly in the reports of official investigations—was overshadowed by continuing propagandist stress on the barbarity of Africa.

Throughout the eighteenth century West Indian pro-slavery propaganda dwelt on the general depravity of African manners and on the specific cruelty of native tyrants. Over the same period abolitionists firmly rejected West Indian portrayals of the slave trade as a rescue operation. But while they made much of the corrupting influence of the trade on Africa, they showed little recognition of native achievement. At one extreme Negroes were victims of European oppression who should be allowed to enjoy an uncontaminated but uniformly primitive existence. At the other extreme they were also the victims of native despotism, which flouted ideals of natural rights as surely as the slave trade.The implication in this latter view, that there was a need for a beneficent re-organization of Negro society on European lines, received more emphasis as economic alternatives to the slave trade were sought. The information about Negro skills in a variety of crafts—which was buried in the hostile accounts of many slave traders—was used by abolitionists merely as a sign of potential, not as evidence of an inherently different, equally valid social system.

Propagandists were both reiterating and accentuating stereotypes long available in numerous secondary accounts of Africa. Some of the larger of such works gave a fair summary of reporters' observations: if the complexity and achievement of Negro society received less emphasis than its deficiencies, this was a reflection of the attitudes of such authorities as Bosman, Barbot, and Smith. In other works, notably the *Universal Modern History,* the redeeming aspects of Negro life were more heavily overshadowed by diatribes about ignorance and depravity. In

shorter works there was little space for more than the basic
stereotypes, while the desire to entertain as much as to inform led
to disproportionate stress on colourful, if barely corroborated,
accounts of cannibalism and bloodshed.

Whether an individual reader knew a great deal of the
complexities of West African life or merely retained general
impressions of barbarism depended on personal motivation. But
the imperfections of Negro society were so widely documented on
so many levels that it is clear that the abolitionist poets and
dramatists, whose work has sometimes been seen as important
evidence of racial attitiudes, were not writing in a vacuum of
ignorance. Their attempts to ennoble the Negro character were a
reaction not only to stereotypes about the Negro as a slave but also
to general beliefs about the social and environmental defects of
Africa.

On the other hand, the wealth of information about Africa was
also a major bulwark against pseudo-scientific racism. Edward
Long may have been able to introduce his theory of innate Negro
inferiority with a long account of African failings extracted from
the *Universal Modern History.* But his omission of the
accompanying qualification, that such generalizations were only
applicable to the unimproved interior, was typical of the selectivity
of racialists. David Hume's strictures on Negro cultural sterility
were made in a brief footnote which ignored the message of
numerous contemporary accounts of Africa. And Samuel Estwick
was forced to support his argument about innate moral depravity
partly by reference to customs which no authority attributed to
Negroes. Similarly the racialist references to Negro-ape
affinities—based on a few unstressed passages in a tiny fraction of
the works on Africa—were much less plausible than some writers
have suggested. More typical of the African commentaries as a
whole than those who briefly referred to Negro-ape sexual
connections were those, like William Snelgrave, who placed
unfavourable comments about African manners in the context of
world-wide non-European savagery. Similar perspectives were
explicitly offered by such secondary works as Fenning and
Collyer's *New System of Geography* and implicitly by numerous
shorter works, which presented images of African society
alongside similar portrayals of other non-European areas.

The tendency to see Negroes as culturally backward human
beings, rather than as a separate race, rested on much more than
the often involuntary message of geographical surveys. Opposing
propagandists differed only in their claims about whether the slave
trade was a valid means of enabling Negroes to realize their human

potential. There is no question but that slavery was frequently depicted as a degrading, de-humanizing system and that the Negro's colour and other physical attributes were inextricably associated with a servile condition. But pro-slavery propaganda did not, in any significant measure, make a logical connection between the two stereotypes. Instead of representing Negroes as a subhuman species fit for animal drudgery the great majority defended slavery as a benevolent system giving Negroes an opportunity of human fulfilment denied them in the savage African wilderness. If the late eighteenth century abolition debate produced a handful of pro-slavery racialists, it witnessed far more—equally committed in defence of slavery—who pointedly rejected racialism.

The only way in which slavery was rationalized in racial terms was in the argument about tropical labour. The belief that only Negroes could work in extreme heat was widely promulgated, by abolitionists as well as defenders of slavery, yet its continuing vagueness underlines a lack of interest in racial difference which was fundamental to the thought of the period. Even the most uninhibited defenders of slavery failed to analyze the Negro's tropical constitution or advance claims of racial immunity to disease. Charles White's solitary pseudo-scientific exposition ran counter to every contemporary medical orthodoxy. It was equally symptomatic of his intellectual isolation that the evidence which most explicitly refuted his theories had been assembled by men examining slavery rather than evaluating racialist theories.

The virtual absence of such theories reflects the essential conservatism of contemporary thought as much as the priorities of propaganda. The eighteenth century produced many explanatory theories of racial difference but, within Britain, no anatomical investigations of the Negro until Charles White's belated and limited exercise. The predominant environmental theories were a denial of racist theory in their specific emphasis on the mutability of human difference. They were also symptomatic of an attitude which rejected empirical investigation in favour of untested assumptions. The most basic assumption of all—about the unity of mankind—was often stated in terms of the fashionable scientific definition of species but a more basic influence was a continuing acceptance of scriptural monogenesis. Polygenetic theories were rare and their exponents nearly always struggled to avoid heresy. The plausibility of their attempts to re-interpret the Old Testament must be judged by the same rigorous criteria which rejected racial interpretations of the curse of Ham through textual analysis.

The predominance of monogenesis and environmentalism effectively undermined the commonest intellectual device employed by racialists, the concept of gradation. But there were additional reasons why the Chain of Being, while recurring in so many fields of eighteenth century thought, was applied to race by so few. Undoubtedly it offered a superficially convenient way of explaining the Negro's physical and cultural separateness from whites. But for many reasons the Chain of Being was a means of rationalization rather than an active influence in itself. In stressing the closeness of savage and animal behaviour it impelled scrutiny of evidence which placed Negro culture in a relatively advanced stage of barbarism. In stressing physical similarity between man and ape the great majority of the exponents of gradation argued the decisive importance of man's spiritual qualities, a process which again raised Negroes some distance above merely brutal savagery. And if, on the crudest level of physical appearance, gradation helped to formalize the Negro's remoteness from Europeans, it also helped to emphasize the essential similarity of black and white for those who referred to numerous intermediate stages of barely definable difference.

One can make only hesitant claims for the wider significance of the racial and cultural attitudes discussed in this book. It is clear, for instance, that they were part of the atmosphere of the abolition debate but not a cause of that debate nor a major influence on its outcome. British contacts with West Africa were so well known that it is impossible to see the abolition attack as the result of sudden revelation about the slave trade. With so many assumptions about the Negro shared by pro- and anti-slave trade writers, it is impossible to see the success of that attack as a victory for one racial attitude over another.

If this book sheds any light on the question of why the slave trade was so long tolerated or why it was eventually overthrown, it can only be in its emphasis on the vicarious nature of the British racial experience. Perhaps the arrival of greater numbers of Negroes in England in the 1770s and 1780s, and the attendant publicity, made the long-established descriptions and stereotypes of the travel and geographical publications at last seem urgently real. But it seems clear that this could only be a factor subordinate to a combination of quite profound changes in economic and social attitudes. New industrial trends and new commercial opportunities made the economic imperatives supporting the slave trade more clearly a question of sectional rather than national expediency. And growing compassion for the African was merely part of a wider humanitarianism which was softening an earlier tendency to social cruelty at home as well as in the barbarous outposts of the first British Empire.

These changes are major issues still being explored by a number of historians. If a survey of racial attitudes makes a minor contribution in that field, its main significance must be as monument to an unhappy past and signpost to equally turbulent nineteenth century interracial experiences. Abolition in 1807 was to be followed by many issues involving the Negro: the policing of the slave trade, exploration, trade, and colonial administration in Africa; emancipation, apprenticeship, and associated problems in the West Indies. Each of these issues generated its own pressures: but, for those who would comprehend them fully, it is important to understand that, in the period before the dramatic innovations of Darwinian evolutionary thought, the Negro was seen as a man, certainly, but as a wild, untutored cousin rather than a brother.

NOTES

PREFACE

1. Winthrop D. Jordan, *White Over Black: American Attitudes toward the Negro 1550–1812*, Pelican (1970); Eric Williams, *Capitalism and Slavery*, 2nd ed. 1964. Here, and in all subsequent footnotes, works were published in London, unless otherwise stated.

CHAPTER TWO

1. Such assumptions are pervasive even in James Walvin's *Black and White: the Negro and English Society, 1555–1945* (1973): see especially Chapter 2, "The Impact of Africa".
2. The first edition was published in 1942. Subsequent references are to the second edition (New York, 1969).
3. *Guinea's Captive Kings*, pp. 29–37; Richard Hakluyt, *Principall Navigations, Voiages etc of the English Nation*, 1589, 2 vols. (Cambridge, 1965); John Barbot, *A Description of the Coasts of North and South Guinea*, Churchill, V, 1–668.
4. Philip D. Curtin, *The Image of Africa: British Ideas and Action, 1780–1850* (1965), pp. 9–13; David B. Davis, *The Problem of Slavery in Western Culture*, Pelican (1970), pp. 498–500; James Walvin, *The Black Presence: a Documentary History of the Negro in England, 1555–1860* (1971), pp. 7, 21–22, 62–63, 66–74, 115–16; Jordan, *White Over Black*, pp. 3–43, 101.
5. Some of these pamphlets are discussed in later chapters and many cited in the Bibliography under 'Slave Trade'.
6. *A Journal of a Voyage made in the Hannibal of London, 1693, 1694 . . .* Churchill, VI, 171–239—hereafter cited as Phillips, *Journal*.
7. *New Voyage to Guinea* (1744).
8. Francis Moore, *Travels into the Inland Parts of Africa . . .* (1738); William Snelgrave, *A New Account of Some Parts of Guinea, and the Slave Trade . . .* (1734).
9. *A Voyage to Guinea, Brasil, and the West-Indies . . .* (1735); *The Navy Surgeon; or, A Practical System of Surgery . . .* (1734).
10. *A Voyage to Senegal, the Isle of Gorée and River Gambia . . .* (1759).
11. *A Voyage to the River Sierra Leone . . .* 1788, reprinted (1966).
12. *The History of Dahomy, an Inland Kingdom of Africa* (1793).
13. *A Voyage to the Coast of Africa in 1758* (1759).
14. *An Account of the Slave Trade on the Coast of Africa* (1788).
15. *Dahomy*, pp. 216–21.

16. *Some New and Accurate Observations, Geographical, Natural and Historical of the Coast of Guinea so far as relates to the Improvement of that Trade for the Advantage of Great Britain in general, and the Royal African Co. in particular* (1725).

17. Anthony Benezet, *Some Historical Account of Guinea* . . . , 2nd ed., 1788, reprinted (1968); Ralph Sandiford, *The Mystery of Iniquity* . . . *postscript, the Injury this trading in Slaves doth the Commonwealth* . . . 2nd ed. (1730); *Works of John Woolman*, 2nd ed. (1775).

18. *Problem of Slavery*, pp. 187–220.

19. *The World Surveyed, or the famous voyages and travailes of Vincent le Blanc* (1660), pp. 405.

20. Sypher, *Guinea's Captive Kings*, pp. 108–22.

21. *Ibid.*, pp. 124–25.

22. *Letter from a Merchant at Jamaica to a M.P. in London, touching the African Trade. To which is added a speech made by a Black at Gardaloupe, at the funeral of a Fellow-Negro* (1709).

23. See, for example, *Gentleman's Magazine*, V (1735), 21–23; X (1740), 341; XVI (1746), 479; *London Magazine*, IX (1740), 493–94.

24. Some of Sharp's works are listed in the Bibliography.

25. *The Negro's and Indian's Advocate, suing for their Admission into the Church* (1680).

26. Richard Ligon, *A True and Exact History of the Island of Barbados*, 2nd ed. (1673); Edward Long, *The History of Jamaica*, 3 vols. (1774); Griffith Hughes, *The Natural History of Barbados* (1750); Bryan Edwards, *The History Civil and Commercial of the British West Indies*, 2 vols. (1793).

27. *A Voyage to the Islands of Madera, Barbados, Neves, St. Christophers, and Jamaica* . . . , 2 vols. (1707–25), I, lvii.

28. Abbé Guillaume Thomas Raynal, *A Philosophical and Political History of the Settlements and Trade of the Europeans in the East and West Indies*, trans J. Justamond, 3rd ed., 5 vols. (1777)—hereafter cited as Raynal.

29. *Hakluytus Postumus or Purchas his Pilgrimes*, 1625, 20 vols. (Glasgow, 1905) —hereafter cited as *Hakluytus Postumus*.

30. Full title in List of Abbreviations.

31. Comprehensive lists of the titles in this category and in the other broad categories discussed below are contained in the Bibliography.

32. These six were: Samuel Clarke, *A Mirrour or Looking-Glasse both for Saints and Sinners* . . . *whereunto are added A Geographical Description of all the Countries in the Knowne World* . . . (1657, 4th ed., 1671); Robert Fage, *A Description of the Whole World* . . . (1658, 4th ed., 1671); Edmund Bohun, *A Geographical Dictionary* . . . *of the Whole World* (1688, 6th ed., 1710); Laurence Eachard, *A Most Complete Compendium of Geography, General and Special* (1691, 8th ed., 1713); Robert Morden, *Geography Rectified; or, a Description of the World* . . . (1680, 4th ed., 1700); Patrick Gordon, *Geography Anatomis'd; or, the Geographical Grammar* . . . (1693, 20th ed., 1754).

33. See, for example, note 40 below.

34. The main African material was contained in the Modern section, vols. XIV–XVIII (1760)—hereafter referred to as *The Universal Modern History.* But the Ancient section, especially Volume I (1747) also contained material on the Negro's racial characteristics—hereafter cited as *Universal Ancient History.*

35. S. J. Curtis, *History of Education in Great Britain*, 7th ed (1967), pp. 110–14.

36. Francis Brokesby, *Of Education with respect to Grammar Schools, and the*

Universities . . . (1701), pp. 89–90; *An Essay Upon Education* (1711), p. 20; John Clarke, *An Essay Upon the Education of Youth in Grammar Schools* (1720), pp. 11–12; James Buchanan, *A Plan of an English Grammar-School Education* (Edinburgh, 1770), p. 115; George Chapman, *A Treatise on Education with a Sketch of the Author's Method*, 2nd ed. (1774), pp. 102–03, 194, 221; George Croft, *A Plan of Education Delineated and Vindicated* (Wolverhampton, 1784), pp. 35–37.

37. "The Rugby Curriculum" in Samuel Butler, *The Life and Letters of Dr. Samuel Butler*, 2 vols. (1896), I, 28, 36; Croft, *Plan of Education*, pp. 35–36.

38. Joseph Priestley, *An Essay on a Course of Liberal Education for Civil and Active Life* (1765), p. 67; Joseph Priestley, *A Syllabus of a Course of Lectures in the Study of History* (Warrington, n.d.), Lecture XIII; John Boswell, *A Method of Study, or, an Useful Library, in Two Parts* (1738), p. 22; William Smith, *The Student's Vade Mecum* (1770), p. 256; Curtis, *History of Education*, pp. 115–16.

39. Daniel Lysons, comp. *Collectanea: or, a Collection of Advertisements and Paragraphs from the Newspapers relating to various subjects*, 2 vols. (n.d.), II, 15b, 16, 18, 18b, 19—hereafter cited as Lysons B.

40. William Guthrie, *A New Geographical, Historical and Commercial Grammar* . . . (1770, 21st ed., 1801). For Eachard and Gordon see note 32 above. For the recommendations of educationists and others see: *Directions for a Proper Choice of Authors to form a Library, which may both Improve and Entertain the Mind and be of real Use in the Conduct of Life* (1766), pp. 2–3, 17–18, 20–25; "School Books" in *A Modern Catalogue of Books printed in Great Britain and published in London, since the year MCCLXXXV to the Present Time* (1791), p. 23; *Newbery's Catalogue of Instructive and Amusing Publications for Young Minds* (1800), passim; Croft, *Plan of Education*, p. 36; Chapman, *Treatise*, p. 221; Smith, *Vade Mecum*, p. 256.

41. For example, Richard Blome, *Cosmography and Geography in Two Parts* (1683), p. 460; Clarke, *Mirrour*, pp. 68–69.

42. *A Briefe Description of the Whole World*, 2nd ed. (1600).

43. In addition to *Hakluytus Postumus* he wrote *Purchas His Pilgrimage or Relations of the World and the Religions observed in all Ages and Places* (1614).

44. *Cosmographie, in four books*, 2nd ed. (1657).

45. Daniel Fenning, Joseph Collyer and others, *A New System of Geography or a General Description of the World* . . . 2 vols. (1766, 1765). As examples of its plagiarism compare I, 394 (printed in error as 382), 402, 408–10, 433–55 with, respectively, *Universal Modern History*, XVI, 102–103 note L, 376, 387–96, 249–92.

46. XVI, 102–103, note L.

47. II, 505–506.

48. For example, Fenning and Collyer, *New System*, I, 394 (382 in error), II, 700–701; Charles Theodore Middleton, *A New and Complete System of Geography* . . . , 2 vols. (1777–78), I, 336–37, 537–39, II, 469, 474.

49. Walvin, *Black and White*, pp. 105–43; see also Kenneth Lindsay Little, *Negroes in Britain: A Study of Racial Relations in English Society* (1947), pp. 165–90; Eldred Jones, *Othello's Countrymen: The African in English Renaissance Drama* (1965), pp. 12–13.

50. XVII, 95.

51. *Observations on Slavery: particularly with a view to its effects on the British Colonies, in the West-Indies* (Manchester, 1787), pp. 34–35,

52. Gomer Williams, *History of the Liverpool Privateers and Letters of Marque with an Account of the Liverpool Slave Trade* (1897), pp. 475, 479, *Gentleman's Magazine*, XXXVI (1766), 403; *Notes and Queries*, Ser. 5, X (1878), 338, 453, Ser. 12, V (1919), 81, CXLVIII (1925), 413; Extract of letter from Dublin, *Morning Chronicle*, 7th June 1786, 3a; Margaret Priestley, *West African Trade and Coast Society: A Family Study* (1969), p. 27. *Boswell's Life of Johnson*, ed. George Birkbeck Hill, rev. and enlarged, ed. L. F. Powell, 6 vols. (Oxford, 1934–64), III, 212–13, 214 note.

53. Long, *History of Jamaica*, II, 475–76; *An Inquiry into the Origin, Progress and Present State of Slavery with a Plan for the Gradual, Reasonable and Secure Emancipation of the Slaves* (1789), pp. 26–27; *Gentleman's Magazine*, XLI (1771), 595–96.

54. Job is the subject of a biography: Douglas Grant, *The Fortunate Slave: An Illustration of Slavery in the Early Eighteenth Century* (1968); for references to Montagu's patronage, see pp. 106–07.

55. *Letters of Ignatius Sancho, an African: to which are prefixed Memoirs of his Life by Joseph Jekyll, Esq. M.P.*, 5th ed., 1803 (reprinted, 1968, with an Introduction by Paul Edwards), Introduction, iv, xv.

56. *Diary*, 29th July 1789, 3c; *Whitehall Evening Post*, 28–30th July 1789, 2; *Morning Post*, 1st August, 1789, 3a; 8th December 1789, 3a; 21st December 1789, 3c; *English Chronicle*, 5th–8th December 1789.

57. Long, *History of Jamaica*, II, 476.

58. Grant, *Fortunate Slave*, pp. 90, 95, 99–101; *Life of Sancho*, Introduction, xv.

59. Although he has escaped the notice of historians of the period, he achieved a section in the *Dictionary of National Biography*, ed. Leslie Stephen (1886), VI, 323–24.

60. *Diary*, 29th July 1789 3c: *Morning Post*, 1st August 1789, 3a.

61. *Diary, loc. cit.*; *Morning Post*, 8th December 1789, 3a; *English Chronicle*, 5th–8th December, 1789.

62. Daniel Lysons, comp. *Collectanea; or, a Collection of Advertisements and Paragraphs from the Newspapers relating to various subjects*, 5 vols. (n.d.), I, 107—hereafter cited as Lysons A.

63. Copy of the Report of the Board of Trade on the Memorial of Bullfinch Lambe, 6th July 1731, P.R.O., C.O. 267/5, ff. 305–306; The Case of Adamo Tomo, *ibid.*, f. 207.

64. Astley, II, 496–97.

65. *New Account*, pp. 68–72.

66. *Dahomy*, pp. 45–46.

67. *Gentleman's Magazine*, XIX (1749), 89–90; *London Magazine*, XVIII (1749), 94; Middleton, *New and Complete System*, I, 325.

68. *The Royal African: or, Memoirs of the Young Prince of Annamaboe* (c. 1750), Preface, iii–iv.

69. African Committee to Thomas Melvil, 21st August 1751, P.R.O. T70/143, f. 101; Committee's Minutes, 23rd October 1751, *Ibid.*, ff. 107, 110.

70. *Gentleman's Magazine*, XIX (1749), 90.

71. Copy of letter from Ansah to Halifax, P.R.O. CO. 267/5, ff. 36–41; Melvil to Committee, *ibid.*, ff. 6–7.

72. Thomas Thompson, *An Account of Two Missionary Voyages by the Appointment of the Society for the Propagation of the Gospel . . .* (1758), pp. 66–67; *Abstract of the Proceedings of the Society for the Propagation*

of the Gospel . . . (1755), pp. 58–59; (1757), p. 60; (1759), pp. 72–73; (1766), p. 43; (1767), p. 70.

73. *An Account of the Colony of Sierra Leone from its first establishment in 1793, being the substance of a report delivered to the Proprietors* (1795), pp. 213–21; *Annual Register,* XXXVI (1794), *Chronicle,* 1–2.
74. C.O. 267/9—Sierra Leone Correspondence, Unbound Papers, 10 October 1790.
75. Account by Wadstrom, *loc. cit.*
76. *Accounts and Papers,* XXVI, 646a, Part I, Detached Pieces of Evidence, No. 4; Matthews, *Voyage to Sierra Leone,* pp. 170–1.
77. Priestley, *Trade and Coast Society,* p. 27.
78. *Annual Register, loc. cit.*
79. Account by Wadstrom, *loc. cit.*; Matthews, *loc. cit.*
80. *Accounts and Papers, loc. cit.*
81. See Chapters Three, Four, and Five.
82. *Notes and Queries,* Ser. 2, VIII (1859), 58.
83. *Ibid.,* Ser. 2, II (1856), 187; Ser. 1, IX (1854), 99; Williams *Liverpool Privateers,* p. 477.
84. *Black Presence,* pp. 12–16.
85. C. W. Chitty, "Aliens in England in the Sixteenth Century", *Race,* VIII (October, 1966), 129–46.
86. Public Record Office, *Acts of the Privy Council* (1890–95), 21st February 1573–74, 26th October 1574, 1st July 1574, 8th November 1574.
87. *Ibid.,* 27th September 1573.
88. A. V. Judges, ed., *The Elizabethan Underworld* (1965), p. 496; *Acts of the Privy Council,* 7th July 1562, 8th August 1562, 13th June 1573, 10th March 1576.
89. For numerous letters and articles on crime in 1785, the year when the Black Poor first appeared, see the following issues of the *Public Advertiser:* 25th June, 2c–d, 4a; 30th June, 2a–b; 5th July, 1d; 20th July, 1d–2a; 21st July, 1c–2a; 23rd July, 2a–d; 26th August, 2a; 30th August, 4a–b; 3rd September, 1a–b; 29th September, 2a–b.
90. For example, *General Advertiser,* 8th February 1786, 4a–b; *St. James Chronicle,* 14th–17th January 1787, 4; *Morning Chronicle,* 20th July 1786, 2b.
91. *General Advertiser,* 22nd March 1786, 3c.
92. *Morning Herald,* 10th April 1786, 3b.
93. *Public Advertiser,* 29th June, 1786, 4a.
94. *Ibid.,* 16th March 1785, 2d. This and the references cited below disprove Little's claim that the plight of Lascars went unnoticed until the nineteenth century: *Negroes in Britain,* p. 186.
95. *Public Advertiser,* 6th December 1785, 3c; 21st December, 1785, 1c.
96. *Ibid.,* 5th January 1786, 4c.
97. *Ibid.,* 9th January 1786, 3b; 10th January 1786, 4c; 12th January 1786, 4d.
98. *Ibid.,* 16th January 1786, 4d.
99. *Morning Chronicle,* 28th January 1786, 1c.
100. *Public Advertiser,* 6th December 1785, 3c; 9th January 1786, 3b.
101. *Ibid.,* 21st December, 1785, 1c.
102. *Ibid.,* 7th January 1786, 2b, 4b.
103. *Ibid.,* 17th February 1786, 2b.
104. *Ibid.,* 19th January 1786, 3b.
105. *Morning Chronicle,* 28th January 1786, 1c; 3rd February 1786, 1b; *Public Advertiser,* 11th February 1786, 2b–c; 17th February 1786, 1d, 2b;

Morning Herald, 14th February 1786, 3a. See also the favourable comments
of the Negro spokesman, Olaudah Equiano, who was chosen by the
Committee to accompany the settlers to Sierra Leone: Olaudah Equiano,
*Interesting Narrative of the Life Of Olaudah Equiano, or Gustavus Vassa,
the African, written by himself,* 2 vols. (1789), II, 230–31.

106. *Morning Chronicle,* 24th February 1786, 2a.
107. Chapter Four.
108. For references to these centres see *Public Advertiser,* 16th January 1786,
4; 11th February 1786, 2b–c; *Morning Chronicle,* 28th January 1786, 1c.
109. 3rd January 1787, 4b.
110. 8th January 1787, 4a.
111. 9th January 1787, 2b.
112. *Morning Post,* 30th December 1786; Samuel Estwick, *Considerations on
the Negro Cause by a West Indian,* 1st ed. (1772), pp. 43–44; Edward Long,
Candid Reflections upon the Negro Cause (1772), p. 49. The racialist
theories of Long and Estwick are discussed in detail in the next chapter
and referred to throughout this book.
113. *A Short Rejoinder to the Rev. Mr. Ramsay's Reply* . . . (1787), pp. 99–100
note.
114. For example, John Scattergood, *An antidote to Popular Frenzy, particularly
to the present Rage for the Abolition of the Slave Trade.* . . . (1792), p. 24;
Philip Thicknesse, *Memoirs and Anecdotes,* 2 vols. (1788), I, 282.
115. James Tobin, *Cursory Remarks upon the Rev. Mr. Ramsay's Essay on the
Treatment and Conversion of African Slaves* . . . (1785), p. 118 and note;
The Newgate Calendar, 1782–86, P.R.O., H.O. 77/1.
116. *Public Advertiser,* 18th January 1785, 4b.
117. *Morning Chronicle,* 14th January 1786, 3d.
118. *Cursory Remarks,* p. 117.
119. For example, *Morning Chronicle,* 4th January 1786, 3c; 14th January 1786,
3d; *London Chronicle,* 3rd–5th January 1786, 11b; 12–14th January 1786,
46b; *General Advertiser,* 14th January 1786, 3a; *Morning Herald,* 16th
January 1786, 3c; *London Recorder and Sunday Gazette,* 15th January
1786, 3a–b; *St. James Chronicle,* 14th–17th January, 1786, 3b.
120. For example, *Public Advertiser,* 7th January 1786, 4b.
121. *Observations,* p. 36.
122. *The Repository,* I (1788), 59.
123. *Gentleman's Magazine.* XXXIV (1764), 493.
124. Estwick, *Considerations,* 1st ed., pp. 43–44; Long, *Candid Reflections,*
p. 47; Samuel Martin, *An Essay Upon Plantership,* 5th ed. (1773) Preface,
xv.
125. Hoare, *Memoirs of Sharp,* Appendix II, vi.
126. Estwick, *Considerations,* 1st ed., p. 43; Long, *Candid Reflections,*
pp. 75–76; Tobin, *Cursory Remarks,* p. 117.
127. *Candid Reflections,* pp. 51, 75–76.
128. *Observations,* p. 35.
129. See, for example, *Morning Chronicle,* 20th July 1786, 2b; *Public Advertiser,*
30th November 1785, 3a; 29th June 1786, 4a; 2nd September 1786, 3b;
23rd February 1788, 3.
130. *Public Advertiser,* 18th April, 1786, 2a.
131. *History of Jamaica,* II, 328–29, 332.
132. *Candid Reflections,* pp. 47–49.

133. Granville Sharp, *A Representation of the Injustice and dangerous Tendency of Tolerating slavery* . . . (1769), p. 109; Tobin, *Cursory Remarks*, p. 118; Thomas Atwood, *The History of Dominica (1791), p. 212;* Long, *Candid Reflections,* p. 49; Scattergood, *Antidote,* p. 24; Martin, *Plantership,* Preface, xv; Thicknesse, *Memoirs,* I, 282.

134. Middleton, *New And Complete System,* I, 325–26; *A Narrative of the Most Remarkable Particulars in the Life of James Albert Ukawsaw Gronniosaw, an African Prince, as related by himself,* (Bath, 1770?), p.39.

135. Ottobah Cugoano, *Thoughts and Sentiments on the Evil and Wicked Traffic of the Slavery and Commerce of the Human Species* . . . (1787), p. 140; Equiano, *Interesting Narrative,* II, 234–38, 243–48.

CHAPTER THREE

1. *Notes on the State of Virginia* (1787), pp. 229–40.

2. *XVII,* 290.

3. Clarke, *Mirrour,* pp. 53, 73; *Encheiridion Geographicum,* H 3; Duval, *Geographia Universalis,* p. 87; *Thesaurus Geographicus,* (1695), p. 457; Dionysius Petavius, *The History of the World . . . with a Geographical Description* . . . (1659), p. 106.

4. Phillips, *Journal,* 219; Godwyn, *Negro's and Indian's Advocate,* pp. 20–21; Henry Home, Lord Kames, *The Elements of Criticism,* 2nd ed. 3 vols. (1763), II, 113.

5. *History of the Earth,* II, 77, 232.

6. Jones, *Present State of Virginia,* p. 3; William Strachey, *Historie of Travell into Virginia Britannia* (1612), *Hakluyt Society Publications,* Ser. 2, CIII (1953), p. 72; Robert Beverley, *The History and Present State of Virginia* (1705), Book III, pp. 1–2; John Seller, *A New Systeme of Geography* (1685), p. 97.

7. Johann Rheinhold Forster, *Observations made during a Voyage round the World . . .* (1778), pp. 229–36; *Hakluytus Postumus,* IV, 11, 14.

8. *Travels in Europe, Asia, and Africa,* 2 vols. (1782), I, 450.

9. Astley, II, 561; Robert Burton (*alias* Nathaniel Crouch), *The English Acquisitions in Guinea and East India,* 4th ed. (1728), p. 10.

10. Moore, *Travels into the inland,* pp. 29–30; *Universal Modern History,* XVII, 289–90; Lindsay, *A Voyage to the Coast,* pp. 76–77.

11. Comte de Buffon (George Louis Le Clerc), *Natural History, General and Particular,* 2nd ed. trans. William Smellie, 8 vols. 1785, III, 141.

12. Job Ludolphus, *A New History of Ethiopia: being a Full and Accurate Description of the Kingdom of Abbassinia . . . ,* trans. J. P. Gent. (1682), p. 71; Fenning and Collyer, *New System,* I, 329; de Fer, *Short and Easy Method,* p. 281; Morden, *Geography Rectified,* p. 516; Thomas Salmon, *The Modern Gazetteer: or a Short View of the Several Nations of the World . . . ,* 3rd ed. (1756), see "Ethiopia"; *Thesaurus Geographicus,* p. 459.

13. William Brenchley Rye, *England as Seen by Foreigners in the days of Elizabeth and James the First* (1865), pp. 262–63, note 118; Paul Hentzner, *Travels in England during the Reign of Queen Elizabeth,* 1612 (1889), pp.47–49.

14. *Annals of the First Four Years of the Reign of Queen Elizabeth* (n.d.) Camden Society Publications, O.S. VII (1840), 7.

15. Lysons B, I, 94b, 95, 98, 103, 104.

16. Kenneth J. Gergen, "The Significance of Skin Colour in Human Relations", *Daedalus*, Spring (1967), 395; Philip Mason, *Common Sense About Race* (1961), pp. 89–91; G. R. Dunstan, R. F. Hobson, "A Note on an early Ingredient of Racial Prejudice in Western Europe; with a psychiatrist's comment, *Race*, VI (April, 1965), 337; Davis, *Problem of Slavery*, pp. 481–82; Jones, *Othello's Countrymen*, pp. 27–36.

17. *Journal,* 219.

18. *A Plan for Improving the Trade at Senegal* (1763), p. 13.

19. *The Works of Sir Thomas Browne,* ed. Charles Sayle, 3 vols. (1904). II, 380–83.

20. *The Anthropological Treatises of J. F. Blumenbach . . . and the Inaugural Dissertation of John Hunter, M.D. on the Varieties of Man,* trans. from Latin by T. Bendyshe (1865), p. 363. Hereafter referred to as Hunter.

21. *White Over Black,* pp. 228, 252–54.

22. *A Philosophical Account of the Works of Nature,* 2nd ed. (1739), p. 231.

23. *The Animal Kingdom, or Zoological System, of the Celebrated Sir Charles Linnaeus: Vol. I part I . . . with numerous additions from more recent Zoological writers by Robert Kerr . . .* (1792), 46; Charles Bonnet, *The Contemplation of Nature,* trans. from French, 2 vols. (1766), I, 68–69.

24. Davis, *Problem of Slavery,* pp. 493–95; Walvin, *Black Presence,* pp. 115–16.

25. *The Great Chain of Being: a Study of the History of an Idea* (Cambridge, Mass., 1936).

26. "On the Varieties of the Human Species", *London Magazine,* XIX (1750), 316–18; Richard Turner, *A View of the Earth, being a short, but comprehensive system of modern geography,* 2nd ed. (1766), p. 15 note; W. Knox, *Three Tracts respecting the conversion and instruction of the free Indians and negroe slaves in the colonies* (1768), p. 14.

27. *Considerations on the Negroe Cause Commonly so called, address'd to the Rt. Honourable Lord Mansfield by a West Indian,* 2nd ed. (1772), pp. 70–82: hereafter references to Estwick, *Considerations,* are to this edition.

28. *History of Jamaica,* II, 353–56; *Universal Modern History,* XIV, 17, 21.

29. *History of Jamaica,* II, 356, 375.

30. *Ibid.* 372–75.

31. See, for example, George Edwards, *Essays upon Natural History and other Miscellaneous Subjects* (1770), p. 66.

32. *Orang-Outang, sive Homo Sylvestris: Or, the Anatomy of a Pygmie compared with that of a Monkey, an Ape, and a Man . . .* (1699), Epistle Dedicatory; pp. 2–15, 51–55.

33. *Ibid.* p. 43.

34. "The Natural History of Animals that most nearly approach Humanity", *Universal Magazine,* LXXI (1782), 189–94, 238–44, 363–68; Thomas Boreman, *A Description of Some Curious and Uncommon Creatures* (1739), pp. 1–11; Oliver Goldsmith, *The History of the Earth and Animated Nature,* 8 vols. (1774), IV, 195; Richard Brookes, *A New and Accurate System of Natural History,* 6 vols. (1763), I, 127–29; George Edwards, *Gleanings of Natural History* (1758), pp. 6–8; Ray, *Wisdom of God,* pp. 364–65.

35. For example, Goldsmith, *loc. cit.*; Brookes, *loc. cit.*; Description of "Man of the Woods", *Universal Magazine,* XXIV (1759), 29–30.

36. Buffon, *Natural History,* II, 360–63; VIII, 80–81, 97–104.

37. John Gregory, *A Comparative View of the State and Faculties of Man with those of the Animal World* (1765), pp. 8–9; cf. review of *The Posthumous Works of Jeremiah Seed, Monthly Review,* II (1749), 426; "An Inquiry into

the Nature and Destination of Brutes'', *Universal Magazine*, XLII (1768), 369.

38. Review of Hermann Samuel Reimer, *Observations Physiques* . . . , *Monthly Review*, XLV (1772), 533–49; ''The Natural History of Animals that most nearly approach Humanity'', 367; Letter on instinct and reason, *Universal Magazine*, XLIX (1771), 102–103.

39. *Contemplation of Nature*, I, 57–58, 65.

40. Bonnet, *Contemplation*, I, 67; Gregory, *Comparative View*, p. 10; Review of Francis Hutcheson, *A System of Moral Philosophy*, Monthly Review, XIII (1755), 163.

41. Gregory, *Comparative View*, 63; ''On the Importance of an Inquiry into the Human Mind'', *Universal Magazine*, XXXIV (1764), 286; Bonnet, *Contemplation*, I, 68–69; James Dunbar, *Essays on the History of Mankind*, 2nd ed. (1781), pp. 4–5, 13–15, 43–44, 63–64, 161–62, 165; Jean-Jacques Rousseau, *Discourse Upon the Origin and Foundation of the Inequality Among Mankind* (1761), pp. 34, 37, 39, 219–220; Richard Bradley, *A Philosophical Account of the Works of Nature*, 2nd ed. (1739), p. 231; John Miller, *The Origin of The Distinction of Ranks*, 3rd ed. (1779), pp. 3, 6.

42. Estwick, *Considerations*, pp. 74–82; Long, *History of Jamaica*, II, 377.

43. Arthur O. Lovejoy, ''Buffon and the Problems of Species'', in Bentley Glass, Owsei Temkin, William L. Straus, Jr., eds., *Forerunners of Darwin: 1745–1859* (Baltimore, 1959), pp. 93–95.

44. *History of Jamaica*, II, 335.

45. *Image of Africa*, p. 44.

46. For example, Godwyn, *Negro's and Indian's Advocate*, p. 23; Thomas Bacon, *Four Sermons upon the Great and Indispensible Duty of all Christian Masters and Mistresses to Bring up their Negro Slaves in the Knowledge and Fear of God* (1750), xvi; Johann Rheinhold Forster, *Observations*, p. 257.

47. *Natural History*, VII, 392.

48. *History of Jamaica*, II, 358; the notes for Long's unpublished second edition of this work show him grappling with this problem with a draft attack on Buffon's environmentalism, especially as it related to dogs: B.M., Add. MS. 12405, f. 277. The work of Charles White is discussed in some detail in Chapter Nine (below).

49. For example, Buffon, *Natural History*, III, 163–64; Bonnet, *Contemplation* I, 69.

50. For example, William Whiston, *A New Theory of the Earth* . . . , 2nd ed., (1708); Patrick Cockburn, *An Enquiry into the Truth and Certainty of the Mosaic Deluge* (1749); John Jackson, *Chronological Antiquities* . . . (1753); Jacob Bryant, *A Treatise on the Authenticity of the Scriptures* (1793).

51. *Men before Adam . . . translated from the Praeadamitae of de la Préyère (1656)*, pp. 248 ff.; *Co-Adamitae* . . . (1732), pp. 1–22; *London Magazine*, XIX (1750), 316–18; Curtin, *Image of Africa*, pp. 42–43.

52. *White Over Black*, pp. 235–36.

53. *History of Jamaica*, II, 360, 364, 370.

54. *Ibid.*, 363–64; Lord Monboddo (James Burnet), *Of the Origin and Progress of Language*, 6 vols. (1773–92), I, 239.

55. *Inequality among Mankind*, pp. 219–36.

56. *Origin and Progress*, I, 234–35.

57. Benoit de Maillet, *Telliamed, or Discourses between an Indian Philosopher and a French Missionary* (1750), xxix, 219–25, 231–52, 260–74; *Monthly Review*, II (1749), 37–38.

58. *White Over Black*, pp. 28–35.

59. *Ibid.*, p. 31; Clarke, *Mirrour*, p. 52; *Thesaurus Geographicus*, pp. 448, 456; Morden, *Geography rectified* p. 466; Pierre Duval, *Geographia Universalis, The present state of the World, giving an Account of the several Religions, Customs and Riches, of each People* . . . (1685), p. 64.

60. See for example, Abbot, *Briefe Description*, pp. 175–76, 314; *Purchas his Pilgrimage*, p. 395, 561, 659; Heylyn, *Cosmographie*, p. 876.

61. Salmon, *Universal Traveller*, II, 388. A suggestion that African albinoes might be the offspring of ape-negro liaisons was consistent with this theme, since it was inspired by the report that the albinoes were infertile: *Universal Modern History*, XVI, 293–94 note.

62. *White Over Black*, p. 32.

63. *Purchas His Pilgrimage*, p. 662.

64. *White Over Black*, p. 32.

65. Discussed more fully in Chapter Seven.

66. Lysons A., I, 82, 82b, 83, 84b, 85, II, 18b.

67. Lysons A, II, 4.

68. *Ibid.*, 8.

CHAPTER FOUR

1. For example, Elsa V. Goveia, "The West Indian Slave Laws of the Eighteenth Century," in Laura Foner, Eugene D. Genovese, eds. *Slavery in the New World* (Englewood Cliffs, N. J., 1969), 113–37; Orlando Patterson, *The Sociology of Slavery* (1967).

2. *A Plan for the Abolition of Slavery in the West Indies* (1772), pp. 8–9.

3. *Essays*, p. 407.

4. Herman Moll, *A System of Geography* . . . (1701), p. 103; Rev. —. Paschoud, *Historico-Political Geography* . . . 2nd ed. (1724), p. 275.

5. Review of M. Le Gentil, *Voyage dans les Mers de L'inde* . . . , *Monthly Review*, LXV (1781), 457.

6. Adanson, *Voyage to Senegal*, p. 38; Lindsay, *Voyage to the Coast*, pp. 76–77; Jones, *Present State of Virginia*, p. 3; Phillips, *Journal*, 214; cf. Barbot, 100.

7. Paschoud, *Historico-Political Geography*, pp. 320–21; Peter Marsden, *An Account of the Island of Jamaica* (Newcastle, 1788), p. 9; newspaper cited in Williams, *Liverpool Privateers*, p. 479.

8. Henry Home (Lord Kames), *Sketches of the History of Man*, 2nd ed. 4 vols. (1778), I, 23; "Rules for the Preservation of Health on the Coast of Africa", *Gentleman's Magazine*, XXVIII (1758), 461; H. E. Holder, *A Short Essay on the Subject of Negro Slavery* . . . (1788), pp. 26–27.

9. *An Essay on the Causes of the Variety of Complexion and Figure in the Human Species* . . . (1788), pp. 180–182.

10. "A Short Account of the British . . . West Indies," *London Magazine*, XXVII (1758), 168, 396, 625.

11. *White Over Black*, pp. 262–64.

12. *Mystery of Iniquity*, p. 21.

13. Long, *Candid Reflections*, pp. 21, 50, 63; *Plan for Abolition in the West Indies*, pp. 4–9.

14. pp. 2–4.

15. *The Universal Dictionary of Trade and Commerce*, 4th ed. (1774), 'Africa'.

16. Letter from Leeward Islands, *Gentleman's Magazine*, XI (1741), 145–47.

17. *The Importance of Jamaica to Great Britain, consider'd* . . . (1774), pp. 8–9,

15; Long, *History of Jamaica*, I, 375; Richard Blome, *A Description of the Isle of Jamaica, with the other Isles and Territories in America, to which the English are related . . .* , 3rd ed. (1687), p. 22.

18. *Image of Africa*, p. 83.
19. *The Civil and Natural History of Jamaica* (1756), p. 25.
20. p. 329.
21. *An Essay on the Natural History of Guiana . . .* (1769), pp. 385–86.
22. Thomas Trapham, *Discourse on the State of Health in Jamaica* (1679), pp. 113–20; Fenning and Collyer, *New System*, II, 669.
23. Leslie, *Account of Jamaica*, p. 329; William Hillary, *Observations on the Changes of the Air and the Concomitant Epidemical Diseases in the Island of Barbados (1752)*, p. 227.
24. Hillary, *op. cit.*, pp. 304–305, 336; Richard Towne, *A Treatise of the Diseases most frequent in the West Indies . . .* (1726), pp. 184, 188.
25. Jordan, *White Over Black*, pp. 259–60; John Quier, *Letters and Essays on the Small-Pox and Inoculation, the Measles, . . . of the West Indies . . .* (1778), pp. 11–12 note, 54–55, 70, 105–106; "Essays on Smallpox," *Universal Magazine*, XX (1757), 16.
26. *Negro's and Indian's Advocate*, pp. 3, 12, 14.
27. Pierre Duval, *Geographia Universalis . . .* (1685), p. 87; Paschoud, *Historico-Political Geography*, p. 275; *Thesaurus Geographicus*, p. 457; Morden, *Geography Rectified*, p. 506.
28. For example, Janet Schaw, *Journal of a Lady of Quality . . .* ed. Evangeline W. Andrews (New Haven, Conn. 1921), p. 127.
29. Morden, *Geography Rectified*, pp. 572–73; Blome, *Cosmography*, p. 460; Clarke, *Mirrour*, pp. 67–68; quotation from Moll, *System*, pp. 191–92.
30. George Fox, *To the Ministers, Teachers, and Priests, so called, and so stileing your Selves, in Barbadoes* (1672), pp. 5, 77; Richard Baxter, *Christian Directory* (1673), p. 557; Godwyn, *Negro's and Indian's Advocate*, p. 9; William Beveridge, *Anniversary Sermon preached before the S.P.G.* (1706), pp. 20–21; George Stanhope, *Anniversary Sermon preached before the S.P.G.* (1714), p. 23; Sandiford, *Mystery of Iniquity*, p. 39; Anthony Hill, *Afer Baptizatus or: the Negro turn'd Christian . . .* (1702), *passim*; *Abstracts of the Proceedings of the S.P.G.* (1736–37), pp. 41–42, 44, 45; (1740), pp. 44, 47, 50–51, 56, 57; (1741), pp. 52, 53, 58, 59, 60, 61, 66.
31. See for example the following S.P.G. *Anniversary Sermons:* William Fleetwood (1711), pp. 15–22; Richard Smalbrooke (1733), p. 38; Thomas Secker (1741), pp. 7, 18–20; also Bacon, *Four Sermons*, pp. xxiv–xxv, 59–62; Hill, *Afer Baptizatus*, pp. 28–31; Stephen Hales, *A Sermon preached before the Trustees for Establishing the Colony of Georgia . . .* (1734), pp. 13–15.
32. *A Letter to the Right Reverend, the Lord Bishop of London from an Inhabitant of . . . Leeward-Caribee Islands . . . concerning the Conversion of the Negro Slaves*, p. 32.
  This writer's proposal for a simplified Christianity was a reflection of the fact that the main objections to evangelism in the 18th century were based on plantocratic fears that the literacy, which thorough-going Protestant conversion would bring, would make slaves more aware and resentful of their condition.
33. "The African Slave Trade Defended . . .", *London Magazine*, IX (1740), 493–94; *The National and Private Advantages of the African Trade Considered . . .* (1746), p. 4; *Gentleman's Magazine*, V (1735), 91; Griffith Hughes, *The Natural History of Barbados* (1750), p. 17.
34. *The British Empire in America . . .* , 2 vols. (1708), II, 119–21.

35. *Considerations on the Present Peace, as far as it is relevant to the Colonies, and the African trade* (1763), pp. 36–37.

36. 5th ed. (1773), Preface—title page, v.

37. Thomas Jefferys, *The Natural and Civil History of the French Dominions in North and South America* (1760), p. 187; *A Soldier's Journal* (1770), pp. 100, 105, 108–110; cf. Fenning and Collyer, *New System*, II, 672.

38. *Soldier's Journal*, p. 111.

39. Andrew Burnaby, *Travels Through the Middle Settlements in North America* (1775), pp. 18–19; Peter Kalm, *Travels into North America*, 3 vols. (Warrington, 1770–71), I, 391–92; William Burke, *An Account of the European Settlements in America*, 2nd ed. 2 vols. (1758), II, 124.

40. Martin, *Plantership*, pp. 2–3; James Grainger, *An Essay on the More Common West India Diseases and the Management of Negroes* (1764), pp. 69–70.

41. *History of Jamaica*, II, 441–72.

42. For example, Leslie, *Account of Jamaica*, pp. 321, 362–63; *Plan for Abolition in West Indies*, pp. 12–14; *London Magazine*, XIV (1745), 495–96; XV (1746), 324–25; XXVII (1758), 167–68.

43. *Soldier's Journal*, p. 111; Bancroft, *Guiana*, p. 367; *Plan for Abolition in West Indies*, pp. 12–13.

44. Especially Long, *History of Jamaica*, II, 441–72.

45. John Fielding, *Extracts from the Penal Laws* (1769), pp. 144–45; Martin, *Plantership*, Preface, xiv–xvi; Knox, *Three Tracts*, pp. 15–16.

46. Long, *History of Jamaica*, II, 405–406, 491; Martin, *Plantership*, Dedication, xi; *An Essay Concerning Slavery and the danger Jamaica is exposed to from the too great number of slaves* (1746), pp. 18–23.

47. John Atkins, *A Voyage to Guinea, Brazil, and the West Indies . . .* (1735), p. 208; "Short Account of British . . . West Indies", *London Magazine*, XXVII (1758), 168; Oldmixon, *British Empire*, II, 14, 47; *Great Newes from Barbadoes* (1676), pp. 9–10.

48. *London Magazine*, IV (1735), 50, V (1736), 583; John Campbell, *Candid and Impartial Considerations on the Nature of the Sugar Trade . . .* (1763), pp. 95–105; Raynal, *Philosophical and Political History*, IV, 356–64; *The Present State of the West Indies* (1778), p. 59; Leslie, *Account of Jamaica*, pp. 362–63; Long, *History of Jamaica*, II, 334–50; Atkins, *Voyage*, p. 245.

49. Descriptions of West Indian slavery and the lives of the slaves are to be found in numerous works, including Patterson, *Sociology of Slavery*; Elsa V. Goveia, *Slave Society in the British Leeward Islands at the end of the Eighteenth Century* (New Haven, Conn., 1965); Wesley Frank Pitman, "Slavery on the British West India Plantations in the 18th Century," *Journal of Negro History*, XI (1926), 584–668.

50. *Monthly Review*, LVIII (1778), 142–44; Oldmixon, *British Empire*, II, 123; Edward Thompson, *Sailor's Letters . . .*, 2nd ed. 2 vols. (1767), II, 19, 24–25, 30–32; *Soldier's Journal*, pp. 108–10; Leslie, *Account of Jamaica*, pp. 322–23.

51. Hughes, *Barbados*, pp. 15–16; Jefferys, *Natural and Civil History*, p. 192; Hans Sloane, *A Voyage to the Islands of Madera, Barbados, Nieves, St Christophers and Jamaica . . . with a Natural History of the last of those Islands . . .*, 2 vols. (1707–25), I, xlviii.

52. Wesley, *Journal*, in *Works*, II, 337–38; *Letters from the Reverend Samuel Davies . . . showing, the State of Religion in Virginia, South Carolina, &c., particularly among the Negroes*, 2nd ed. (1757), p. 12; Knox, *Three Tracts*,

p. 37; *Instructions for Missionaries,* p. 8; Raynal, *Philosophical and Political History,* III, 423.

CHAPTER FIVE

1. For example, Jordan, *White Over Black,* pp. 253–54; Walvin, *Black and White,* p. 167; Curtin, *Image of Africa,* p. 42.
2. Lynn Thorndike, *The Sphere of Sacrobosco and its Commentators* (Chicago, 1949), pp. 129, 137; George Sampson, ed., *The Utopia of Sir Thomas More* (1910), p. 27.
3. For example, Duval, *Geographia Universalis,* p. 59.
4. Africanus, III, 830–31; cf. Blome, *Cosmography,* p. 380.
5. Chapters 6, 7, and 8 (below) deal in some detail with this new reporting.
6. The most thorough analysis of causal theories is in Jordan, *White Over Black, passim* but especially pp. 11–20, 239–52, 497–502, 512–38.
7. Caius Secundus Plinius (Pliny), *Natural History,* 10 vols., trans M. Rackham (1947), II, 251; *The Geography of Strabo,* 8 vols., trans. H. L. Jones (1917), VIII, 147; Arthur Golding, *The Excellent and Pleasant Worke of Iulius Solinus Polyhistor,* 1587 (Gainesville, Florida, 1955), Cap. XLIII; *Medieval Lore from Bartholomaeus Anglicus,* ed. Robert Steele (London and Boston, 1907), pp. 88–89; "Voyage to Guinea, 1554–55", in Hakluyt, *Principall Navigations,* I, 94–95.
8. J. R. Forster, *Observations,* pp. 260–61; Godwyn, *Negro's and Indian's Advocate,* p. 60; Goldsmith, *History of the Earth,* II, 233–34; Buffon, *Natural History,* III, 188–92; *Monthly Review,* XLII (1770), 523; Stanhope Smith, *Essay,* pp. 13–19; William Robertson, *History of America,* 2 vols. (1777), I, 299.
9. Goldsmith, *History of the Earth,* II, 234; "Observations on the Causes of the Black Complexion of the Negroes", *Universal Magazine,* XCVII (1795), 319–20; Letter signed 'J.S.H.', *ibid.,* LXVIII (1781), 254; Stanhope Smith, *Essay,* pp. 25–32, 57–58, 72–76.
10. Hunter, pp. 363–76; Buffon, *Natural History,* III, 163, 205; VII, 396. cf. Bacon, *Four Sermons,* xv; Stanhope Smith, *Essay,* p. 76; Turner, *View of the Earth,* p. 15 note; John Ray, *Philosophical Letters* (1718) pp. 344–46.
11. Buffon, *Natural History,* III, 162–65, 205–206; Stanhope Smith, *Essay,* p. 76; Barbot, 36–37; Burton, *English Acquisitions,* pp. 11–12; Atkins, *Voyage to Guinea,* p. 180; Astley, II, 266, 275; *Universal Modern History,* XVII, 276; Salmon, *Universal Traveller,* II, 358.
12. Dunbar, *Essays,* pp. 382–84; Gregory, *Comparative View,* pp. 30–31; Richard Blome, *The Present State of His Majesties Isles and Territories in America* (1687), pp. 97, 142–43; Burke, *European Settlements,* I, 168.
13. Buffon, *Natural History,* III, 203–206; VII, 396; Stanhope Smith, *Essay,* pp. 84–89; Goldsmith, *History of the Earth,* II, 236–39; Forster, *Observations,* pp. 252–56; Hunter, pp. 375–76, 387.
14. Robert Boyle, *Experiments and Considerations Touching Colours* (1664), pp. 260–61; Charles Sayle, ed. *The Works of Sir Thomas Browne,* 3 vols. (1904), II, 370–71; Astley, II, 269; Long, *History of Jamaica,* II, 351–52 note.
15. Matthew Hale, *The Primitive Origination of Mankind, considered and examined according to the Light of Nature* (1677), p. 201; Godwyn, *Negro's and Indian's Advocate,* p. 22; Forster, *Observations,* pp. 271–72; Buffon,

Natural History, III, 163–65, 201; VII, 395. Jordan, *White Over Black*, p. 243.

16. Buffon, *Natural History*, VII, 394; Jobson, *Golden Trade*, p. 28; Moore, *Travels into the Inland*, p. 29; *Universal Modern History*, XVII, 226; Middleton, *New and Complete System*, I, 303; Salmon, *Universal Traveller*, II, 360.

17. Cornelius de Pauw, *Recherches Philosophiques sur les Americains . . . 2 vols. (Paris, 1768–69)*, I, *184–86; Monthly Review*, XLII (1770), 523–24; Goldsmith, *History of the Earth*, II, 228–29; Buffon, *Natural History*, III, 163–64; Equiano, *Interesting Narrative*, I, 40–42; Stanhope Smith, *Essay*, pp. 40 note, 90–93; Johann Georg Adam (George) Forster, *A Voyage Round the World in his Britannic Majesty's Sloop, Resolution, commanded by Capt. James Cook . . .*, 2 vols. (1777), I, 34–5.

18. See, for example, Boyle, *Experiments*, pp. 163–64; Samuel Haworth, *Anthropologia: or a Philosophic Discourse Concerning Man* (1680), pp. 80–81; Isbrand de Diemerbroeck, *The Anatomy of Human Bodies*, trans. William Salmon (1689), p. 10; William Cowper, *The Anatomy of Human Bodies* (1698), Table 4, fig. 6.

19. Thomas Gibson, *The Anatomy of Human Bodies Epitomized* (1682), pp. 9–10; James Keill, *The Anatomy of the Human Body*, abridged (1698), pp. 11–13—12th edition published in 1759.

20. Pierre Dionis, *The Anatomy of Human Bodies improved* (1703) pp. 98–100; James Drake, *Anthropologia Nova or, a New System of Anatomy*, 2 vols. (1707), I, 18; Samuel Foart Simmons, *Elements of Anatomy and the Animal Oeconomy*, from the French of O. Person (1775), p. 128; William Cheselden, *The Anatomy of the Human Body*, 11th ed. (1778), p. 135; William Hogarth, *The Analysis of Beauty* (1753), p. 114.

21. Astley, II, 270; Goldsmith, *History of the Earth*, II, 235; Forster, *Observations*, pp. 258–59; Hunter, p. 368; Bacon, *Four Sermons*, xiv.

22. *Gentleman's Magazine*, XII (1742), 279; Long, *History of Jamaica*, II, 351–52 note; *Universal Modern History*, XIV, 20.

23. Drake, *Anthropologia Nova*, I, 18; Cheselden, *Anatomy*, p. 135.

24. Hughes, *Barbados*, p. 14; Oldmixon, *British Empire in America*, II, 125–26; Bacon, *Four Sermons*, xiv–xv.

25. Jordan, *White Over Black*, p. 244; Buffon, *Natural History*, III, 206–207; Stanhope Smith, *Essay*, pp. 134–35; George Edwards, *Gleanings of Natural History* (1758), pp. 3–5.

26. *Works of Browne*, II, 375; Goldsmith, *History of the Earth*, II, 227, 233, 238; Diemerbroeck, *Anatomy*, pp. 196–97; Daniel Turner, *De Morbis Cutaneis: a Treatise of Diseases Incident to the Skin*, 3rd ed. (1726), pp. 155–90; Daniel Turner, *The Force of the Mother's Imagination upon her Foetus . . . still further considered* (1730), passim; James Augustus Blondel, *The Power of the Mother's Imagination Examined* (1729); John Henry Mauclerc, *Doctor Blondel Confuted* (1747); Buffon, *Natural History*, II, 330–31; Bradley, *Works of Nature*, pp. 229–31; cf. "Of the Influences which the Passions of the Mother have on the Foetus", *Universal Magazine*, LII (1773), 74–75; *Universal Modern History*, XVI, 294; Mocquet, *Travels*, pp. 227–29.

27. I, 99.

28. Royal Society, *Philosophical Transactions*, XIX (1729), 781; LI (1760), 759; LV (1764), 45.

29. *White Over Black*, pp. 249–52.

30. For example, Robertson, *History of America*, I, 301; Buffon, *Natural*

History, III, 178–80; "An Account of the White Negro . . ." *Universal Magazine*, XXXIX (1766), 207; *Gentleman's Magazine*, XXXVI (1766), 403; *Monthly Review*, XXXV (1766), 449–50; Stanhope Smith, *Essay*, pp. 156–57.

31. Boyle, *Experiments*, pp. 166–67; Ogilby, *Africa*, pp. 508–09; Hunter, p. 388; Mocquet, *Travels*, pp. 227–29; *Gentleman's Magazine*, XXXVI (1766), 403; *Monthly Review*, XXV (1766), 449–50; Stanhope Smith, *loc. cit.*, note.

32. Robertson, *History of America*, 1, 301–302; Ogilby, *Africa*, p. 509; Buffon, *Natural History*, III, 181–82; "Account of the Natives of the Friendly Islands", *Annual Register*, XXVII (1784–85), 2; Review of F. Bussi, *Dissertatione Storico-Anatomico . . .* , *Monthly Review* (1785), 523; Review of M. van Iperen, *A Description of a white Negro in the Isle of Bali*, *Monthly Review*, LXV (1781), 543; *Universal Magazine*, XXXIX (1766), 207; Stanhope Smith, *loc. cit.*

33. *Purchas His Pilgrimage*, pp. 655–65; Abbot, *Briefe Description*, pp. 261–62; Heylyn, *Cosmographie*, p. 1016; Hunter, p. 388.

34. For example, Goldsmith, *History of the Earth*, II, 232; Clarkson, *Essay on Slavery and Commerce*, p. 203; Buffon, *Natural History*, III, 200; Hunter, p. 372; Ramsay, *Essay on Treatment and Conversion*, p. 216.

35. For example, Peter Kolb, *The Present State of the Cape of Good Hope: or, a Particular Account of the Several Nations of the Hottentots . . .* , trans. Guido Medley, 2 vols. (1731), I, 55—referring here to Negroes, not Hottentots; Salmon, *Universal Traveller*, II, 358; Astley, II, 270; *Universal Modern History*, XIV, 20; Morden, *Geography Rectified*, p. 516.

36. Atkins, *Voyage to Guinea*, p. 39; Astley, II, 270.

37. Hoxie Neale Fairchild, *The Noble Savage: A Study in Romantic Naturalism* (New York, 1928), pp. 8–15.

38. "Decades of the New World", in Edward Arber, ed., *The First Three English Books on America 1511–1555 A.D. Being Chiefly Translations, Compilations etc. by Richard Eden* (Birmingham, 1885), pp. 78, 159, 191.

39. Hakluyt, *Principall Navigations*, II, 643H.

40. Caption to drawings of John White in David Beers Quinn, ed. *The Roanoke Voyages 1584–90*, Hakluyt Soc. Pubs., Ser. 2, CIV, CV (1955), I, 435.

41. *Purchas His Pilgrimage*, p. 30; John Keble ed., *The Works of Richard Hooker*, 3 vols. (Oxford, 1836) I, 284.

42. James F. Anderson, *Natural Theology: The Metaphysics of God* (Milwaukee, 1962), pp. 4–7.

43. *Purchas His Pilgrimage*, p. 31; Heylyn, *Cosmographie*, p. 1016; Ogilby, *Africa*, p. 318; *A Key into the Language of America* (1643), ed. J. Hammond Trumbull, in *The Complete Writings of Roger Williams*, 7 vols. (New York, 1963), I, 162.

44. Roger Bastide, "Color, Racism, and Christianity", *Daedalus*, Spring 1967, 320; Williams, *Key*, 153.

45. See, for example, *Hakluytus Postumus*, II, 405, 445, 454, III, 530, 538; Hakluyt, *Principall Navigations*, II, 548, 561.

46. *Briefe Description*, p. 253.

47. *The Historie of the World, in five bookes* (1614), pp. 273, 284–87.

48. *Works of R. Hooker*, I, 300.

49. Heylyn, *Cosmographie*, p. 1016; Abbot, *Briefe Description*, pp. 94–96; *Purchas His Pilgrimage*, pp. 435–37.

50. Clarke, *Mirrour*, p. 76; Morden, *Geography Rectified*, p. 538; *Thesaurus Geographicus*, p. 465; Blome, *Cosmography*, p. 421.

51. Brokesby, *Of Education*, pp. 84, 86, 87, 154–55, 193; *London Magazine*, I, (1732), 393–94, 461.

52. *The Travels of a Philosopher*, trans. from French (1769), pp. 6–8, 182.

53. *London Magazine*, I (1732), 461.

54. J. Ewer, *Anniversary Sermon preached before the Society for the Propagation of the Gospel* (1767), pp. 3–4; cf. Anthony Hill, *Afer Baptizatus: or the Negro Turn'd Christian* . . . (1702), pp. 12, 18; Bryant, *Authenticity of Scriptures*, pp. 13–14, 18; Hughes, *Barbados*, pp. 18–19; William Ten Rhyne, *An Account of the Cape of Good Hope and the Hottentots*, Churchill, IV, 838; "Letter from J. Hippisley, Cape Coast Castle . . .", *Annual Register*, IV, (1761), 159–60.

55. "On the Importance of an Inquiry into the Human Mind", *Universal Magazine*, XXXIV (1764), 286.

56. For example, C. A. Helvetius, *A Treatise on Man, His Intellectual Faculties and His Education*, trans. William Hooper, Vol. I (1777), 154 (note by W. Hooper); Millar, *Origin of the Distinction of Ranks*, p. 3; "Dissertation on the Treatment of the Negro Race", *Universal Magazine*, LXVIII (1781), 3–4; *London Magazine*, VII (1738), 449.

57. David Beers Quinn, ed. *The Voyages and Colonising Enterprises of Sir Humphrey Gilbert*, 2 vols. Hakluyt Soc. Pubs., Ser. 2, LXXXIII and LXXXIV (1940), II, 388, 455–57; Richard Eburne, *A Plain Pathway to Plantations* (1624), ed. Louis B. Wright (Ithaca, New York, 1962), p. 28.

58. Estwick, *Considerations*, pp. 78–80, Forster, *Observations*, pp. 295, 300–301; William Guthrie, *A New Geographical, Historical and Commercial Grammar*, 17th ed. (1798), pp. 30–36; Middleton, *New and Complete System*, I, 241; Fenning and Collyer, *New System*, I, 307; Emmanuel Bowen, *A Complete System of Geography*, 2 vols. (1747), II, 381; Fresnoy, *Geography for Children* . . . , 22nd ed. (1800), p. 5; Tobias Smollett, *The Present State of all Nations*, 8 vols. (1768–69), VIII, 62–63.

59. William Falconer, *Remarks on the Influence of Climate* . . . *and Way of Life on* . . . *Mankind* (1781), p. 178; Dunbar, *Essays*, p. 257; Adam Smith, *An Inquiry into the Nature and Causes of the Wealth of Nations*, 6th ed., ed. Edwin Cannan, 2 vols. (1950), I, 22–23.

60. *Hakluytus Postumus*, I, 1–39, XIX, 218–23; Quinn, *Humphrey Gilbert*, II, 455–57.

61. For example, George Gregory, *Essays, Historical and Moral*, 2nd ed. (1788), pp. 48, 59.

62. See for example, *Alfred's 'Orosius'*, in R. Pauli, *The Life of Alfred the Great* (1857), p. 259; Ranulf Higden, *Polychronicon Ranulphi Higden*, ed. Churchill Babington (1865), I, 51.

63. Curtin, *Image of Africa*, p. 65.

64. Adam Ferguson, *An Essay on the History of Civil Society* (Edinburgh, 1767), pp. 166, 171; Falconer, *Remarks on the Influence of Climate*, p. 69; "On Two Italian Dancers", *Gentleman's Magazine*, XI (1741), 29–30; "A Traveller's Opinion of the English in General", *Annual Register*, IX (1766), 219; J. H. Bernardin de Saint-Pierre, *A Voyage to the Island of Mauritius* . . . *the Isle of Bourbon, the Cape of Good Hope*, trans. from French by John Parish (1775), pp. 266–67.

65. Long, *History of Jamaica*, III, 476–77; *Universal Modern History*, XVI, 399.

66. John Wesley, *Thoughts Upon Slavery,* in *The Works of John Wesley,* 3rd ed., 14 vols. 1872, reprinted (Grand Rapids, Michigan, n.d.) XI, 64.
    Forster, *Observations,* pp. 36, 293; Hunter, p. 390; Robertson, *History of America,* I, 314–16, 347; Dunbar, *Essays,* p. 223; Falconer, *Remarks on the Influence of Climate,* p. 185; Monboddo, *Origin and Progress of Language,* I, 251–52; Rousseau, *Inequality Among Mankind,* pp. 41–42.
67. *Remarks on the Influence of Climate,* pp. 117–20, 130, 135.
68. *Origin of the Distinction of Ranks,* pp. 9–12.

CHAPTER SIX

1. Jordan, *White Over Black,* p. 253.
2. *Universal Modern History,* XIV, 17.
3. *Guiana,* pp. 339–40.
4. Duval, *Geographia Universalis,* pp. 64–65; *Encheiridion Geographicum,* G. 4; Blome, *Cosmography,* pp. 247, 336; Eachard, *Compendium,* p. 115; *Thesaurus Geographicus,* p. 448.
5. Barbot, 324, 327–28; Bosman, pp. 338–39; Phillips, *Journal,* 214–15; *Universal Modern History,* XVI, 395–96; Smith, *New Voyage to Guinea,* pp. 194–95.
6. Phillips, *loc. cit.;* Bowen, *Complete System,* II, 475; Smollett, *Present State,* VIII, 153–54; Bosman, pp. 340, 348–50; Barbot, 328–32; Middleton, *New and Complete System,* I, 330; Fenning and Collyer, *New System,* I, 409–10; *Universal Modern History,* XVI, 398, 404.
7. Atkins, *Voyage to Guinea,* pp. 61–62; Astley, II, 535.
8. Adanson, *Voyage to Senegal,* pp. 52–54; Benezet, *Some Historical Account,* p. 13; Wesley, *Thoughts Upon Slavery,* 63; *Thoughts on the Slavery of the Negroes* (1784), pp. 9–10.
9. *Voyage to Senegal,* pp. 36–37, 43, 50; Jobson, *Golden Trade,* p. 60.
10. For example, Angelo and Carli, Churchill, I, 620–21; Merolla, *ibid.,* 718; *Universal Modern History,* XVI, 45–46, 107–110, 111–12, 275.
11. Blome, *Cosmography,* p. 399; Duval, *Geographia Universalis,* p. 95; Morden, *Geography Rectified,* pp. 522–23.
12. Barbot, 96; see also *Encheiridion Geographicum,* I. 4.
13. Bosman, p. 147; Barbot, 306; Fenning and Collyer, *New System,* I, 422; *Universal Modern History,* XIV, 17–18; Salmon, *Universal Traveller,* II, 385.
14. Blome, *Cosmography,* p. 380; Clarke, *Mirrour,* p. 506; Bowen, *Complete System,* II, 460.
15. Africanus, III, 825; Ogilby, *Africa,* p. 323; Bowen, *Complete System,* II, 464.
16. Clarke, *Mirrour,* p. 53; Duval, *Geographia Universalis,* p. 86; Middleton, *New and Complete System,* I, 290; Morden, *Geography Rectified,* p. 506; de Fer, *Short and Easy Method,* p. 277; Petavius, *History,* p. 106; *Sir William Monson's Naval Tracts,* Churchill, III, 441, 473, 480–81.
17. *Universal Modern History,* XVII, 420; Payne, *Universal Geography,* I, 457.
18. Barbot, 62; Petavius, *History,* p. 106.
19. Barbot, 58–59, 62; Jobson, *Golden Trade,* pp. 61–82; Astley, II, 302–303; *Universal Modern History,* XIV, 24, 325; Moore, *Travels into Inland,* pp. 39, 144–45.
20. Atkins, *Voyage to Guinea,* p. 60; cf. *A Letter to the Right Reverend the Lord Bishop of London from an Inhabitant of . . . the Leeward-Caribee Islands, . . . In which is inserted a Short Essay concerning the Conversion*

of the Negro Slaves . . . (1730), p. 32; Fenning, *Geography*, I, 435; *Universal Modern History*, XIV, 29.

21. *Ibid.*, XVII, 211–12; Bosman, p. 131; Lindsay, *Voyage to the Coast*, p. 55; Astley, II, 563.

22. Houstoun, *Observations*, pp. 16, 18–33; Atkins, *Voyage to Guinea*, pp. 75, 188; Thomas Thompson, *An Account of Two Missionary Voyages* (1758), p. 47; *Royal African or Memoirs of the Young Prince of Annamaboe* . . . (c. 1750), pp. 21–40; 46–47, John Hippisley, *Essays* . . . (1764), p. 26.

23. Atkins, *Voyage to Guinea*, p. 172; Phillips, *Journal*, 217–19; Barbot, 325–27; Bosman, pp. 363–363a; *The Trade to Africa Considered, and Demonstrated to be Improved to the Nation's Benefit over a Million a Year by Separate Traders* (n.d.), p. 3; *A Letter from a Merchant in Bristol, touching the Trade to Africa* . . . (1711?), p. 1.

24. For example, *The Destructive Consequences of a Regulated Trade to Africa as promoted by the Separate Traders* (n.d.), p. 1; *Several Reasons proving that our Trade to Africa cannot be preserved and carried on effectively by any other Method, than that of a Considerable Joint-Stock, with exclusive Privileges* (1709?), p. 4; *A Memorial Touching the Nature and State of the Trade to Africa* (1709), p. 2.

25. For example, *Trade to Africa Considered*, p. 3; *The Improvement of the African Trade Further Demonstrated by Separate Traders* . . . (n.d.), p. 3; *Considerations on the Present Trade to Africa, answer'd paragraph by paragraph* (n.d.), p. 1.

26. Atkins, *Voyage to Guinea*, pp. 158–68; Astley, II, 562–63; Salmon, *Universal Traveller*, II, 393.

27. *A Scheme for an Additional Stock to the Royal African Company by Subscription* (1713–14), p. 1; *A Short and True Account of the Importance and Necessity of Settling the African Trade,* . . . (1711), pp. 1, 4.

28. Atkins, *Voyage to Guinea*, p. 185; Houstoun, *Observations*, pp. 11, 24; Raynal, III, 394; see also Bosman, pp. 86–87.

29. Astley, II, 145–58.

30. *The National and Private Advantages of the African Trade Considered* (1746) *passim;* Malachy Postlethwayt, *The Importance of the African Expedition Considered* (1758), pp. 52–60.

31. Astley, II, 150; Postlethwayt, *Universal Dictionary of Trade and Commerce*, see under 'Gold'; Bosman, p. 86; Smith, *New Voyage to Guinea*, p. 138.

32. Atkins, *Voyage to Guinea*, p. 184; Astley, II, 150, 564, 703; Houstoun, *Observations*, pp. 18, 22; Raynal, III, 393; Phillips, *Journal*, 206; Bosman, pp. 82–3; Ogilby, *Africa*, p. 460; Postlethwayt, *Importance of The African Expedition*, p. 72.

33. Barbot, 339; Benezet, *Some Historical Account*, pp. 2, 22–26.

34. Barbot, 365; Fenning, *New System*, I, 389.

35. Jobson, *Golden Trade*, p. 121; Barbot, 41.

36. Middleton, *New and Complete System*, I, 318; *Universal Modern History*, XVII, 52; Atkins, *Voyage to Guinea*, p. 99; Bosman, p. 128; Barbot, 262.

37. Barbot, 42, 262; Salmon, *Universal Traveller*, II, 371.

38. Ogilby, *Africa*, p. 323; Blomc, *Cosmography*, p. 399; de Fer, *Short and Easy Method*, p. 285; Phillips, *Journal*, 220; Astley, II, 524–25; Dalzel, *Dahomy*, Introduction, xxiv–xxv.

39. Houstoun, *Observations*, pp. 10–11.

40. XIV, 31.

41. Jobson, *Golden Trade*, pp. 38–39; Clarke, *Mirrour*, p. 67; Ogilby, *Africa*, pp. 456–57.

42. Moore, *Travels into the Inland*, pp. 34–35; Barbot, 39–40; Angelo and Carli, Churchill, I, 629; Salmon, *Universal Traveller*, II, 359; *Universal Modern History*, XVI, 25, 174, 287; Atkins, *Voyage To Guinea*, p. 50.

43. *Golden Trade*, pp. 125–26.

44. Adanson, *Voyage to Senegal*, p. 117; *Universal Modern History*, XVI, 24–25.

45. Barbot, 110; Bosman, pp. 193, 199; Smith, *Voyage to Guinea*, p. 100 note; Snoeck, *Tooth and Grain Coasts*, Bosman, p. 475; Jobson, *Golden Trade*, pp. 38–39; *Universal Modern History*, XIV, 30; Astley, II, 274–75, 536; Paschoud, *Historico-Political Geography*, p. 280.

46. For example, Bosman, pp. 125, 189–90, 199; Barbot, 110, 292.

47. Barbot, 258, 292-95; Bosman, pp. 120, 132-33, 178–87.

48. Barbot, 265–66; Bosman, pp. 7, 17, 61, 391.

49. *Some Historical Account*, pp. 22–26.

50. *Universal Modern History*, XVII, 303.

51. Jefferys, *History of the French Dominions*, pp. 187, 190–91; Grainger, *West India Diseases*, p. 7; Long, *History of Jamaica*, II, 403–404; Hughes, *Barbados*, p. 14; *The Alarm-Bell: or, Considerations on the present dangerous state of the Sugar Colonies* (1749), p. 8; *Answer to the Objections Against the Proposals of the Royal African Company for Settling the Trade to Africa in a Second Letter to a M.P.* (1748), pp. 2–3; *Papers Laid before the Honourable House of Commons by the Commissioners for Trade and Plantations . . . for the better Securing . . . the Trade to Africa* (1750), pp. 7, 51; *The Argument touching Security . . . for carrying on the African Trade, demonstrated to be Groundless* (1710), p. 2; Barbot, 339; Phillips, *Journal*, 214; Atkins, *Voyage to Guinea*, p. 179; Salmon, *Universal Traveller*, II, 392; *Thesaurus Geographicus*, p. 463.

52. Godwyn, *Negro's and Indian's Advocate*, p. 16; J. Hillier, *Two Letters from Cape Corse* (1687–88, 1688) in *Miscellanea Curiosa . . . containing a Collection of Some of the Principal Phenomena in Nature . . . read to the Royal Society*, 2nd ed. 3 vols. (1708), III, 359–60; Astley, II, 33.

53. John D. Fage, *A History of West Africa*, 4th ed. of 'An Introduction to West Africa' (Cambridge, 1969), pp. 35–37; Moore, *Travels into Inland*, p. 30; Astley, II, 62–64, 262; *Universal Modern History*, XVII, 278, 302; *London Magazine*, VII (1738), 449; *Gentleman's Magazine*, VIII (1738), 473; Buffon, *Natural History* III, 140; Wesley, *Thoughts Upon Slavery*, 62; Benezet, *Some Historical Account*, p. 9; Jobson, *Golden Trade*, pp. 33–35.

54. Moore and Labat both quoted in *Universal Modern History*, XVII, 273–74; see also *ibid.*, XVI, 25; Barbot, 235–36; Bosman, p. 118.

55. Jobson, *Golden Trade*, p. 105; Raynal, III, 422; *Monthly Review*, XXVI (1762), 356.

56. Astley, II, 541–42; Adanson, *Voyage to Senegal*, pp. 11–13, 289.

57. *Black Presence*, pp. 21–22.

58. Adanson, *Voyage to Senegal*, pp. 253–54; Atkins, *Voyage to Guinea*, p. 82.

59. Bohun, *Dictionary*, II, "Negro"; Barbot, 77, 157, 262, 268–69, 273; Atkins, *Voyage to Guinea*, pp. 99, 180; Angelo and Carli, Churchill, I, 621; Blome, *Cosmography*, p. 399; *Thesaurus Geographicus*, p. 464; Salmon, *Universal Traveller*, II, 400–402.

60. "The Speech of Moses Ben Saam", *Gentleman's Magazine*, V (1735), 21; "Some Reflections on the Trade of Buying and Selling Negroes", *London Magazine*, VII (1738), 129–31.

61. Beattie's views quoted at length in *Gentleman's Magazine*, XLI (1771), 594–95.

62. Gordon, *Geography Anatomiz'd*, p. 321; *Universal Modern History*, XIV, 17, 32.
63. "A Description of the River Sanaga . . . from the latest Accounts", *London Magazine*, XXVII (1758), 359–61; Smollett, *Present State*, VIII, 58–59; *Considerations on the Present Peace*, p. 26; Lindsay, *Voyage to the Coast*, pp. 95–101.
64. Pp. 2–12.
65. See for example, *Universal Dictionary of Trade and Commerce*, 'Africa', 'Gold'; *Importance of the African Expedition Considered*, pp. 52–60; also two articles in the *Universal Magazine*, which used his arguments: XX (1757), 97–105; XXXIII (1763), 57–60.
66. *Universal Dictionary of Trade and Commerce*, 'Africa'; *Importance of the African Expedition*, pp. 85–99.

CHAPTER SEVEN

1. Eldred Jones, *Othello's Countrymen*, pp. 37–119; Golding, *Solinus Polyhistor*, Cap. XLII; Hakluyt, *Principall Navigations*, I, 94; *The Golden Coast* (1665), pp. 20–45; Blome, *Cosmography*, p. 379; Clarke, *Mirrour*, p. 53; Duval, *Geographia Universalis*, p. 87; de Fer, *Short and Easy Method*, p. 277.
2. Angelo and Carli, Churchill, I, 613, 629.
3. Fenning and Collyer, *New Systems*, I, 388, 394 (printed in error as 382); Bosman, p. 385.
4. Adanson, *Voyage to Senegal*, pp. 56–67.
5. Blome, *Cosmography*, p. 382; Morden, *Geography Rectified*, p. 507; Barbot, 138, 331, 347–48, 363, 377, 393; Phillips, *Journal*, 219; Houstoun, *Observations*, p. 34. Bosman, p. 345; Snoeck, in *ibid.*, p. 484. *Universal Modern History*, XVII, 220; Burton, *English Acquisitions*, pp. 10–11.
6. Barbot, 110, 240; Bosman, p. 199; Salmon, *Universal Traveller*, II, 371–72; Snoeck, Bosman, p. 475; Middleton, *New and Complete System*, I. 331.
7. Barbot, 248; Bosman, pp. 193, 203; Astley, II, 62–64.
8. Discussed by J. D. Fage in Bosman, p. 534.
9. Barbot, 246, 277; Bosman, p. 211; Burton, *English Acquisitions*, pp. 12–13.
10. Ogilby, *Africa*, p. 457; Barbot, 246, 248, 333, 363, 377; Bosman, p. 212.
11. *History of Jamaica*, II, 383.
12. *Ibid.*, 385; Bosman, pp. 198–200; Barbot, 241; Hippisley, *Essays*, p. 14; Jobson, *Golden Trade*, p. 54.
13. Jobson, *Golden Trade*, p. 53; Barbot, 245, 333, 337, 348, 352, 372; Bosman, pp. 205, 344, 357–58; Atkins, *Voyage to Guinea*, p. 52; Merolla, Churchill, I, 718; Blome, *Cosmography*, p. 401; Middleton, *New and Complete System*, I, 332; Salmon, *Universal Traveller*, II, 358.
14. *New Voyage to Guinea*, pp. 243–49.
15. Jobson, *Golden Trade*, p. 54; Burton, *English Acquisitions*, p. 13; Moll, *System*, pp. 119, 123.
16. Lindsay, *Voyage to the Coast*, pp. 77–78; Smith, *New Voyage to Guinea*, pp. 250–51; Goldsmith, *History of the Earth*, II, 74–75.
17. Barbot, 36; Astley, II, 32, 274, 309, 322–33; Buffon, *Natural History*, III, 141–42; Smith, *New Voyage to Guinea*, p. 100 note; Moore, *Travels into the Inland*, p. 121.
18. Barbot, 252; Bosman, pp. 51–52, 141–43; *Universal Modern History*, XVII, 98–99; Salmon, *Universal Traveller*, II, 365.

19. Atkins, *Voyage to Guinea*, pp. 93–94; Phillips, *Journal*, 209–10.
20. Barbot, 157, 170–71, 239.
21. Davis, *Problem of Slavery*, p. 503; Atkins, *Voyage to Guinea*, p. 40, *Navy Surgeon*, Appendix, pp. 7–8; Phillips, *Journal*, 201–203, 208; Bosman, p. 52; Report from Philip Quaque, *Abstract of Proceedings of S.P.G.* (1768), pp. 65–66; Salmon, *Universal Traveller*, II, 364–65.
22. *Letter to Bishop of London*, p. 11; Holder, *Short Essay on Slavery*, pp. 34–35; Long, *History of Jamaica*, II, 432, 436; Bancroft, *Guiana*, pp. 372–73.
23. *History of Jamaica*, II, 327–28, 330, 333, 335.
24. *Ibid.*, 353; Estwick, *Considerations*, pp. 74–76.
25. *Ibid.*, pp. 80–81, Kolb, *Cape of Good Hope*, I, 28; Bowen, *Complete System*, II, 498; *Universal Modern History*, XV, 487; Astley, III, 331 note.
26. Estwick, *Considerations*, pp. 80–81; Long, *History of Jamaica*, II, 353; Hippisley's views in *Annual Register*, IV, (1761), 160; Villault cited in Astley, II, 631; *Letter to Bishop of London*, p. 9.
27. Bancroft, *Guiana*, p. 260; Long, *History of Jamaica*, II, 382 note; Snelgrave, *New Account*, Preface, A3–A4.
28. *Golden Coast*, p. 39; Duval, *Geographia Universalis*, p. 64; Blome, *Cosmography*, p. 400; Paschoud, *Historico-Political Geography*, p. 282; *Thesaurus Geographicus*, p. 463; Merolla, 746.
29. Clarke, *Mirrour*, pp. 53, 72; *True Travels, Adventures, Observations of Captain John Smith*, Churchill, II, 397; *Thesaurus Geographicus*, p. 462; Ogilby, *Africa*, p. 518.
30. Churchill, I, 666–67, 672, 676, 680, 726, 729.
31. Atkins, *Voyage to Guinea*, p. 131; Ward, *Natural History*, p. 124; *Universal Magazine*, LXXI (1782), 242.
32. *Universal Modern History*, XVI, 194–95, 350; Monboddo, *Origin and Progress*, I, 209 note; *History of Jamaica*, II, 373.
33. Kames, *Sketches*, I, 65; *Thesaurus Geographicus*, pp. 461–62; Barbot, 97; Merolla, 653, 729; Roland Oliver and John D. Fage, *A Short History of Africa*, (1966), p. 128; Long, *History of Jamaica*, II, 373. *The Strange Adventures of Andrew Battell of Leigh, in Angola, and the Adjoining Regions*, ed. E. G. Ravenstein, *Hak. Soc. Pubs.*, Ser 2, VI, (1901), 19–35, 82–87; Ogilby, *Africa*, pp. 519–20; *Universal Modern History*, XVI, 10–18, 321–50.
34. XLIII (1768), 186.
35. *Monthly Review*, LV (1777), 526–27.
36. *New System*, I, 430.
37. *Voyage to Guinea*, pp. xii–xxv, 37, 57, 123.
38. Phillips, *Journal*, 197; Snoeck in Bosman, p. 487; Astley, II, 561; *Universal Modern History*, XVII, 205; Smith, *New Voyage*, p. 110 note; *Universal Modern History*, *loc. cit.*; Middleton, *New and Complete System*, I, 312; Barbot, 144.
39. Atkins, *Voyage to Guinea*, p. 129; *Universal Modern History*, XVI, 102; *Monthly Review*, XLVIII (1773), 45; *Letter to the Bishop of London*, p. 8; Bosman, p. 365; Snoeck, in *ibid.*, 489; Atkins, *Voyage to Guinea*, p. 130.
40. Snelgrave, *New Account*, pp. 19–53; this account is summarized and discussed by Grant, *Fortunate Slave*, pp. 129–31.
41. Blome, *Cosmography*, p. 384; Clarke, *Mirrour*, p. 72; *Universal Modern History*, XIV, 21; Barbot, 296, 381; Gemelli, Churchill, IV, 216.

42. Salmon, *Universal Traveller*, II, 397–99; Atkins, *Voyage to Guinea*, pp. 126–31; Astley, II, 495.
43. *Some Historical Account*, xiv–xv.
44. Astley, II, 482–85.
45. Hughes, *Barbados*, p. 17; Long, *History of Jamaica*, II, 389, 397–99; Barbot, 284.
46. *Essays*, p. 13.
47. For example see *Monthly Review*, XLVIII (1773), 45.
48. Millar, *Origin and Distinction of Ranks*, pp. 302–04; Seller, *New Systeme*, p. 92; Merolla in Churchill, I, 653, 743; Ogilby, *Africa*, pp. 366, 396, 457, 510; Smith, *New Voyage*, p. 143; Thompson, *Two Missionary Voyages*, p. 57; Hillier, *Two Letters from Cape Corse*, p. 356.
49. *New Account*, Introduction (no. p. nos), pp. 101–104.
50. Astley, II, 545–46.
51. Bosman, pp. 230–32; Barbot, 284.
52. Long, *History of Jamaica*, II, 373, 389, 397–99; Martin, *Plantership*, iii–iv.
53. Thomas Secker, *Anniversary Sermon . . .* (1741), pp. 6–7; Moll, *System*, pp. 103, 120; Middleton, *New and Complete System*, I, 540; Salmon, *Universal Traveller*, II, 364–65; Angelo and Carli, Churchill, I, 631; cf. Houstoun, *Observations*, pp. 33–34.
54. For modern criticisms see Bosman, p. 531. Blome, *Cosmography*, p. 384. Le Blanc, *World Surveyed*, p. 322. Ogilby, *Africa*, p. 402; Barbot, 304; Bosman, p. 146; Thompson, *Two Missionary Voyages*, pp. 43–44; Astley, II, 440, 540, 663–76; Smollett, *Present State*, VIII, 142; *Universal Modern History*, XVII, 126; Middleton, *New and Complete System*, I, 303; Salmon, *Universal Traveller*, II, 376.
55. Fenning and Collyer, *New System*, I, 422; John Toland, *Letters to Serena* (1704), p. 124; Bosman, p. 147; Barbot, 306.
56. Bosman, p. 156; Thompson, *Two Missionary Voyages*, pp. 44–45; Astley, II, 442.
57. Barbot, 58, 340; Bosman, pp. 367 a, 368a; Atkins, *Voyage to Guinea*, p. 83; *Universal Modern History*, XVI, 376; Moll, *System*, p. 120.
58. Barbot, 51; Matthews, *Voyage to Sierra Leone*, pp. 64–73, 123–30, 130–36; Smollett, *Present State*, VIII, 180.
59. Geoffrey Parrinder, *Religion in Africa*, Penguin ed. (1969), p. 27; *Universal Modern History*, XVI, 376.
60. *Two Missionary Voyages*, pp. 38, 40, 69–73.
61. Phillips, *Journal*, 207, 225; Barbot, 58; Bosman, pp. 149, 154.
62. Jobson, pp. 108, 116–18; Phillips, *Journal*, 207; Barbot, 51, 59; Oldmixon, *British Empire*, II, 124.
63. Barbot, 59; Smollett, *Present State*, VIII, 142; Salmon, *Universal Traveller*, II, 376.
64. Granville Sharp, *The Just Limitation of Slavery in the Laws of God . . .* (1776), p. 26 note; Godwyn, *Negro's and Indian's Advocate*, p. 34; Atkins, *Voyage to Guinea*, pp. 80, 83–84, 106.
65. Bosman, pp. 80, 376; Barbot, 341–42; Phillips, *Journal*, 224; Adanson, *Voyage to Senegal*, pp. 228, 229, 310.
66. Bosman, pp. 148–50; Phillips, *Journal*, 193; Atkins, *Voyage to Guinea*, p. 52; Thompson, *Two Missionary Voyages*, pp. 59–62; Thompson, *Sailor's Letters*, II, 30–31; Hughes, *Barbados*, p. 15; Leslie, *Jamaica*, p. 323.
67. Ogilby, *Africa*, pp. 368, 391; Barbot, 51; Astley, II, 540; Bosman, p. 152; Angelo and Carli, 631.

CHAPTER EIGHT

1. *Problem of Slavery*, pp. 501–502.
2. Hakluyt, *Principall Navigations*, I, 94–96; cf. *Medieval Lore from Bartholomaeus Anglicus*, p. 89. *Purchas His Pilgrimage*, p. 644; *Golden Coast*, pp. 20–45.
3. Astley, II, 32–33.
4. Africanus, III, 823–27.
5. Blome, *Cosmography*, pp. 380–81; Clarke, *Mirrour*, pp. 66–67; Petavius, *History*, p. 106.
6. Blome, *loc. cit.*; Clarke, *loc. cit.*; de Fer, *Short and Easy*, p. 278; Le Blanc, *World Surveyed*, p. 179; Seller, *New Systeme*, p. 90; Africanus, III, 827.
7. Ogilby, *Africa*, pp. 399, 462; Burton, *English Acquisitions*, p. 23.
8. *The Falsities of the Private Traders to Africa discover'd, and the Mischiefs they occasion demonstrated* . . . (n.d.), p. 1; similar statements in *Several Reasons proving, that our Trade to Africa cannot be preserved* . . . *by any other Method than that of a Considerable Joint-Stock*, p. 4.
9. *Memorial Touching Nature and State of Trade to Africa*, p. 5; *Several Reasons proving, that our Trade to Africa cannot be preserved* . . . p. 4; Charles D'Avenant, *Reflections upon the Constitution and management of the trade to Africa* . . . (1709), in *The Political and Commercial Works* . . . *of Charles D'Avenant*, 5 vols. (1771), V, 136.
10. For example, *A Plain Account of the Loss, this Nation has sustain'd, by laying open the Trade to Africa* (n.d.), p. 1; *Reasons, Shewing that the Trade to Guinea* . . . *cannot be preserved without Forts and Castles* . . . (n.d.) p. 1; *Destructive Consequences of Regulated Trade to Africa by Separate Traders*, p. 1; *Memorial Touching the Nature and State*, p. 2; D'Avenant, *Reflections*, p. 94–95.
11. For example, *The Trade to Africa Considered, and Demonstrated to be improved near a Million a Year*, p. 3; *Improvement of the African Trade farther demonstrated by Separate Traders*, p. 3; *Considerations on Present Trade, answer'd paragraph by paragraph*, p. 1; *Letter from merchant in Bristol*, p. 1.
12. *The Case of the Creditors of the Royal African Company of England* (n.d.), p. 2.
13. *Trade to Africa Considered*, p. 3.
14. *Letter from a Merchant in Bristol*, p. 1.
15. For example, Fenning and Collyer, *New System*, I, 423; *Universal Modern History*, XVII, 75; Salmon, *Universal Traveller*, II, 390; "Some Observations on the Trade at the Forts on the Gold Coast of Africa", *Gentleman's Magazine*, XXXIII (1763), 330–31; Smith, *Wealth of Nations*, II, 223.
16. Bosman, pp. 132–37; Le Maire, p. 103; Barbot, 57.
17. *Journal*, 191, 218–19.
18. Bosman, pp. 117–18.
19. Atkins, *Voyage to Guinea*, pp. 198–99. For similar ridicule see *ibid.*, pp. 64–65; Lindsay, *Voyage to the Coast*, pp. 72–73; Thompson, *Two Missionary Voyages*, pp. 31–32.
20. pp. 132–33, 135–37.
21. *Journal*, 218–19.
22. Barbot, 56; Le Maire, pp. 40, 47, 97, 103.
23. *Ibid.*, p. 103; Phillips, *Journal*, 193; Atkins, *Voyage to Guinea*, p. 52.
24. For example, Astley, II, 267–68, 482–84, 538–39, 552.
25. *Ibid.*, 257–59.

26. *Universal History*, XVI, 393–404; much the same passage in Fenning and Collyer, *New System*, I, 409–10; Middleton, *New and Complete System*, I, 320, 332.
27. Astley II, 482–84, 488; Salmon, *Universal Traveller*, II, 394–99.
28. *Ibid.*, II, 373.
29. *New System*, I, Preface.
30. *New and Complete System*, I, 539–40.
31. *Gentleman's Magazine*, VIII (1738), 472–73; *London Magazine*, VII (1738) 448–50, cf. Moore, *Travels into the Inland*, p. 87.
32. *New System*, I, 394 (misprinted as 382); cf. *Universal Modern History*, XVI, 101–103.
33. *New and Complete System*, I, 538; Raynal, III, 433.
34. Review of *A System of the Principles of the Laws of Scotland* in *Monthly Review*, XXIII (1760), 191.
35. *Letter from a Merchant at Jamaica . . . speech by a Black at Gardaloupe* p. 19.
36. Wynne, *British Empire in America*, II, 539.
37. *London Magazine*, XXVII (1758), 359–61.
38. Benezet, *Some Historical Account*, pp. 82–83; Woolman, *Works*, p. 284.
39. Blome, *Cosmography*, p. 381; Le Blanc, *World Surveyed*, p. 323; Paschoud, *Historico-Political Geography*, pp. 248, 275; de Fer, *Short and Easy*, p. 277; Fenning and Collyer, *New System*, I, 408; *Universal Modern History*, XVI, 8–9; Astley, II, 558; Salmon, *Universal Traveller*, II, 369; Middleton, *New and Complete System*, I, 243, 327; Barbot, 47; Le Maire, 35, 39–40; Atkins, *Voyage to Guinea*, pp. 53, 74, 88, 151, 172, 176–80.
40. *Letter to the Bishop of London*, pp. 7–8.
41. *Gentleman's Magazine*, V (1735), 91–92, XI (1741), 146, IX (1740), 493–94.
42. Ligon, *Barbados*, p. 46. Martin, *Plantership*, pp. iii, 3.
43. Walter Rodney, "African slavery and other forms of social oppression on the Upper Guinea coast in the context of the Atlantic slave trade," *Journal of African History*, VII (1966).
44. Thomas Cooper, *Letters on the Slave Trade first published in Wheeler's Manchester Chronicle* (Manchester, 1787), p. 30; Barbot, 364, 368; Bosman, p. 430.
45. For example, Gordon, *Geography Anatomiz'd*, p. 324; *Universal Modern History*, XVI, 103; Middleton, *New and Complete System*, I, 291, 331; Knox, *Three Tracts*, pp. 19–21; *Plan for Improving Trade At Senegal*, p. 16.
46. *Thesaurus Geographicus*, p. 464; Bosman, pp. 391–92; Barbot, 47–48; Le Maire, p. 51; Astley, II, 256; *Universal Modern History*, XVII, 111–12; Salmon, *Universal Traveller*, II, 369; *Letter from a Merchant . . . speech by a Black*, p. 18.
47. Astley, II, 267; *Universal Modern History*, XVII, 276; Middleton, *New and Complete System*, I, 291; Salmon, *Universal Traveller*, II, 357; Moore, *Travels in the Inland*, p. 43; Hippisley, *Essays*, pp. 11–12; Barbot, 292; Bosman, p. 191.
48. Long, *History of Jamaica*, II, 289, 384, 388, 400; Hippisley, *Essays*, pp. 11–12; *Universal Modern History*, XVII, 111–12, 355–56.

CHAPTER NINE

1. *Hints for a Specific Plan for the Abolition of the Slave Trade, and for the relief of the negroes in the British West Indies* (1788), pp. 6–7; *Morning Chronicle*, 18th February, 1788, 2a–c.

2. *Notes on the Two Reports from the Committee of the Honourable House of Assembly of Jamaica, appointed to examine . . . the allegations . . . contained in the several petitions . . . presented to the British House of Commons, on the . . . Slave Trade, and the Treatment of the Negroes . . . (1789),* pp. 13–14.

3. Peter Peckard, *Am I not a man and a brother?* (Cambridge, 1788), p. 2; John Gardner Kemeys, *Free and Candid Reflections Occasioned by the Late Additional Duties on Sugars and Rum . . .* (1788), pp. 72–80 note. Kemeys also wrote privately to Long about the Negroes in question: B.M. Add. MS. 12431, ff. 205–07.

4. *European magazine and London Review,* XIII (1788), 75–76. Long read this article but made no public comment: B.M. Add. MS. 12405, f. 296.

5. *Diary,* 25th April 1789, 1c–2a; Thomas Clarkson, *An Essay on the Slavery and Commerce of the Human species, particularly the African . . .* (1786), pp. 164, 187–99; James Ramsay, *An Essay on the Treatment and Conversion of African Slaves in the British Sugar Colonies* (1784), pp. 211–14, 219–31; Review of Clarkson's *Essay, London Chronicle,* 9–12 September 1786, 249b; "On Slavery", *General Advertiser,* 13th September 1786, 4a; 'J.T.' "A Single Argument on the Impossibility of the Africans being an inferior Species", *Morning Chronicle,* 22nd March 1788, 2b; Letter signed 'H', *Public Advertiser,* 24th March 1788, 1d.

6. William Dickson, *Letters on Slavery* (1789), viii; Peckard, *Am I not a Man?,* p. 3 note; Thomas Gisborne, *The Principles of Moral Philosophy Investigated, and briefly applied to the constitution of civil society . . .* (1795), p. 172.

7. *Black Presence,* pp. 21, 27–30.

8. See the following numbers of the *Morning Chronicle,* 1788; 5th February, 4a–c, 12th February, 4a; 22nd March, 2b; 23rd June, 4a–c; 1st July, 1a–2b; 11th July, 1d; 19th August, 1c–2b; 25th August, 2a–b; 11th September, 1c–2a; 19th September, 1a–c; 25th September, 1c–2b; 3rd October, 1b–d; 10th October, 1c–2a; 28th October, 1d–2c; 4th November, 1d–2a.

9. Letter signed 'CRISPIN MEND'EM', *London Chronicle,* 1st–4th March, 1788, 222.

10. See for example, the following numbers of the *Diary,* 1789; 16th April, 2a–b; 23rd April, 2a–b; 16th May, 2b–c; 29th May, 2a.

11. *Public Advertiser,* 31st January 1788, 1c.

12. *Gentleman's Magazine,* LIX (1789), 334.

13. Tobin, *Cursory Remarks,* pp. 140–41; William Beckford, Jun., *Remarks on the Situation of the Negroes in Jamaica . . .* (1788), pp. 85–86; *The Repository,* I (1788), 131, 371; Letter signed 'E.W.', *Morning Chronicle,* 25th August 1788, 2a–b.

14. Letter signed 'R.O.', *ibid.,* 7th March 1788, 4c–d; Letter signed 'Humanitas', *ibid.,* 1st July 1788, 1a–2b.

15. *History of Jamaica,* II, 444–472; Letter signed 'Philadelphus'; *Diary,* 23rd April, 1789, 1d–2a; Letter signed 'Old Mingo', *ibid.,* 1st August 1789, 4a–c; *Parliamentary History,* XXIX, cols. 1063, 1108, 1141–43, 1287; XXVIII, cols. 53; XXIX, cols. 268–69.

16. Letter signed 'Libertas', *Diary,* 30th June 1789, 3d; 'Philadelphus', *ibid.,* 23rd April 1789, 1d–2a.

17. *Essay on Treatment and Conversion,* pp. 231, 238.

18. For example, *Parliamentary History,* XXIX, cols. 1141–43; XXVIII, col. 53; "Observations on the Resolutions of the West India Planters . . .", *Diary,* 30th May 1789, 1d–2a.

19. For example, *Parliamentary History*, XXVIII, cols. 53, 59; XXIX, cols. 259, 263, 268–69, 275, 1063, 1287.
20. *Morning Chronicle*, 5th February 1788, 4a–c.
21. Sharp, *Just Limitation*, pp. 27–33 note; Clarkson, *Essay on Slavery and Commerce*, pp. 177 note; Dickson, *Letters on Slavery*, pp. 59, 70.
22. Jordan, *White Over Black*, p. 253; *Morning Chronicle*, 5 Feb. 1788, 4a–c, 19th August, 1788, 1c–2b; *An Inquiry into the Origin, Progress, and Present State of Slavery . . .* (1789), pp. 25–27.
23. J. B. Holroyd, Earl of Sheffield, *Observations on the Project for Abolishing the Slave Trade . . .* (1790), pp. 42–43.
24. Dickson, *Letters on Slavery*, p. 76; Peter Peckard, *Justice and Mercy Recommended, particularly with reference to the slave trade . . .* (Cambridge, 1788), p. 32 note; *Considerations on the Abolition of Slavery and the Slave Trade upon Grounds of Natural, Religious and Political Duty* (Oxford, 1789), p. 131; *Thoughts on the Slavery of the Negroes*, (1784), p. 14.
25. Dickson, *loc.cit.*; Letter signed "Benezet, Jun.", *Morning Chronicle*, 23rd June 1788, 4a–c; *Report of the Society Instituted for the Purpose of Effecting the Abolition of the Slave Trade*, in Arthur Young, ed., *Annals of Agriculture and other Useful Arts*, IX (1788), 82–87; Extracts from M. Brissot de Warville, *New Travels in the U.S.A.*, *Universal Magazine*, XC (1792), 258–59.
26. *Gentleman's Magazine*, XLI (1771), 595–96.
27. *Considerations on the Abolition of Slavery and the Slave Trade*, pp. 135, 139.
28. *Gentleman's Magazine*, LVIII (1788), 1112; *Universal Magazine*, LXXXIII (1788), 306; *ibid.*, XC (1792), 264–67; *Considerations on the Abolition of Slavery and the Slave Trade*, p. 132; Dickson, *Letters on Slavery*, 184–87.
29. *Thoughts on the Slavery of the Negroes*, pp. 12–13; Clarkson, *Essay on Slavery and Commerce*, p. 164; *Hints for Abolition*, p. 10; *Considerations on the Abolition of Slavery and the Slave Trade*, pp. 126–27; Dickson, *Letters on Slavery*, pp. 61, 70.
30. Clarkson, *Essay on Slavery and Commerce*, p. 169; Ramsay, *Essay on Treatment and Conversion*, p. 244; Letter signed 'Oroonoko', *Morning Chronicle*, 25th September, 1788, 1c–2b.
31. *Letters on Slavery*, pp. 74–76.
32. *Letter to Bishop of London*, p. 32; Patrick Barclay, *The Universal Traveller . . .* (1735), p. 279; Fenning and Collyer, *New System*, II, 672, 700; Bacon, *Four Sermons*, p. 91.
33. *Accounts and Papers*, XXXIV, 745, p. 50.
34. *Ibid.*, XXVI, *646a*, Part III, Barbados—Answers 37, 39; St. Christopher and Grenada—Answer 39; "Further evidence . . . from various R.N. Officers".
35. *Hints for a Specific Plan for the Abolition of the Slave Trade . . .* (1788), pp. 16–17; *Thoughts on the Slavery of the Negroes*, p. 17; "Observations on a Resolution of the West India Planters and Merchants", *Diary*, 30th May 1789, 1d–2b; Letter signed "H.N.", *Morning Chronicle*, 8th July 1788, 1c–d; letter signed "J.R.", *ibid.*, 18th July 1788, 2a–d; Letter signed "A West Indian", *ibid.*, 27th August 1788, 1c–2a.
36. For example, Dickson, *Letters on Slavery*, pp. 6–22, 29–38; John Luffman, *A Brief Account of the Island of Antigua . . . in Letters to a Friend . . . 1786, 1787, 1788*, pp. 93–108; Samuel Bradburn, *An Address to the People Called Methodists concerning the Evil of Encouraging the Slave Trade* (Manchester, 1792), pp. 3–4; Peter Marsden, *An Account of the Island of Jamaica, with Reflections on the Treatment . . . of the Slaves . . .* (Newcastle, 1788), p. 41;

Abraham Booth, *Commerce in the Human Species . . . Inimical to the Laws of Moses and the Gospel of Christ. A Sermon . . .* (1792), p. 16.

37. For example, Bradburn, *Address,* pp. 2–3; Booth, *Commerce,* p. 16; Luffman, *Antigua,* p. 81.
38. *Essay on Slavery and Commerce,* pp. 214–15.
39. For example, James Adair, *Unanswerable Arguments Against Abolition of the Slave Trade* (n.d.), p. 177; *A Country Gentleman's Reasons for voting against Mr Wilberforce's Motion . . .* (1789), pp. 33–78 passim; Thomas Maxwell Adams, *A Cool Address to the People of England, on the Slave Trade* (1788), pp. 18–19; *An Appeal to the Candour and Justice of the People of England, on behalf of the West India Merchants and Planters . . .* (1792), pp. 21, 60.
40. Hector M'Neill, *Observations on the Treatment of the Negroes in the Island of Jamaica . . .* (1800?), p. 13; *Considerations Upon the Fatal Consequences of Abolishing the Slave Trade* (1789), p. 6.
41. Bryan Edwards, *A Speech delivered at a Free Conference between the Honourable the Council and Assembly of Jamaica . . . on . . . Mr Wilberforce's Propositions . . .* (1790), pp. 34, 45–58.
42. Luffman, *Antigua,* pp. 126–27; Dickson, *Letters on Slavery,* p. 89; Marsden, *Jamaica,* p. 40; Robert Boucher Nickolls, *A Letter to the Treasurer of the Society Instituted for the Purpose of Effecting the Abolition of the Slave Trade* (1787), pp. 5–6; Peter Peckard, *Justice and Mercy Recommended . . . A Sermon . . .* (Cambridge, 1788), p. 34.
43. See, for example, the passing reference in Davis, *Problem of Slavery,* p. 493.
44. Charles White, *An Account of the Regular Gradation in Man, and in different Animals and Vegetables, and from the former to the latter* (1799), p. 79 and note.
45. *Ibid.,* pp. iii, 41–42.
46. *The Works of the Late Professor Camper, on the Connexion between the Science of Anatomy and the Arts of Drawing, Painting, Statuary &c.&c.* trans. T. Cogan (1794), pp. 32–45.
47. *Ibid.,* pp. 16, 27–28, 59–61.
48. *Ibid.,* x–xi, xi note.
49. "Life of Ignatius Sancho", in *Letters of Sancho,* ix–xi.
50. Review of Blumenbach, *De Generis Humani Varietate Nativa &c.,* 3rd ed., *Monthly Review,* N.S., XXI (1796), 515–23.
51. *Letters of Sancho,* xi.
52. *Gradation,* pp. 42–55.
53. *Ibid.,* p. 129.
54. *The Works of John Hunter, F.R.S., with Notes,* ed. James F. Palmer, 4 vols. (1835–37), IV, 319–330; the salient parts of this pamphlet had been reproduced, before White wrote, in the *Annual Register,* XXIX (1787), 38; XXXI (1789), 41.
55. *Gradation,* pp. 128–29.
56. *Ibid.,* p. 32.
57. *Ibid.,* pp. 133–34.
58. *Ibid.,* pp. 7–10; Richard Watson, *Chemical Essays,* 5 vols. (1781–87), V, 171.
59. *Works of Professor Camper,* p. 32; White, *Graduation,* pp. 26, 27 note.
60. *Gradation,* pp. 59–60, 73–79; the notes for Long's unpublished work show that he intended to advance arguments very similar to White's on such diseases as tetanus, yellow fever and yaws; B.M. Add. MS. 12405, f. 273; 12438, ff. 7–12.
61. *Natural History,* III, 199.

62. Curtin, *Image of Africa*, p. 83.
63. For example, Adair, *Unanswerable Arguments*, pp. 121, 131; Philo-Africanus, *A Letter to William Wilberforce, Esq.* (1790), pp. 5, 36, 41–42; *Appeal to Candour and Justice*, pp. 4, 50; Jesse Foot, *A Defence of the Planters in the West Indies* (1792), pp. 96–101; Gilbert Francklyn, *Observations, occasioned by the attempts made in England to effect the abolition of the slave trade* . . . (1789), pp. 52, 64; M'Neill, *Observations*, p. 40.
64. For example, Ramsay, *Essay*, p. 239; Luffman, *Antigua*, pp. 45–46; Marsden, *Jamaica*, pp. 8–9, 38–39.
65. *Accounts and Papers*, XXVI, *646*, pp. 8, 15; *ibid.*, *646 a*, Part III, Answer 11.
66. *Loc. cit.*; *ibid.*, XXIX, *698*, pp. 250, 262.
67. *Ibid.*, XXVI, *646 a*, Part III, Answers 15, 17.
68. *Ibid.*, XXVI, *646*, p. 16; *646 a*, Part III, Antigua—Answers 11, 16, Jamaica—Appendix 8; *ibid.*, XXIX, *698*, pp. 88–89, 112, 208, 251, 252, 262, 300, 323.
69. *Ibid.*, XXXIV, *745*, pp. 55, 77.
70. *Ibid.*, XXVI, *646 a*, Part III, Jamaica—Appendices 6, 7, 8.
71. *Ibid.*, XXIX, *698*, p. 323.
72. *Ibid.*, XXX, *699*, p. 186.
73. *Unanswerable Arguments*, pp. 114–15, 132.
74. *Notes on the Two Reports of the Honourable House of Assembly of Jamaica* . . . *on the* . . . *Slave Trade* (1789), pp. 51–59.
75. *Public Advertiser*, 6th June 1788; *Morning Chronicle*, 19th January 1788, 2b-d, 1st July 1788, 1d-2a.
76. *Observations*, pp. 34 note, 34–35.
77. Review of *Facts and Observations relative to the* . . . *pestilential Fever* . . . *in Philadelphia* . . . , *Monthly Review*, N.S., XXIX (1799), 452–53; Review of William Lempriere, *Practical Observations on the Diseases of the Army in Jamaica* . . . , *ibid.*, N.S., XXX (1799), 32; Review of Val. Seaman, *An Account of the Epidemic Yellow Fever, as it appeared in New York in 1795*, *ibid.*, N.S., XX (1796), 493–94; James Clark, *A Treatise on the Yellow Fever, as it appeared in the Island of Dominica* . . . *1793–4–5–6* . . . (1797), pp. 1–3; Elliott Arthy, *The Seaman's Medical Advocate* . . . (1798), pp. 2–6, 80; Hector M'Lean, *An Enquiry into the Nature, and Causes of the Great Mortality among the Troops at St. Domingo* . . . (1797), pp. 185–86; James Anderson, *A Few Facts and Observations on the Yellow Fever of the West Indies* (Edinburgh, 1798), *passim*; James Bryce, *An Account of the Yellow Fever with a Successful Method of Cure* (Edinburgh, 1796), pp. 20–21, 37–38.
78. Arthy, *Seaman's Medical Advocate*, pp. 2–6; Bryce, *Yellow Fever*, pp. 20–21; Luffman, *Antigua*, p. 146; "Useful and Salutary Hints for the Regulation of Persons whom Duty or Business may call to the West Indies", *Universal Magazine*, XCVII (1795), 283; Benjamin Moseley, *A Treatise on Tropical Diseases; and on the Climate of the West Indies* (1787), pp. 13, 49, 55.
79. Atkins, *Voyage to Guinea*, p. 39; Matthews, *Voyage to Sierra Leone*, p. 136; C. B. Wadstrom, *Observations on the Slave Trade, and a Description of Some Part of the Coast of Guinea* . . . (1789), p. 51.
80. *Ibid.*, pp. 36, 50–51; "Settlement at Sierra Leone", *Diary*, 29th October, 1789, 4a-c.
81. "African Emigration", *ibid.*, 15th October, 1789, 2c.
82. "The Natural History of Animals that most nearly approach Humanity",

Universal Magazine, LXXI (1782), 189–94, 238–44, 363–68; The Natural History of Beasts (1798), pp. 107–108, 110; A General History of Quadrupeds (Newcastle upon Tyne, 1790), pp. 389–91.

83. John Payne, Universal Geography formed into a New and Entire System, 2 vols., (1791), I, 121; Watson, Chemical Essays, V, 173–74; F. B. von Wurmb, "A Description of the Large Orang outang of Borneo", Philosophical Magazine, I, (1798), 225–31; De Geoffroy, "Observations on the Account of the supposed Orang Outang of the East Indies . . .", ibid., 337–42.

84. "Character, Anecdotes, and Observations of the late Dr. Samuel Johnson", Universal Magazine, LXXVII (1785), 189; "Anecdotes of James Burnet, Lord Monboddo", Annual Register, XLI (1799), 22, 364; "The Man of Method", Annual Register, XXXVIII (1796), 509; Letter signed "Ignotus", Public Advertiser, 16th September, 1786, 1d-2a. Gentleman's Magazine, LXIX (1799), 529;

85. For example, Dunbar, History of Mankind, p. 202; Review of Zimmerman, Geographische Geschichte, Monthly Review, LXXX (1789), 685–86; Forster, Observations, p. 254; Review of Camper, Monthly Review, LXII (1780), 220.

86. John Walker, Elements of Geography and of Natural and Civil History, 3rd ed. (1800), Preface, pp. 135–37, 215–18, 222.

87. (1794), p. 147.

88. James Bentley Gordon, Terraquea: or, a New System of Geography and Modern History, 2nd ed. 4 vols. (Dublin, 1794), I, 167, 169; Walker, Elements of Geography, p. 152.

89. Ibid., p. 153.

CHAPTER TEN

1. Robert Norris, Memoirs of the Reign of Bossa Ahadee, King of Dahomey, (1799).

2. Curtin, Image of Africa, p. 68.

3. Substance of the Report of the Court of Directors of the Sierra Leone Company . . . 19th October 1791 (1791), p. 23; Thomas Clarkson, Letters on the Slave Trade and the State of the Natives . . . contiguous to Fort St. Louis and Gorée (1791), pp. 59–63; Thoughts on the Slavery of the Negroes, p. 15; Dickson, Letters on Slavery, pp. 73–74.

4. 6th ed. (1792), p. 2.

5. Accounts and Papers, XXVI, 646 a., Part I, Produce.

6. Ibid., XXV, 636, pp. 15–16, 35; 637, pp. 50, 61–62, 69; 638, p. 84, 640, pp. 136, 148; 641, p. 174; 643, p. 212.

7. Ibid., XXVI, 646 a., Part I, Produce; Matthews, Voyage to Sierra Leone, p. 11.

8. John Leyden, An Historical and Philosophical Sketch of the Discoveries of the Europeans in North and West Africa . . . (Edinburgh, 1799), pp. 78, 107–25.

9. Luffman, Antigua, pp. 135–36; Ramsay, Essay on Treatment and Conversion, p. 204; Gregory, Essays, Historical and Moral, p. 39.

10. Adair, Unanswerable Arguments, p. 148; Considerations Upon Fatal Consequences of Abolishing Slave Trade, p. 6; Accounts and Papers, XXVI, 646a, Part II, Penny, Norris, Dalzel.

11. For example, ibid., loc. cit., Arnold, Henderson; Fox, Summary of the Evidence, p. 6.

12. Ramsay, *Essay on Treatment and Conversion,* pp. 203–204; Clarkson, *Essay on Slavery and Commerce,* p. 170.
13. Thomas Atwood, *The History of Dominica* (1791), p. 267; Dalzel, *Dahomy,* p. 130.
14. *Ibid.,* Preface, vii, xiii, pp. 34–42, 126, 129, 130, 147, 152–55, 165–66, 173, 178, 188–91, 193, 202, 204–205, 211–13, 225.
15. *Ibid.,* pp. 217–21; Edwards, *Speech at a Free Conference,* p. 12; Knox, *Three Tracts,* p. 21; Matthews, *Sierra Leone,* pp. 6–7; *Accounts and Papers,* XXX, *699,* p. 362.
16. For example, Wadstrom, *Observations,* pp. 79–80; *Remarks on the African Slave Trade,* (1790), pp. 9–10; Clarkson, *Letters on the Slave Trade,* pp. 8–9, 31–32; Fox, *Summary of the Evidence,* p. 3; Gregory, *Essays, Historical and Moral,* pp. 345–46.
17. Cugoano, *Thoughts and Sentiments,* pp. 25–26; Falconbridge, *Account,* pp. 9–10.
18. Oldmixon, *British Empire,* II, 124; Ligon, *Barbados,* p. 46; *A Country Gentleman's Reasons for Voting against Mr. Wilberforce's Motion . . .* (1789), pp. 30, 32; Adams, *Cool Address,* p. 32.
19. Benezet, *Some Historical Account,* pp. 83–84; Wesley, *Thoughts Upon Slavery,* 65; Clarkson, *Essay on Slavery and Commerce,* p. 107 note; Cugoano, *Thoughts and Sentiments,* pp. 27–28; *Thoughts on the Slavery of the Negroes,* pp. 27–28.
20. Blome, *Cosmography,* p. 381; *Thesaurus Geographicus,* p. 457; Moll, *System,* pp. 124–25; Paschoud, *Historico–Political Geography,* p. 275; Salmon, *Universal Traveller,* II, 369; Middleton, *New System,* I, 243.
21. "Some Particulars of a Voyage to Guinea by James Arnold," *Accounts and Paper,* XXVI, *646 a,* Part I, *Slaves; ibid., loc. cit.,* Eldrid (Sierra Leone), Dalzel (Gold Coast); XXIX, *698,* p. 515.
22. *Essay on Slavery and Commerce,* pp. 103–105.
23. *Ibid.,* p. 47.
24. Thomas Day, *Fragment of an Original Letter on the Slavery of the Negroes written . . . in 1776,* in *Four Tracts* (1784), p. 29.
25. For example, *Ibid.,* p. 29; Cugoano, *Thoughts and Sentiments,* pp. 25–27; Equiano, *Interesting Narrative,* I, 45–89; *An Account of the Colony of Sierra Leone . . .* (1795), pp. 97–109, 191–92, 197; Falconbridge, *Account,* pp. 12–18; Gregory, *Essays, Historical and Moral,* pp. 345–46; Leyden, *Historical and Philosophical Sketch,* p. 94; Luffman, *Antigua,* pp. 79–80; *Substance of the Report of the Court of the Directors of the Sierra Leone Company . . . 1791,* pp. 33–40; Wadstrom, *Observations,* pp. 2, 7–12, 16–17; Wesley, *Thoughts Upon Slavery,* 65; *An Address to H.R.H. the Duchess of York against the use of sugar* (1792), p. 7; Fox, *Summary of the Evidence,* pp. 3–4; Thomas Gisborne, *Remarks on the late Decision of the House of Commons respecting the abolition of the slave trade,* 2nd ed. (1792), p. 11; *Observations on the Project for Abolishing the Slave Trade* (1790), p. 15; Peckard, *Justice and Mercy Recommended,* pp. 32–33; *Remarks on the African Slave Trade* (1790), pp. 9–10; *An Address to the Inhabitants of Glasgow, Paisley and Neighbourhood, concerning the African Slave Trade . . .* (Glasgow, 1791). p. 4.
26. *Accounts and Papers,* XXVI, *646 a,* Part I, *Slaves,* Gandy, Matthews, Weuves; *ibid.,* XXIX, *698,* p. 11.
27. E.g. *ibid.,* XXV, *637,* p. 38, Miles; *638,* p. 74, Knox; *640,* p. 129, Weuves.
28. *Ibid.,* XXVI, *646 a,* Part I, *Slaves.*
29. *Ibid., Government, Religion, Manners and Customs.*

30. *Loc. cit.*
31. *Loc. cit.*
32. For example, *ibid., Slaves,* Evidence of William James, Isham Baggs, and James Arnold.
33. *Ibid.,* their evidence was cited in all three sections of Part I.
34. *Loc. cit.; Ibid.,* XXIV, *626,* p. 2; XXIX, *698,* p. 514, Hall, pp. 582–4, 604–7, Falconbridge; XXX, *699,* pp. 81–83, Trotter, 101, Dove.
35. *Ibid.,* XXVI, *646 a,* Part I, *Government, Religion, Manners and Customs.*
36. *Essay on Slave Trade,* pp. 28–29; "Thoughts on the Abolition of the African Slave Trade . . .," *Gentleman's Magazine,* LVIII (1788), 409. McNeill, *Observations on treatment of Negroes in Jamaica,* pp. 15–16, 18; Long, *History of Jamaica,* II, 389–92.
37. *Speech at a Free Conference,* pp. 10–12.
38. *Accounts and Papers,* XXVI, *646 a,* Part I, *Government, Religion, Manners and Customs.*
39. For example, *ibid.,* XXV, *635,* p. 6, Barnes; *637,* p. 39, Miles; *638,* p. 76, Knox; *640, p. 140,* Weuves; *p. 161, Fountain; 643,* p. 207, Littleton; XXIX, *698,* p. 6, Fraser.
40. *Ibid.,* XXV, *637,* p. 47, Miles; *638,* p. 75, Knox; *640,* p. 131, Weuves; *ibid.,* XXVI, *646 a,* Part I, *Slaves,* Eldrid, Dalzell (Whydah and Dahomey).
41. *Loc. cit.*
42. For example, *ibid.,* XXV, *635,* p. 6, Barnes; *637,* pp. 54–56, Miles; *638,* p. 74, Knox; *640,* p. 130, Weuves, p. 160, Fountain.
43. For example, Weuves, *loc. cit.;* Fountain, *loc. cit.;* Barnes, *loc. cit; ibid., 636,* pp. 5, 29, Barnes; *643,* p. 205, Littleton, XXIX, *698,* p. 18.
44. *Ibid.,* XXX, *699,* pp. 81–2.
45. *Ibid.,* XXXIV, *745,* P. 40.
46. *Ibid.,* XXVI, *646 a,* part I, *Slaves.*
47. *Loc. cit.* Baggs; *ibid.,* XXIX, *698,* p. 585, Falconbridge; XXX, *699,* p. 296, Dalrymple; XXXIV, *745,* p. 17, Towne.
48. Benezet *Some Historical Account,* pp. 88–92; Raynal, III, 394–95; *Universal Modern History,* XVI, 8–9, XVII, 354; Salmon, *Universal Traveller,* II, 357, 369, 374–5; Middleton, *New and Complete System,* I, 243, 537–38.
49. John Newton, *Thoughts Upon the African Slave Trade,* pp. 25–28; *Accounts and Papers,* XXVI, *646 a,* Part I, *Slaves;* Equiano, *Interesting Narrative,* I, 5–7.
50. *Letters on Slave Trade and State of Natives,* pp. 39–46.
51. *Accounts and Papers,* XXVI, *646 a,* Part I, *Slaves.*
52. Clarkson, *Letters on the Slave Trade and the state of the natives,* pp. 45–46, 70–71, 76–78; Cugoano, *Thoughts and Sentiments,* p. 12.
53. *Remarks on a Pamphlet written by the Reverend James Ramsay under the Title Thoughts on the Slavery of the Negroes in the American Colonies* (1784), p. 13.
54. Matthews, *Sierra Leone,* pp. 150, 152.
55. Mungo Park, *Travels in the Interior Districts of Africa . . . 1795, 1796, and 1797* (1799), pp. 287–98.
56. "Proposals for Printing a new edition of the Holy Scriptures in Arabic", *Gentleman's Magazine,* LXIX (1799), 369–72.
57. *Annual Register,* XLI (1799), 490.
58. *A Key to Geography,* (Sheffield, 1787), p. 78.
59. *Geography for Youth, or, a Plain and Easy Introduction to the Science of Geography, for the Use of Young Gentlemen and Ladies,* 3rd ed. (1787), p. 165.

60. *Historical and Philosophical Sketch*, *passim* and pp. 237–38.

61. John Free, *Tyrocinium Geographicum Londinense, or the London Geography . . . for . . . Younger Pupils* (1789), pp. 70, 73, 81–82; Walker, *Elements of Geography*, p. 153; John Newbery, *Geography Made Easy for Children, improved from the Circle of the Sciences* (1793), p. 151.

62. *Public Advertiser*, 29th Oct. 1787, 2a; *ibid.*, 3rd Nov. 1787, 2 c–d.

63. Monboddo, *Ancient Metaphysics*, IV, 252; Anderson, *Observations on Slavery*, pp. 36–37; *Review of Selections from M. Pauw with additions by Daniel Webb, Monthly Review*, N.S. XVII, (1795), 132.

NOTES ON BIBLIOGRAPHY

The list of manuscripts below comprises only those actually cited in the foregoing chapters.

On the other hand, because the major themes of this book have been based on the proposition that the Negro, Africa, slavery, and the slave trade were widely publicized in Britain in the relevant period, the lists of publications include a number of works which have been consulted but not cited above. An additional reason for this policy is the hope that much of the material listed might prove useful to scholars interested in other areas of racial and cultural attitudes, since so many of the descriptive works on the Negro and Africa include much wider surveys of the non-European world.

With the exception of some polemical literature about slavery, which is located in the Goldsmith's Library, University of London, all publications listed are in the British Museum.

Headings of Bibliography:

PRIMARY SOURCES

A. MANUSCRIPTS
B. PUBLICATIONS
    I   Official Publications
    II Geographical and Travel Literature
       1. Collections of Voyages
       2. Circumnavigations and other General Voyages
       3. Geographical Treatises
          (a) Classical and Medieval
          (b) School Texts and Other Works for Children
          (c) Large-Scale Surveys
          (d) Gazetteers, Dictionaries, and other Reference Works
       4. Descriptions of Africa and the East Indies
          (a) General and Miscellaneous
          (b) West Africa
          (c) Southern Africa and the East Indies
       5. Descriptions of the New World
          (a) North America
          (b) The West Indies
    III Propaganda on Slavery and the Slave Trade
       1. Economic Aspects
          (a) The African Companies and their Critics
          (b) The West Indian Colonies
       2. Abolitionist Works
       3. Proslavery Works

SECONDARY SOURCES

Listed alphabetically

BIBLIOGRAPHY

PRIMARY SOURCES

A. MANUSCRIPTS

British Museum
Additional Manuscripts: 12402–12440—The Edward Long Papers
12404–406—Notes for a revised edition of Long's *History of Jamaica.*
12431   —Papers on Slavery and the Slave Trade: John Kemeys to Edward
           Long, ff. 205–207.

Public Record Office
Colonial Office Papers
C.O. 267/5—*Sierra Leone Correspondence*
           —Extracts of a Letter from Thomas Melvil, Chief Agent at Cape
           Coast Castle, to African Committee, 11th July 1751: ff. 6–7.
           —Copy of Letter from William Ansah to Earl of Halifax, 20th Feb.
           1752: ff. 36–41.
           —Copy of the Report of the Board of Trade on the Memorial of
           Bullfinch Lambe, 6th July 1731: ff. 305–306.
           —The Case of Adamo Tomo: f. 207.
C.O. 267/9—*Sierra Leone Correspondence (Unbound Papers)*
           —Account by C. E. Wadstrom of the redemption from slavery of
           the son of King Peter of Mesurado, 10th October, 1790.
Home Office Papers
H.O. 77/1 —*The Newgate Calendar, 1782–86*
Treasury Papers
T. 70/143 —*Records of African Companies*
           —Committee to Thomas Melvil, 21st August 1751: f. 101.
           —Committee Minutes, 23rd October 1751: ff. 107, 110.

B. PUBLICATIONS

I   *Official Publications*

The Parliamentary History of England, from the Earliest Period to the Year 1803,
     Vols. XXI–XXIV, 1780–1800. Published 1814–19.
Parliamentary Papers Printed by Order of the House of Commons from the Year
     1731 to 1800.
     —Vol. 82:   *Accounts and Papers,* XXIV, 1789.
                 No. 626 —Statement of Circumstances Relating to the Slave
                         Trade.
                 No. 627 —Propositions Relative to the Slave Trade.

—Vol. 83:   *Accounts and Papers*, XXV, 1789.
            Nos. 635—45
                    —   Minutes of the Evidence Taken before a Com-
                         mittee of the House of Commons . . . to consider
                         the circumstances of the Slave Trade . . .
—Vol. 84:   *Accounts and Papers*, XXVI, 1789.
            No. 646 —Papers received since the Date of the Report of
                     the Committee for Trade, on the Subject of the
                     Trade to Africa, and particularly the Trade in
                     Slaves.
            No. 646a—Report of the Lords of the Committee of the
                     Council appointed for the Consideration of all
                     Matters relating to Trade and Foreign Plantations
                     . . . the Evidence . . . concerning the present state
                     of the Trade to Africa, and particularly the Trade
                     in Slaves . . .
—Vol. 87:   *Accounts and Papers*, XXIX, 1790.
            No. 698 —Minutes of the Evidence taken before the Select
                     Committee appointed for the examination of
                     Witnesses on the Slave Trade. Reported 30th
                     March 1790.
—Vol. 88:   *Accounts and Papers*, XXX, 1790.
            No. 699 —Minutes of the Evidence taken before a Com-
                     mittee of the House of Commons, being a Select
                     Committee Appointed 23rd April 1790. To take
                     examination of the Several Witnesses ordered by
                     the House to attend the Committee . . . to whom
                     it is referred to consider further of the Circum-
                     stances of the Slave Trade.
—Vol. 92:   *Accounts and Papers*, XXXIV, 1790–91.
            No. 745 —Minutes of the Evidence taken before a Com-
                     mittee of the House of Commons . . . respecting
                     the African Slave Trade. Reported 1st March
                     1791.
Public Record Office. *Acts of the Privy Council of England.* New Series,
    I–XXXIII, 1890–1907.

II   *Geographical and Travel Literature*

1.   *Collections of Voyages*

Astley, Thomas (publisher). *A New General Collection of Voyages and Travels.*
    4 vols. 1745–47.
Barrow, John. *A Collection of Authentic, Useful, and Entertaining Voyages and
    Discoveries.* 1765.
Campbell, John. *A Collection of Voyages, originally published by John Harris,
    much enlarged.* 2 vols. 1715.
Churchill, Awnsham and John. *A Collection of Voyages and Travels* . . . vols.
    1–4, 1704, vols. 5–6, 1732, vols. 7–8, 1745.
A Collection of Voyages and Travels, 2 vols. 1709–10.
A Collection of Voyages, 4 vols. 1729.
Drake, Edward Cavendish. *A New Universal Collection of Authentic and
    Entertaining Voyages and Travels* . . . 1768.
Hakluyt, Richard, the Younger. *Principall navigations, Voiages etc. of the English
    Nation.* 2 vols., 1589, reprinted, Cambridge, 1965.

Harris, John. *Navigantium atque Itinerantium Bibliotheca: A Complete Collection of Voyages and Travels . . .* 3rd ed., 1764.
Moore, John Hamilton. *A New and Complete Collection of Voyages and Travels.* 2 vols., 1780.
Purchas, Samuel. *Hakluytus Postumus or Purchas His Pilgrimes.* 20 vols. 1625, reprinted, Glasgow, 1905.
A View of the Universe; or, A New Collection of Voyages and Travels into all Parts of the World. 2 vols. 1710.
Smollett, Tobias. *A Compendium of Authentic and Entertaining Voyages digested in a chronological series . . .* 2nd ed. 7 vols. 1766.

2. *Circumnavigations and other General Voyages*

Careri, John Francis Gemelli. *A Voyage Around the World.* trans. from Italian, Churchill, IV, 1–606.
Dampier, William. *A New Voyage Around the World,* 7th ed., *Collection of Voyages* (1729), I, 536–42.
Forster, Johann Georg Adam (George). *A Voyage Round the World in his Britannic Majesty's Sloop, Resolution, commanded by Capt. James Cook . . .* 2 vols. 1777.
Forster, Johann Reinhold. *Observations made during a Voyage round the World . . .* 1778.
Lockman, John. *Travels of the Jesuits, into Various Parts of the World . . . now first attempted in English . . .* 1743.
Macintosh, William. *Travels in Europe, Asia, and Africa.* 2 vols. 1782.
Mocquet, Jean. *Travels and Voyages into Africa, Asia, and America, the East and West Indies . . .* trans. Nathaniel Pullen, 1696.
Smith, John. *True Travels, Adventures, and Observations of Capt. John Smith, into Europe, Asia, Africa, and America, 1593–1629.* Churchill, II, 371–412.
Thunberg, Carl P. *Travels in Europe, Africa, and Asia.* 4 vols., 1795.

3. *Geographical Treatises*

(a) *Classical and Medieval*

Alfred the Great. *Orosius,* in R. Pauli, *The Life of Alfred the Great.* 1857.
Bartholomaeus Anglicus. *Medieval Lore from Bartholomaeus Anglicus.* ed. Robert Steele, 1907.
Higden, Ranulph. *Polychronicon Ranulphi Higden . . .* ed. Churchill Babington, 1865.
Pliny (Caius Secundus Plinius), *Natural History.* 10 vols. trans. H. Rackham, 1947.
Sacrobosco. *The Sphere of Sacrobosco and Its Commentators.* ed. Lynn Thorndike, Chicago, 1949.
Solinus. *The Excellent and Pleasant Worke of Iulius Solinus Polyhistor.* trans. Arthur Golding, 1587, reprinted, Gainesville, Florida, 1955.
Strabo. *The Geography of Strabo.* 8 vols. trans. N. L. Jones, 1917.

(b) *School Texts and Other Works for Children*

Davidson, Robert. *The Elements of Geography, Short and Plain . . .* 1787.
Demarville,—. *The Young Ladies Geography, or Compendium of Modern Geography.* 1757.
Eachard, Laurence. *A Most Compleat Compendium of Geography, General and Special.* 1691, 8th ed. 1713.
Encheiridion Geographicum, Or, a Manual of Geography . . . Edinburgh, 1704.

Fage, Robert. *A Description of the Whole World with some General Rules touching the use of the Globe* . . . 1658, 4th ed. 1671.

Fairman, William. *A Treatise on Geography.* 1788.

Fer, Nicholas de. *A Short and Easy Method to Understand Geography* . . . c. 1715.

Free, John. *Tyrocinium Geographicum Londinense, or the London Geography, consisting of* . . . *Short Lectures* . . . *for the Use of* . . . *Younger Pupils* . . . 1789.

Geography and Astronomy Familiarized, n.d.

Geography for Youth, or, a Plain and Easy Introduction to the Science of Geography, for the Use of Young Gentlemen and Ladies . . . 3rd ed. 1787.

Gordon, Patrick. *Geography Anatomiz'd: or, the Geographical Grammar* . . . 1693. 20th ed. 1754.

Guthrie, William. *A New Geographical, Historical and Commercial Grammar* . . . 17th ed. 1798, 21st ed. 1801.

————. *A New System of Modern Geography* . . . 1770, 6th ed. 1795.

H. T. *A Short Way to Know the World*, 1712.

Keith, Thomas. *A Short and Easy Introduction to the Science of Geography.* 1787.

Lenglet du Fresnoy, Pierre Nicolas. *Geography for Children; or a Short and Easy Method of Teaching and Learning Geography: designed principally for the use of schools.* 22nd ed. 1800.

Lessons in Geography. 1798.

Lloyd, Evan. *A Plain System of Geography.* 1798.

Loriot, L. *A Short and Easy Method of Geography.* 1797.

Mair, John. *A Brief Survey of the Terraqueous Globe.* 1798.

Moll, Herman. *A System of Geography, a New and Accurate Description of the Earth* . . . 1701.

Montriou, J. A. L. *Elements of Universal History*, n.d.

Moore, Sir Jonas. *A New Systeme of the Mathematics*, 2 vols. 1680–81. (Vol. II includes geography).

Newbery, John. *Geography Made Easy for Children, improved from the Circle of the Sciences*, 1793.

Ouisseau, J. *Practical Geography.* 1794.

Perks, William. *The Youth's General Introduction to Geography.* 1793.

Richardson, John. *A Key to Geography.* Sheffield, 1787.

Salmon, Thomas. *A New Geographical and Historical Grammar.* 6th ed. 1758.

Service, John Paterson. *Recreation for Youth, a Useful Epitome of Geography and Biography.* 1787.

Turner, Richard, the Younger. *An Easy Introduction to the Arts and Sciences* . . . 1787, 9th ed. 1803.

————. *A New and Easy Introduction to Universal Geography in a Series of Letters to a Youth at School.* 1780, 8th ed. 1797.

Tytler, James. *A New and Concise System of Geography.* 1788.

————. *The New Universal Geographical Grammar* . . . *improvement and continuation of Mr. Salmon's grammar* . . . 1788.

Walker, John. *Elements of Geography and of Natural and Civil History.* 3rd ed. 1800.

Wells, Edward. *Treatise of Ancient and Present Geography.* 1701.

(c) *Large-scale Geographical Surveys*

Abbot, George. *A Briefe Description of the Whole World.* 2nd ed. 1600.

Barclay, Patrick. *The Universal Traveller* . . . 1735.

Blome, Richard. *Cosmography and Geography in Two Parts* . . . 1683.

————. *A Geographical Description of the Four Parts of the World.* 1670.

Boemus, Ionnas. *Manners, Laws and Customs of All Nations . . .* trans. Ed. Aston, 1611.

Bowen, Emmanuel. *A Complete System of Geography.* 2 vols. 1747.

Carver, Jonathan. *The New Universal Traveller.* 1779.

Clarke, Samuel. *A Mirrour or Looking-Glasse both for Saints and Sinners . . . whereunto are added A Geographical Description of All the Countries in the Knowne World . . .* 4th ed. 1671.

Duval, Pierre. *Geographia Universalis. The Present State of the World . . .* 1685.

Entick, John. *The Present State of the British Empire in Europe, Asia, Africa, and America,* 4 vols. 1774.

Fenning, Daniel, Collyer, Joseph and others. *A New System of Geography or a General Description of the World . . .* 2 vols. 1766, 1765. For revised ed. 1785 see Hervey, Frederic (below).

The Gentleman's, Trader's, and Traveller's Pocket Library. 1753.

Geography Reformed . . . 1739.

Goldsmith, Oliver. *History of the Earth and Animated Nature.* 8 vols. 1774.

Gordon, James Bentley. *Terraquea; or, a New System of Geography and Modern History,* 2nd ed. 4 vols. Dublin, 1794.

Heron, Robert. *The New Universal Traveller: Travels in Africa and Asia.* 2 vols. 1791–92.

Hervey, Frederic. *A New System of Geography . . .* 1785 (revised ed. of Fenning and Collyer, *New System*).

Heylyn, Peter. *Cosmographie, in four bookes.* 2nd. ed. 1657.

The History of All Nations. 1771.

J., G. *Geography Epitomiz'd . . .* 1718.

Le Blanc, Vincent. *The World Surveyed . . .* trans. Francis Brooks, 1660.

Macfait, Ebenezer. *A New System of General Geography.* 1780.

Middleton, Charles Theodore. *A New and complete System of Geography . . .* 2 vols. 1777–78.

Miège, Guy. *A New Cosmography, or Survey of the Whole World . . .* 1682.

Morden, Robert. *Geography Rectified; or, a Description of the World . . .* 1680, 4th ed. 1700.

Paschoud, Rev. —. *Historico-Political Geography . . . of the several Countries of the World.* 2nd ed. 1724.

Payne, John. *Universal Geography formed into a New and Entire System.* 2 vols. 1791.

Petavius, Dionysius. *The History of the World . . . Together with a Geographicall Description of Europe, Asia, Africa, and America.* 1659.

Poivre, Pierre. *The Travels of a Philosopher, or, Observations on the Manners and Arts of Various Nations in Africa and Asia.* trans from French, 1769.

Purchas, Samuel. *Purchas His Pilgrimage or Relations of the world and the Religions observed in all Ages and Places.* 1614.

Raleigh, Walter. *The Historie of the World in five bookes.* 1614.

Salmon, Thomas. *The Universal Traveller, or a Complete Description of the Several Nations of the World.* 2 vols. 1752–53.

Seller, John. *A New Systeme of Geography.* 1685.

Smollett, Tobias. *The Present State of All Nations.* 8 vols. 1768–69.

Thesaurus Geographicus, A New Body of Geography: or a Compleat Description of the Earth. 1695.

Turner, Richard, the Elder. *A View of the Earth . . .* 2nd ed. 1766, 4th ed. 1787.

Universal History, 65 vols. 1747–60.

(d)   *Gazetteers, Dictionaries, and Other Reference Works*

Bohun, Edmund. *A Geographical Dictionary . . . of the Whole World.* 1688, 6th
     ed. 1710.
————. *The Great Historical, Geographical and Poetical Dictionary* 1694. See
     also Collier, Jeremy (below).
Brice, Andrew, *The Grand Gazetteer.* 1759.
Brookes, Richard. *General Gazetteer.* 1797.
Collier, Jeremy. *The Great Historical, Geographical and Poetical Dictionary.*
     revised ed. of Bohun's work (see above), 1701.
Crutwell, Clement. *The New Universal Gazetteer.* 3 vols. 1798.
A Compendious Geographical Dictionary. 1795.
Eachard, Laurence. *The Gazetteer's or Newsman's Interpreter. The second part
     . . . Being a geographical Index . . .* 1704, 9th ed. 1744.
Geography Epitomiz'd: or, the London Gazetteer. 1718.
Postlethwayt, Malachy. *The Universal Dictionary of Trade and Commerce.* 4th
     ed. 1774.
Salmon, Thomas. *The Modern Gazetteer: or, a Short View of the Several Nations
     of the World.* 3rd ed. 1756, 10th ed. 1782.
Walker, John. *The Universal Gazetteer.* 1798.

4.   *Descriptions of Africa, and the East Indies*

(a)   *General*

Africanus, John Leo. *The History and Description of Africa,* done into English
     by John Pory, 1600, ed. R. Brown, 3 vols. *Hakluyt Society Publications,*
     O.S. XCII/XCIV, 1896.
Burton, Robert (alias Nathaniel Crouch). *The English Acquisitions in Guinea and
     East India.* 4th ed. 1728.
Ludolphus, Job. *A New History of Ethiopia . . .* trans. J. P. Gent. 1682.
Ogilby, John. *Africa, being an accurate description of the regions of Aegypt,
     Barbary, Lybia, and Billedulgerid, the land of Negroes, Guinea, Aethiopia*
     1670.
Park, Mungo. *Travels in the Interior Districts of Africa . . . 1795, 1796, and 1797.*
     1799.

(b)   *West Africa*

Adanson, Michel. *A Voyage to Senegal, the Isle of Goree and River Gambia . . .*
     trans. from French, 1759.
Angelo, Michael and Carli, Denis. *A Voyage to Congo, in the Years 1666 and
     1667 . . .,* trans. from Italian, Churchill, I, 611–50.
Atkins, John. *A Voyage to Guinea, Brazil, and the West Indies . . .* 1735.
Barbot, John. *A Description of the Coasts of North and South Guinea . . .*
     Churchill, V. 1–668.
Battell, Andrew. *The Strange Adventures of Andrew Battell of Leigh, in
     Angola . . .,* ed. E. G. Ravenstein, *Hakluyt Soc. Pubs.* Ser. 2, VI, 1901.
Benezet, Anthony. *Some Historical Account of Guinea . . . and the Slave Trade.*
     2nd. ed. 1788, reprinted 1968.
Bosman, William. *A New and Accurate Description of the Coast of Guinea,*
     1705, new ed. with Introduction by John Ralph Willis and notes by J. D.
     Fage and R. E. Bradbury, 1967.
Dalzel, Archibald. *The History of Dahomy, an Inland Kingdom of Africa . . .*
     1793.

Falconbridge, Anna Maria. *Narrative of Two Voyages to the River Sierra Leone during the Years 1791-2-3.* 2nd ed. 1802.

The Golden Coast; or, A Description of Guinney. 1665.

Hippisley, John. *Essays: (i) on the populousness of Africa; (ii) on the trade at the forts on the Gold Coast; (iii) on the necessity of a fort at Cape Appolonia . . .* 1764.

Houstoun, James. *Some New and Accurate Observations . . . of the Coast of Guinea . . . for the Advantage of Great Britain in general, and the Royal African Company in Particular.* 1725.

Jobson, Richard. *The Golden Trade or a Discovery of the River Gambia, and the Golden Trade of the Aethiopians,* 1623.

Le Maire, Jacques Joseph. *A Voyage of the Sieur Le Maire to the Canary Islands, Cape-Verd, Senegal, and Gamby . . .* in Duquesne, *New Voyage to the East Indies.* 1796, (see under section (c) below).

Leyden, John. *An Historical and Philosophical Sketch of the Discoveries of the Europeans in North and West Africa . . .* Edinburgh, 1799.

Lindsay, John. *A Voyage to the Coast of Africa in 1756.* 1759.

Matthews, John. *A Voyage to the River Sierra Leone Containing an Account of the Trade and Productions of the Country and of the Civil and Religious Customs and Manners of the People. With an Additional Letter on the African Slave Trade.* 1788, reprinted 1966.

Merolla da Sorrento, Jerome. *A Voyage to Congo and Several other Countries, chiefly in Southern-Africk.* trans. from Italian, Churchill, I, 651-76.

Monson, William. *Sir William Monson's Naval Tracts. From an Original Manuscript never before published.* Churchill, III, 154-560.

Montefiore, Joshua. *An Authentic account of the late expedition to Bulam on the coast of Africa; with a description of the present settlement of Sierra Leone and the adjacent country.* 1794.

Moore, Francis. *Travels into the Interior Parts of Africa: containing a Description of the Several Nations for the Space of Six Hundred Miles up the River Gambia . . .* 1738.

Norris, Robert. *Memoirs of the Reign of Bossa Ahadee. King of Dahomey.* 1789.

Phillips, Thomas. *A Journal of a Voyage made in the 'Hannibal' of London, 1693, 1694 . . .* Churchill, VI, 171-256.

Roberts, John. *Cursory Observations on the Trade to Africa.* 1778.

Royal African; or, Memoirs of the young prince of Annamaboe . . . with several historical remarks on the commerce of the European nations whose subjects frequent the coast of Guinea . . . c. 1750.

Sierra Leone Company. *An Account of the Colony of Sierra Leone from its first establishment in 1793, being the substance of a report delivered to the proprietors.* 1795.

———. *Substance of the Report of the Court of Directors . . .* 1791.

Smeathman, Henry. *Plan of a Settlement to be made near Sierra Leone.* 1786.

Smith, William. *A New Voyage to Guinea . . .* 1744.

Snelgrave, William. *A New Account of Some Parts of Guinea and the Slave Trade . . .* 1734.

(c) *Southern Africa and the East Indies.*

Anson, George. *An Account of the Expedition of George Anson, Esq . . .* Harris, *Navigantium atque Itinerantium,* 1, 362–.

Baldaeus, Philip. *A True and Exact Description of the most Celebrated East-India Coasts.* trans. from Dutch, Churchill, III, 561–.

Beaulieu, Commodore—. *Expedition of Commodore Beaulieu to the East Indies.* Harris, *Navigantium atque Itinerantium,* I, 721–.

Beeckman, Daniel. *A Voyage to and from the Island of Borneo in the East Indies.* 1718.

Dellon, Charles. *A Voyage to the East Indies . . .* trans. from French, 1698.

Duquesne, Abraham. *A New Voyage to the East Indies . . .* trans. from French, 1696.

Glanius, —. *A New Voyage to the East Indies.* 1682.

Jourdain, John. *The Journal of John Jourdain 1608–1617.* ed. William Foster, *Hakluyt Society Publications*, Ser. 2, XVI, 1905.

Kindersley, Jemima, *Letters from the Island of Teneriffe, Brazil, the Cape of Good Hope, and the East Indies.* 1777.

Kolb, Peter. *The Present State of the Cape of Good Hope: or, a Particular Account of the Several Nations of the Hottentots . . .* trans. Guido Medley, 2 vols. 1731.

Le Vaillant, François. *Travels into the Interior parts of Africa, by the Way of the Cape of Good Hope, 1780–85,* trans. from French, 2 vols. 1790.

Maxwell, John. *A Discourse Concerning God . . . to which is subjoin'd . . . a short Account of the Cape of Good Hope,* 1715.

Nieuhoff, John. *Voyages and Travels into Brazil and the East Indies.* trans. from Dutch, Churchill, II, 1–369.

Ovington, John. *A Voyage to Suratt, 1689, giving . . . a Description of Madiera . . . the Cape of Good Hope . . .* 1696.

Paterson, William. *A Narrative of Four Journeys into the Country of the Hottentots and Caffraria in 1777–79.* 1789.

Roggewein, Captain —. *An Account of Captain Roggewein's Expedition,* Harris, *Navigantium atque Itinerantium,* I, 310–12.

Saint-Pierre, J. H. Bernardin de. *A Voyage to the Island of Mauritius . . . the Isle of Bourbon, the Cape of Good Hope . . .* trans. John Parish, 1775.

Sparrman, Andreas. *A Voyage to the Cape of Good Hope . . . chiefly into the Country of the Hottentots and Caffres, 1772–76.* trans. from Swedish, 2 vols. 1785.

Tachard, Gui. *A Relation of the Voyage to Siam performed by Six Jesuits, sent by the French King to the Indies and China in the year 1685 . . .* trans. from French, 1688.

Tavernier, Jean-Baptiste. *Collections of Travels through Turky into Persia, and the East Indies . . .* 2 vols. 1684.

Ten Rhyne, William. *An Account of the Cape of Good Hope and the Hottentots . . .* trans. from Latin, Churchill, IV, 829–46.

5. *Descriptions of the New World*

(a) *North America*

Beverley, Robert. *The History and Present State of Virginia.* 1705.

Burke, W. *An Account of the European Settlements in America.* 2nd ed. 2 vols. 1758.

Burnaby, Andrew. *Travels through the Middle Settlements in North America.* 1775.

Catesby, Mark. *The Natural History of Carolina, Florida, and the Bahama Islands.* 2 vols. 1731–43.

Eden, Richard. *The First Three English Books on America 1511–1555 A.D. Being Chiefly Translations, Compilations etc. by Richard Eden.* ed. Edward Arbor, Birmingham, 1885.

Gilbert, Humphrey. *The Voyages and Colonizing Enterprises of Sir Humphrey Gilbert.* ed. David Beers Quinn, 2 vols. *Hakluyt Society Publications,* Ser. 2, LXXXIII–IV, 1940.

Hewitt, Alexander. *An Historical Account of the Rise and Progress of the Colonies of South Carolina and Georgia.* 1779.

Jefferson, Thomas. *Notes on the State of Virginia.* 1787.

Johnston, George Milligan. *A Short Description of the Province of South-Carolina.* 1770.

Jones, Hugh. *The Present State of Virginia.* 1724.

Kalm, Peter. *Travels into North America.* 3 vols. Warrington, 1770–71.

Lawson, John. *The History of Carolina.* 1714.

The Roanoke Voyages 1584–90, 2 vols. ed. David Beers Quinn, *Hakluyt Society Publications,* Ser. 2, CIV-V, 1955.

Robertson, William. *History of America.* 2 vols. 1777.

Strachey, William. *Historie of Travell into Virginia Britannia,* 1612. *Hakluyt Society Publications,* Ser. 2, CIII, 1953.

Wynne, J. H. *A General History of the British Empire in America.* 2 vols. 1770.

(b) *The West Indies*

Atwood, Thomas. *The History of Dominica.* 1791.

Bancroft, Edward. *An Essay on the Natural History of Guiana in several Letters from a Gentleman of the Medical Faculty.* 1769.

Blome, Richard. *A Description of the Isle of Jamaica, with the other Isles and Territories in America, to which the English are related . . .* 3rd ed. 1687.

Browne, Patrick. *The Civil and Natural History of Jamaica.* 1756.

Burton, Robert (alias Nathaniel Crouch). *The English Empire in America: or a Prospect of His Majesties Dominions in the West-Indies . . .* 1685.

Edwards, Bryan. *The History Civil and Commercial of the British West Indies.* 2 vols. 1793.

Frere, C. *A Short History of Barbados.* 2nd ed. 1768.

Hickeringill, E. *Jamaica Viewed.* 3rd ed. 1705.

Hughes, Griffith. *The Natural History of Barbados.* 1750.

The Importance of Jamaica to Great Britain Consider'd. With some account of that Island . . . 1774.

Jefferys, Thomas. *The Natural and Civil History of the French Dominions in North and South America.* 1760.

Leslie, C. *A New and Exact Account of Jamaica.* 3rd ed. 1740.

Ligon, Richard. *A True and Exact History of the Island of Barbados.* 2nd ed. 1673.

Long, Edward. *The History of Jamaica.* 3 vols. 1774.

Luffman, John. *A Brief Account of the Island of Antigua . . . in Letters to a Friend Written . . . 1786, 1787, 1788.* n.d.

Marsden, Peter. *An Account of the Island of Jamaica: with Reflections on the Treatment, Occupation, and Provisions of the Slaves . . .* Newcastle, 1788

Martin, Samuel. *An Essay on Plantership.* 5th ed. with many additions and a Preface on the Slavery of the Negroes in the British Colonies. 1773.

Oldmixon, John. *The British Empire in America . . . Vol. I Newfoundland . . . Vol. II West Indies . . .* 2 vols. 1708.

The Present State of the West Indies. 1778.

Raynal, (Abbé) Guillaume Thomas. *A Philosophical and Political History of the Settlements and Trade of the Europeans in the East and West Indies.* trans. J. Justamond, 3rd ed. 5 vols. 1777.

Schaw, Janet. *Journal of a Lady of Quality . . .* ed. Evangeline W. Andrews, New Haven, Conn. 1921.

Sloane, Hans. *A Voyage to the Islands of Madera, Barbados, Nieves, St. Christophers, and Jamaica . . . with a Natural History of the last of those Islands . . .* 2 vols, 1707–25.

A Soldier's Journal. 1770.
Thompson, Edward. *Sailor's Letters . . .* 2nd ed. 2 vols. 1767.

III   *Propaganda on Slavery and the Slave Trade*

1. *Economic Aspects*

    (a)   *The African Companies and their Critics*

D'Avenant, Charles. *Reflections upon the constitution and management of the trade to Africa . . .* 1709, in *The Political and Commercial works of . . . Charles D'Avenant,* 5 vols. 1771. V.
Postlethwayt, Malachy. *The Importance of the African Expedition Considered . . .* 1758.
——. *The National and Private Advantages of the African Trade considered . . .* 1746.
Wilkinson, William. *Systema Africanum: or, A Treatise Discovering the Intrigues and Arbitrary Proceedings of the Guiney Company . . .* 1690.

Anonymous Works in chronological order:

Reasons . . . Against the Bill for Settling the Trade in Africa. 1698.
A Memorial Touching the Nature and State of the Trade to Africa. 1709.
Several Reasons proving, that our Trade to Africa cannot be preserved and carried on effectively by any other Method, than that of a considerable Joint-Stock, with exclusive Privileges. 1709?
The Argument touching Security . . . for carrying on the African Trade, demonstrated to be groundless. 1710.
A Letter from a Merchant in Bristol, touching the trade to Africa . . . 1711?
A Plain Account of the Loss, this Nation has sustain'd, by laying open the Trade to Africa. 1711.
A Scheme for an additional Stock to the Royal African Company by Subscription. 1713–14.
An Answer to the Objections against the Proposals of the Royal African Company for Settling the Trade to Africa in a second letter to a M.P. 1748.
Papers Laid before the Honourable House of Commons by the Commissioners for Trade and Plantations . . . for the better Securing . . . the Trade to Africa. 1750.

Undated Anonymous Works:

The Case of the Creditors of the Royal African Company of England.
Considerations on the Present Trade to Africa, answer'd paragraph by paragraph.
The Destructive Consequences of a Regulated Trade to Africa as promoted by the Separate Traders.
The Falsities of the Private Traders to Africa discover'd, and the Mischiefs they occasion demonstrated . . .
The Improvement of the African Trade farther Demonstrated by Separate Traders . . .
Reasons, Showing that the Trade to Guinea . . . cannot be preserved without Forts and Castles . . .
Some Considerations . . . against Granting the Sole Trade to Guinea . . . to a Company with a Joint-Stock.
The Trade to Africa Considered, and Demonstrated to be Improved to the Nation's Benefit near a Million a Year by Separate Traders.

(b) · The West Indian Colonies

Campbell, John. *Candid and Impartial Considerations on the Nature of the Sugar Trade, the Comparative Importance of the British and French Islands in the West Indies . . . 1763.*

Kemeys, John Gardner. *Free and Candid Reflections, Occasioned by the Late Additional Duties on Sugars and Rum . . . 1788.*

Littleton, E. *The Groans of the Plantations: or an Account of the Hardships Relating to Barbados.* 1698.

Anonymous Works in chronological order:

The Groans of Jamaica. 1714.

The Present State of the British Sugar Colonies consider'd, In a letter from a Gentleman of Barbadoes to his friend in London. 1731.

An Essay Concerning Slavery, and the danger Jamaica is expos'd to from the too great number of slaves. 1746.

The Alarm-Bell; or, Considerations on the present dangerous state of the Sugar Colonies. 1749.

Considerations which may tend to promote the settlement of our new West-India Colonies, by encouraging individuals to embark in the undertaking. 1764.

The Privileges of the Island of Jamaica Vindicated. 1766.

2. *Abolitionist Works*

Agutter, William. *The Abolition of the Slave Trade considered in a religious point of view. A Sermon . . . 1788.*

Anderson, James. *Observations on Slavery, particularly with a view to its effects on the British colonies, in the West-Indies.* Manchester, 1789.

Booth, Abraham. *Commerce in the Human Species, and the Enslaving of Innocent Persons, Inimical to the Laws of Moses and the Gospel of Christ. A Sermon . . . 1792.*

Bradburn, Samuel. *An Address to the People Called Methodists concerning the evil of encouraging the slave trade.* Manchester, 1792.

Clarkson, Thomas. *An Essay on the Slavery and Commerce of the Human Species, particularly the African . . . 1786.*

———. *Letters on the Slave Trade and the State of the Natives . . . contiguous to Fort St. Louis and Goree.* 1791.

Cooper, Thomas. *Letters on the Slave Trade first published in Wheeler's Manchester Chronicle.* Manchester, 1787.

Cugoano, Ottobah. *Thoughts and Sentiments on the Evil and Wicked Traffic of the Slavery and Commerce of the Human Species, humbly submitted to the Inhabitants of Great-Britain.* 1787.

Day, Thomas. *Fragment of an Original Letter on the Slavery of the Negroes written . . .1776, in Four Tracts.* 1784.

Dickson, William. *Letters on Slavery . . . 1789.*

Dore, James. *A Sermon on the African Slave Trade, preached at Maze-Pond, Southwark . . . 1789.*

Falconbridge, Alexander. *An Account of the Slave Trade on the Coast of Africa.* 1788.

Fox, William. *A Summary of the Evidence produced before a Committee of the House of Commons relating to the slave trade.* 6th ed. 1792.

Gisborne, Thomas. *Remarks on the late decision of the House of Commons respecting the abolition of the slave trade.* 2nd ed. 1792.

Hargrave, Francis. *An Argument in the Case of James Sommersett, a negro* . . . 1772.

Jamieson, John. *The Sorrows of Slavery.* 1789.

Liddon, J. *Cruelty the natural and inseparable consequence of slavery.* 1792.

Newton, John. *Thoughts Upon the African Slave Trade.* 1788.

Nickolls, Robert Boucher. *A Letter to the Treasurer of the Society Instituted for the Purpose of Effecting the Abolition of the Slave Trade.* 1787.

Peckard, Peter. *Am I not a man and a brother?* Cambridge, 1788.

———. *Justice and Mercy Recommended, particularly with reference to the Slave Trade: a sermon* . . . Cambridge, 1788.

Philmore, J. *An Essay on the Man-Trade.* 1760.

Preston, William. *A Letter to Bryan Edwards, Esquire, containing observations on some passages in his History of the West Indies.* 1795.

Ramsay, James. *An Essay on the Treatment and Conversion of African Slaves in the British Sugar Colonies.* 1784.

———. *An Inquiry into the Effects of Putting a Stop to the African Slave Trade and of granting Liberty to the Slaves in the British Sugar Colonies.* 1784.

Sandiford, Ralph. *The Mystery of Iniquity* . . . *postscript, the Injury this trading in Slaves doth the Commonwealth* . . . 2nd ed. 1730.

Sharp, Granville. *The just limitation of slavery in the laws of God, compared with the unbounded claims of the African traders and British American slave-holders.* 1776.

———. *A Representation of the injustice and dangerous tendency of tolerating slavery, or of admitting the least claim of private property in the persons of men in England* . . . 1769.

Society for the Abolition of the Slave Trade. *Report of the Society* . . ., in Arthur Young, ed. *Annals of Agriculture and other Useful Arts,* IX, 1788, 82–87.

Stanfield, James Field. *Observations on a Guinea-Voyage. In a Series of Letters addressed to the Rev. Thomas Clarkson.* 1788.

Wadstrom, C. B. *Observations on the Slave Trade, and a Description of Some Part of the Coast of Guinea* . . . 1789.

Wesley, John. *Thoughts Upon Slavery,* 1776, in *The Works of John Wesley,* 3rd ed. 14 vols. 1872, reprinted Grand Rapids, Michigan, n.d., XI.

Woolman, John. *The Works of John Woolman.* 2nd ed. 1775.

Young, Arthur. *On the Abolition of Slavery in the West Indies,* 1788, in Young, *Annals of Agriculture,* IX, 1788, 88–96.

Anonymous works in chronological order:

A Letter from a Merchant at Jamaica to a M.P. in London, touching the African Trade. To which is added a speech made by a Black at Gardaloupe, at the funeral of a Fellow-Negro. 1709.

A Plan for the Abolition of Slavery in the West Indies. 1772.

Thoughts on the Slavery of the Negroes. 1784.

Hints for a Specific Plan for the Abolition of the Slave Trade . . . 1788.

An Inquiry into the Origin, Progress, and Present State of Slavery with a Plan for the Gradual, Reasonable, and Secure Emancipation of Slaves. 1789.

Considerations on the Abolition of the Slave Trade, upon Grounds of Natural, Religious, and Political Duty. Oxford, 1789.

Notes on the Two Reports of the Honourable House of Assembly of Jamaica, appointed to examine . . . *the allegations* . . . *contained in the several petitions* . . . *presented to the British House of Commons, on the* . . . *Slave Trade, and the Treatment of the Negroes* . . . By a Jamaica Planter, 1789.

Remarks on the African Slave Trade. 1790.

An Address to the Inhabitants of Glasgow, Paisley, and the Neighbourhood, concerning the African slave trade by a Society in Glasgow. Glasgow, 1790.
An Address to H.R.H. the Dutchess of York against the use of sugar. 1792.
No rum! No sugar! or, the Voice of Blood. 1792.
Thoughts on Civilization and the gradual abolition of slavery in Africa and the West Indies. n.d.

3. Pro-slavery Works

Adair, James. *Unanswerable Arguments Against the Abolition of the Slave Trade . . .* n.d.
Adams, Thomas Maxwell. *A Cool Address to the people of England, on the slave trade*. 1788.
Beckford, William, Jun. *Remarks Upon the Situation of Negroes in Jamaica, impartially made from a local experience of nearly thirteen years in that island*. 1788.
Edwards, Bryan. *A Speech delivered at a Free Conference between the Honourable the Council and Assembly of Jamaica . . . On the Subject of Mr Wilberforce's Propositions in the House of Commons, concerning the Slave Trade*. 1790.
Estwick, Samuel. *Considerations on the Negro Cause, commonly so called . . .* 1st ed. 1772, 2nd ed. with corrections, enlargements, and notes, 1772.
Foot, Jesse. *A Defence of the Planters in the West-Indies*. 1792.
Francklyn, Gilbert. *Observations, occasioned by the attempts made in England to effect the abolition of the slave trade . . .* 1789.
Harris, E. *Scriptural Researches on the licitness of the Slave Trade, shewing its conformity with the principles of natural and revealed religion*. 1778.
Holder, H. E. *A Short Essay on the Subject of Negro Slavery with a particular reference to the island of Barbadoes*. 1788.
Holroyd, J. B., Earl of Sheffield. *Observations on the Project for Abolishing the Slave Trade . . .* 1790.
Knox, W. *A letter from W. K. Esq. to William Wilberforce Esq*. 1790.
Long, Edward. *Candid Reflections upon the Negro Cause*. 1772.
McNeill, Hector. *Observations on the treatment of the negroes in the island of Jamaica . . .* 1800?
Norris, Robert. *A Short Account of the African Slave-Trade*. New ed. 1789.
Philo-Africanus, pseud. *A Letter to William Wilberforce, Esq*. 1790.
Scattergood, John. *An Antidote to Popular Frenzy, particularly to the present Rage for the Abolition of the Slave Trade . . .* 1792.
Thompson, Thomas. *The African Trade for Negro Slaves consistent with Humanity and Revealed Religion*, n.d.
Tobin, James. *Cursory Remarks upon the Rev. Mr. Ramsay's Essay on the Treatment and Conversion of African Slaves in the British Sugar Colonies*. 1785.
———. *A Short Rejoinder to the Rev. Mr. Ramsay's Reply*. 1787.
Turnbull, Gordon. *An Apology for Negro Slavery: or the West India Planters Vindicated from the Charge of Inhumanity*. 2nd ed. 1786.

Anonymous works in chronological order:

Considerations on the Present Peace, as far as it is relative to the Colonies and the African Trade. 1763.
Remarks on a Pamphlet written by the Rev. James Ramsay under the Title Thoughts on the Slavery of the Negroes in the American Colonies. 1784.
A Letter to Philo-Africanus upon Slavery, in Answer to his of the 22nd November in the General Evening Post. 1788.

A Short Account of the African Slave Trade. Liverpool, 1788.

Considerations on the Emancipation of Negroes and on the Abolition of the Slave Trade by a West India Planter. 1788.

An Essay on the Slave Trade. 1788.

Commercial Reasons for the Non-Abolition of the Slave Trade, in the West India Islands, by a Planter and Merchant of Many Years Residence in the West-Indies. 1789.

Considerations Upon the Fatal Consequences of Abolishing the Slave Trade in the Present Situation of Great Britain. 1789.

A Country Gentleman's Reasons for voting against Mr. Wilberforce's Motion . . . 1789.

An Appeal to the Candour and Justice of the People of England, in behalf of the West India Merchants and Planters, founded on plain facts and incontrovertible arguments. 1792.

Arguments from Scripture for and against the slave trade. Glasgow, 1792.

Substance of a Speech intended to have been made on Mr. Wilberforce's motion for the abolition of the slave trade. 1792.

The True State of the Question, Addressed to the Petitioners for the Abolition of the Slave Trade by a Plain Man who signed the petition at Derby. 1792.

IV Science

1. Anatomy

Camper, Petrus. *The Works of the Late Professor Camper, on the Connexion between the Science of Anatomy and the Arts of Drawing, Painting, Statuary, &c. &c.* trans. from Dutch by T. Cogan. 1794.

Cheselden, William. *The Anatomy of the Human Body.* 11th ed. 1778.

Cowper, William. *The Anatomy of Human Bodies.* 1698.

Diemerbroeck, Isbrand de. *The Anatomy of Human Bodies.* trans. William Salmon, 1689.

Dionis, Pierre. *The Anatomy of Human Bodies improved.* trans. from French, 1703.

Drake, James. *Anthropologia Nova; or, a New System of Anatomy.* 2 vols. 1707.

Gibson, Thomas. *The Anatomy of Human Bodies epitomized.* 1682.

Haworth, Samuel. *Anthropologia: or, a Philosophic Discourse Concerning Man.* 1680.

Keill, James. *The Anatomy of the Human Body,* abridged. 1698. 12th ed. 1759.

Simmons, Samuel Foart. *Elements of Anatomy and the Animal Oeconomy.* 1775.

2. Tropical Medicine and Related Works

Anderson, James. *A Few Facts and Observations on the Yellow Fever of the West Indies.* Edinburgh, 1798.

Arthy, Elliott. *The Seaman's Medical Advocate . . .* 1798.

Astruc, John. *A Treatise of the Venereal Disease . . .* trans. from Latin by William Barrowby, 2 vols. 1787.

Atkins, John. *The Navy Surgeon: or, a Practical System of Surgery . . . also an Appendix . . . on the Heat, Moisture, and Density of the Air on the Coast of Guiney . . .* 1734.

Aubrey, T. *The Sea-Surgeon, or the Guinea Man's Vade Mecum.* 1729.

Brocklesby, Richard. *Economical and Medical Observations . . . with an Appendix on the Climate and Diseases of Africa . . . by Mr. Boone.* 1764.

Bryce, James. *An Account of the Yellow Fever, with a Successful Method of Cure.* Edinburgh. 1796.

Chalmers, Lionel. *An Account of the Weather and Diseases of South Carolina.* 2 vols. 1776.

Clark, James. *A Treatise on the Yellow Fever, as it appeared in the Island of Dominica . . . 1793–4–5–6 . . .* 1797.

Grainger, James. *An Essay on the More Common West India Diseases . . .* 1764.

Hillary, William. *Observations on the Changes of the Air and the Concomitant Epidemical Diseases in the Island of Barbados . . .* 1752.

Lind, James. *An Essay on Diseases incidental to Europeans in Hot Climates.* 1777.

M'Lean, Hector. *An Enquiry into the Nature, and Causes of the Great Mortality among the Troops at St. Domingo.* 1797.

Moseley, Benjamin. *A Treatise on Tropical Diseases; and on the Climate of the West-Indies.* 1787.

Quier, John. *Letters and Essays on the Small-Pox and Inoculation, the Measles, the Dry Belly-Ache, the Yellow, and Remitting, and Intermitting Fevers of the West Indies . . . by Different Practitioners.* 1778.

Robinson, Nicholas. *A New Theory of Physick and Diseases.* 1725.

Rollo, John. *Observations on the Diseases which appeared in the Army on St. Lucia in 1778 and 1779.* 1781.

Rymer, James. *A Description of the Island of Nevis, with an account of its principal diseases . . .* 1775.

Towne, Richard. *A Treatise of the Diseases most frequent in the West Indies . . .* 1726.

Trapham, Thomas. *A Discourse of the State of Health in Jamaica.* 1679.

Turner, Daniel. *De Morbis Cutaneis: A Treatise of Diseases incident to the Skin.* 3rd ed. 1726.

Warren, Henry. *A Treatise concerning the malignant fever in Barbados.* 1740.

3. *Natural History*

Boreman, Thomas. *A Description of Some Curious and Uncommon Creatures . . .* 1739.

———. *A Description of Three Hundred Animals . . .* 1730.

Bradley, Richard. *A Philosophical Account of the Works of Nature.* 2nd ed. 1739.

Brookes, Richard. *A New and Accurate System of Natural History.* 6 vols. 1763–72.

Buffon, Comte de (George Louis LeClerc). *Natural History, General and Particular.* 2nd ed. trans. William Smellie, 8 vols. 1785.

D'Obsonville, Foucher. *Philosophic Essays on the Manners of Various Animals.* trans. Thomas Holcroft, 1784.

Edwards, George. *Essays Upon Natural History and other Miscellaneous Subjects.*

———. *Gleanings of Natural History.* 1758.

A General History of Quadrupeds. Newcastle-upon-Tyne. 1790.

Hunter, John (surgeon). *The Works of John Hunter, F.R.S. with notes.* ed. J. F. Palmer, 4 vols. 1835–37.

Linnaeus, Charles. *The Animal Kingdom, or Zoological System, of the celebrated Sir Charles Linnaeus; Vol. I part I . . . with numerous additions from more recent zoological writers by Robert Kerr . . .* 1792.

The Natural History of Beasts. 1798.

Ray, John. *Philosophical Letters.* 1718.

———. *The Wisdom of God manifested in the Works of the Creation.* 12th ed. 1759.

Tyson, Edward. *Orang-Outang, sive Homo Sylvestris: or, the Anatomy of a Pygmie compared with that of a Monkey, an Ape, and a Man* . . . 1699.

Waller, Richard. *The Natural History of Animals, containing the Anatomical Description of Several Creatures dissected by the Royal Academy of Sciences at Paris.* 1702.

Ward, Samuel. *A Modern System of Natural History.* 12 vols. 1775–76.

Watson, Frederick. *The Animal World Displayed* . . . 1754.

4.　General and Miscellaneous Scientific Works

Boyle, Robert. *Experiments and Considerations Touching Colours.* 1664.

Blondel, James. *The Power of the Mother's Imagination over the Foetus examined.* 1729.

Mauclerc, John Henry. *Dr. Blondel Confuted.* 1747.

Royal Society. *Miscellanea Curiosa* . . . *Containing a Collection of Some of the Principal Phenomena in Nature* . . . *being Discourses* . . . *read to the Royal Society.* 2nd ed. 3 vols. 1708.

Royal Society. *Philosophical Transactions.* 1665–1800.

Watson, Richard. *Chemical Essays.* 5 vols. 1781–87.

V　Social and Racial Theory

Armstrong, John. *The Influence of Climate Upon Genius.* 1770.

Beattie, James. *An Essay on the Nature and Immutability of Truth; in opposition to sophistry and scepticism.* 1770.

Blackmore, Richard. *The Lay-Monastery* . . . 2nd ed. 1714.

Bonnet, Charles. *The Contemplation of Nature.* trans. from French, 2 vols. 1766.

Browne, Thomas. *The Works of Sir Thomas Browne.* 3 vols. ed. Charles Sayle, 1904.

Bryant, Jacob. *A Treatise Upon the Authenticity of the Scriptures, and the Truth of the Christian Religion.* 1791.

Co-Adamitae: or, an essay to prove the two following paradoxes. viz. I. That there were other men created at the same time with Adam. II. That the angels did not fall . . . 1732.

Cockburn, Patrick. *An Enquiry into the Truth and certainty of the Mosaic Deluge.* Newcastle-upon-Tyne. 1750.

Doig, David. *Two Letters on the Savage State, addressed to Lord Kames.* 1792.

Dunbar, James. *Essays on the History of Mankind.* 1780.

Eburne, Richard. *A Plain Pathway to Plantations* (1624) ed. Louis B. Wright, Ithaca, N.Y. 1962.

Falconer, William. *Remarks on the Influence of Climate, Situation, Nature of Country, Population, Nature of Food, and Way of Life on the Disposition, and Temper, Manners and Behaviour* . . . *of Mankind.* 1781.

Ferguson, Adam. *An Essay on the History of Civil Society.* Edinburgh. 1767.

Fletcher, Giles. *The English Writings of Giles Fletcher the Elder.* ed. Lloyd E. Berry, Madison, Wisconsin, 1964.

Gisborne, Thomas. *The Principles of Moral Philosophy investigated, and briefly applied to the constitution of Civil society* . . . 1795.

Gregory, George. *Essays, Historical and Moral.* 2nd ed. 1788.

Gregory, John. *A Comparative View of the State and Faculties of Man with those of the Animal World.* 1765.

Hale, Matthew. *The Primitive Origination of Mankind, considered and examined according to the light of nature.* 1677.

Helvetius, C. A. *A Treatise on Man, His Intellectual Faculties and His Education.* trans. William Hooper, Vol. I, 1777.

Hogarth, William. *The Analysis of Beauty.* 1753.
Hooker, Richard. *The Works of Richard Hooker.* 3 vols. ed. John Keble, Oxford, 1836.
Hume, David. *Essays, Moral, Political, and Literary.* ed. T. H. Green and T. Grose, 2 vols. 1875.
Hunter, John (army physician). *The Anthropological Treatises of Johann Friedrich Blumenbach . . . and the Inaugural Dissertation of John Hunter, M.D. on the Varieties of Man.* trans. from Latin by T. Bendyshe, 1865.
Jackson, John. *Chronological Antiquities . . .* 1753.
Jones, Rowland. *The Origin of Languages and Nations.* 1764.
Kames, Lord (Henry Home). *Elements of Criticism.* 3 vols. 1762.
———. *Sketches of the History of Man.* 2nd ed. 4 vols. 1778.
Maillet, Benoît de. *Telliamed, or Discourses between an Indian Philosopher and A French Missionary.* trans. from French, 1750.
Millar, John. *The Origin of the Distinction of Ranks.* 3rd. ed. 1779.
Monboddo, Lord (James Burnet). *Antient Metaphysics; or, The Science of Universals . . .* 6 vols. 1779–99.
———. *Of the Origin and Progress of Language,* 6 vols. 1773–92.
Newton, Thomas. *Dissertations on the Prophecies which have been fulfilled and at this time are fulfilling in the world.* 2 vols. 1754.
The Origin and Progress of Despotism in the Oriental and other Empires, of Africa, etc. 1764.
Paley, William. *Essays, Historical and Moral.* 2nd ed. 1783.
Pauw, Cornelius de. *Recherches Philosophiques sur les Americains . . .* 2 vols. Paris, 1768–69.
Préyère, Isaac de la. *Men Before Adam . . . trans. from the Praeadamitae of de la Préyère.* 1656.
Rousseau, Jean-Jacques. *A Discourse upon the Origin and Foundation of the Inequality among Mankind.* trans. from French, 1761.
Ryan, Edward. *The History of the Effects of Religion on Mankind, in Countries, Ancient and Modern, Barbarous and Civilized.* 1788.
Smith, Adam. *An Inquiry into the Nature and Causes of the Wealth of Nations.* 1776. 6th ed. 2 vols. ed. Edwin Cannan, 1950.
Stanhope Smith, Samuel. *An Essay on the Causes of the Variety of Complexion and Figure in the Human Species . . .* 1788.
Whiston, William. *A new Theory of the Earth . . .* 2nd ed. 1708.
White, Charles. *An Account of the Regular Gradation in Man, and in different Animals and vegetables, and from the former to the latter.* 1799.
Williams, Roger. *The Complete Writings of Roger Williams.* 7 vols. New York, 1963.

VI. *The Propagation of the Gospel*

1. *Works Published by The Society for the Propagation of the Gospel in Foreign Parts.*

Abstracts of the Proceedings of the S.P.G. 1738–70.
Anniversary Sermons Preached before the S.P.G. by the following:
Bearcroft, Philip. 1744.
Benson, Martin. 1740
Beveridge, William. 1707.
Drummond, Robert. 1754.
Ellis, Anthony. 1759.
Ewer, John. 1767.

Fleetwood, William, 1711.
Green, John. 1768.
Hayter, Thomas. 1755.
Keene, Edmund. 1757.
Lisle, Samuel. 1748.
Lowth, Robert. 1771.
Newton, Thomas. 1769.
Osbaldeston, Richard. 1752.
Porteous, Beilby. 1783.
Secker, Thomas. 1741.
Smallbrooke, Richard. 1733.
Stanhope, George. 1714.
Warburton, William. 1766.

2. Other Works

Bacon, Thomas. *Four Sermons, upon the Great and Indispensible Duty of all Christian Masters and Mistresses to Bring up their Negro Slaves in the Knowledge and Fear of God . . . 1750.*

Baxter, Richard. *Christian Directory.* 1673.

Church of England. *Instructions for Missionaries in the West India Islands.* 1795.

Davies, Samuel. *The Duty of Christians to Propagate their Religion Among Heathens, Earnestly Recommended to the Masters of Negro Slaves in Virginia.* 1758.

————. *Letters from the Rev. Samuel Davies . . . shewing the state of religion in Virginia, South Carolina, etc., particularly among the negroes.* 2nd ed. 1757.

Fox, George. *To the Ministers, Teachers, and Priests, so called, and so stileing Your selves, in Barbadoes.* 1672.

Gibson, Edmund (Bishop of London). *Two Letters . . . to the Masters and Mistresses of Families in the English Plantations abroad . . . to the Missionaries there . . .* 1727.

Godwyn, Morgan. *The Negro's and Indian's Advocate, suing for their admission into the Church.* 1680.

Hales, Stephen. *A Sermon preached before the Trustees for Establishing the Colony of Georgia . . . and before the Associates of the late Rev. Dr. Thomas Bray, for Converting the Negroes in British Plantations . . .* 1734.

Hill, Anthony. *Afer Baptizatus: or, the Negro Turn'd Christian . . .* 1702.

Knox, W. *Three Tracts respecting the Conversion and instruction of the free Indians, and negroe slaves in the colonies.* 1768.

A letter to the Right Reverend the Lord Bishop of London from an Inhabitant of . . . Leeward-Caribee Islands . . . In which is inserted a Short Essay concerning the Conversion of the Negro-Slaves in our Sugar Colonies . . . 1730.

Society of Friends in Barbados. *A Short Account of the manifest hand of God . . . upon several Marshals . . . who have made great spoil . . . of the goods of the . . . Quakers.* 1696.

Thompson, Thomas. *An Account of Two Missionary Voyages . . .* 1758.

Winslow, Edward. *The Glorious Progress of the Gospel, amongst the Indians in New England, Mass. Hist. Soc. Colls.* Ser. 3, IV, 1834.

VII. The Theory and Practice of Education

Barclay, James. *A Treatise on Education.* 1743.

Boswell, John. *A Method of Study, or an Useful Library in Two Parts,* 1738.

Brokesby, Francis. *Of Education with respect to Grammar Schools and the Universities.* 1701.

Buchanan, James. *A Plan of an English Grammar-School Education.* Edinburgh. 1770.

Burgess, D. *The Entertainer; or, Youth's Delightful Preceptor.* Berwick, 1759.

Butler, Samuel. "The Rugby Curriculum" in *The Life and Letters of Dr. Samuel Butler,* 2 vols. 1896, I, Chapter Three.

Chapman, George. *A Treatise on Education with a Sketch of the Author's Method.* 2nd ed. 1774.

Clarke, John. *An Essay upon the Education of Youth in Grammar Schools.* 1720.

Croft, George. *A Plan of Education Delineated and Vindicated.* Wolverhampton, 1784.

Directions for a Proper Choice of Authors to form a Library, which may both Improve and Entertain the Mind and be of Real Use in the Conduct of Life. 1766.

An Essay Upon Education. 1711.

Hirst, William. *The Necessity and Advantages of Education.* 1728.

A Modern Catalogue of Books printed in Great Britain and published in London, since the Year MCCLXXXV to the Present Time. 1791.

Newbery's Catalogue of Instructive and Amusing Publications for Young Minds. 1800.

Priestley, Joseph. *An Essay on a Course of Liberal Education for Civil and Active Life.* 1765.

———. *A Syllabus on a Course of Lectures in the Study of History.* Warrington. n.d.

Smith, William. *The Student's Vade Mecum.* 1770.

VIII Biography and Memoirs

Albert, James. *A Narrative of the Most Remarkable particulars in the Life of James Albert Ukawsaw Gronniosaw, an African Prince, as related by himself.* Bath, 1770?

Boswell, James. *Boswell's Life of Johnson.* ed. George Birbeck Hill, revised and enlarged, ed. L. F. Powell, 6 vols. Oxford, 1934–64.

Equiano, Olaudah. *Interesting Narrative of the Life of Olaudah Equiano, or Gustavus Vassa, the African, written by himself.* 2 vols. 1789.

Hayward, John. *Annals of the First Four Years of the Reign of Queen Elizabeth.* n.d. *Camden Society Publications,* O.S. VII, 1840.

Hentzner, Paul. *Travels in England during the Reign of Queen Elizabeth.* 1612. new ed. 1889.

Sancho, Ignatius. *Letters of the Late Ignatius Sancho, an African, To which are prefixed Memoirs of his Life, by Joseph Jekyll, Esq. M.P.* 5th ed. 1803, reprinted 1968, with an Introduction by Paul Edwards.

Thicknesse, Philip. *Memoirs and Anecdotes.* 2 vols. 1788.

Toland, John. *Letters to Serena.* 1704.

Wesley, John. *Journal,* in *Works of John Wesley,* II.

IX Newspapers and Newspaper Cuttings

Most of the newspapers in the following list have been sampled at various periods in the eighteenth century and read in continuous runs from 1770–72 and from 1783–90.

The Diary; or, Woodfall's Register (this began publication only in March 1789).

The English Chronicle; or, Universal Evening Post

The Gazetteer and New Daily Advertiser
The General Advertiser
The General Evening Post (London)
The London Chronicle
The London Recorder and Sunday Gazette
The Morning Chronicle and London Advertiser
The Morning Herald and Daily Advertiser
The Morning Post and Daily Advertiser
The Public Advertiser
The St. James Chronicle
The Whitehall Evening Post
The World, or Fashionable Advertiser
Newspaper Cuttings:
Cullum, J. comp. *Miscellaneous Cuttings from Newspapers* . . . 1712–85.
Lysons, Daniel, comp. *Collectanea: Or, a Collection of Advertisements and Paragraphs from the Newspapers relating to Various Subjects.* 5 vols. n.d. (Referred to in the text as Lysons A. British Museum Press-mark: 1889 e. 5).
———. *Collectanea: Or, a Collection of Advertisements and Paragraphs from the Newspapers relating to Various Subjects.* 2 vols. n.d. (Lysons B. B.M. 1881 b. 6).

X   Periodicals

Annals of Agriculture and Other Useful Arts
Annual Register
European Magazine and London Review
General Magazine and Impartial Review
Gentleman's Magazine
London Magazine
Monthly Review
Philosophical Magazine
The Repository
The Spectator. Everyman's Library. No. 164, 4 vols. 1950.
Universal Magazine

SECONDARY SOURCES

Anderson, James F. *Natural Theology; the Metaphysics of God,* Milwaukee, 1962.
Banton, Michael. *Race Relations.* 1967.
Bastide, Roger. "Color, Racism, and Christianity", *Daedalus,* Spring, 1967, 312–27.
Benedict, Ruth. *Race and Racism.* 1942.
Botsford, Jay Barrett. *English Society in the Eighteenth Century, as influenced from Oversea.* New York, 1924.
Chitty, C. W. "Aliens in England in the Sixteenth Century", *Race,* VIII, October, 1966, 129–46.
Cox, Edward Godfrey. *A Reference Guide to the Literature of Travel.* 3 vols. Seattle, 1935.
Curtin, Philip D. *The Image of Africa: British Ideas and Action, 1780–1850.* 1965.
Curtis, S. J. *The History of Education in Great-Britain.* 7th ed. 1967.
Davies, Kenneth Gordon. *The Royal African Company.* 1957.

Davis, David Brion. *The Problem of Slavery in Western Culture.* Pelican ed. 1970.

Degler, Carl N. *Out of our Past.* New York, 1962.

Dictionary of National Biography. ed. Leslie Stephen, 1886.

Dingwall, Eric John. *Racial Pride and Prejudice.* 1946.

Dykes, Eva Beatrice. *The Negro in English Romantic Thought, or a Study of Sympathy for the Oppressed.* Washington. 1942.

Fage, John D. *A History of West Africa: an Introductory Survey.* 4th ed. of 'An Introduction to the History of West Africa', Cambridge, 1969.

Fairchild, Hoxie Neale. *The Noble Savage: A Study in Romantic Naturalism.* New York, 1928.

Foner, Laura and Genovese, Eugene D. *Slavery in the New World: a reader in Comparative History.* Englewood Cliffs, 1969.

George, Katherine. ''The Civilized West looks at Primitive Africa, 1400–1800''. *Isis,* XLIX, 1958, 63–72.

Gergen, Kenneth J. ''The Significance of Skin Color in Human Relations'', *Daedalus,* Spring 1967, 390–406.

Glass, Bentley; Temkin, Owsei; Straus, William R. eds. *Forerunners of Darwin: 1745–1859.* Baltimore, 1959.

Handlin, Oscar. *Race and Nationality in American Life.* New York, 1957.

Hanke, Lewis Ulysses. *Aristotle and the American Indians: A Study of Race Prejudice in the Modern World.* 1959.

Hoare, Prince. *Memoirs of Granville Sharp, Esq.* 1820.

Hecht, Joseph Jean. *Continental and Colonial Servants in Eighteenth Century England.* 1954.

Hobson, R. F. and Dunstan, G. R. ''A Note on an Early Ingredient of Racial Prejudice in Western Europe: with a psychiatrist's comment'', *Race,* VI, April 1965, 334–39.

Jones, Eldred. *Othello's Countrymen: the African in English Renaissance Drama.* 1965.

Jordan, Winthrop Donaldson. *White Over Black: American Attitudes towards the Negro, 1550–1812.* Pelican ed. 1971.

Judges, A. V. ed. *The Elizabethan Underworld.* 1965.

Little, Kenneth Lindsay. *Negroes in Britain: A Study of Racial Relations in English Society.* 1948.

Lovejoy, Arthur Oncken. *The Great Chain of Being: A Study of the History of an Idea . . .* Cambridge, Mass. 1936.

Martin, Eveline C. *The British West African Settlements 1750–1821: A Study in Local Administration.* 1927.

Mason, Philip. *Common Sense About Race.* 1961.

———. *Race Relations,* 1970.

Notes and Queries. 1850.

Oliver, Roland and Fage, John D. *A Short History of Africa.* 1966.

Parrinder, Geoffrey. *Religion in Africa.* Penguin, 1969.

Patterson, Orlando. *The Sociology of Slavery.* 1967.

Priestley, Margaret. *West African Trade and Coast Society: A Family Study.* 1969.

Rye, William Brenchley. *England as Seen by Foreigners in the Days of Elizabeth and James I.* 1965.

Schapera, I. *The Early Cape Hottentots described in the Writings of Olfert Dapper (1668), William Ten Rhyne (1686), and Johannes Gulielmus Grevenbroeck (1695) . . .* 1934.

Shakespeare's England: An Account of the Life and Manners of His Age. 2 vols. Oxford, 1932.

Snowden, Frank M. Jun. *Blacks in Antiquity: Ethiopians in the Greco-Roman Experience.* Cambridge, Mass. 1970.

Sypher, Wylie. *Guinea's Captive Kings: British anti-slavery literature of the eighteenth century.* 2nd ed. New York, 1969.

Thompson, H. P. *Into All Lands: The History of the Society for the Propagation of the Gospel in Foreign Parts, 1701–1950.* 1951.

Walvin, James. *Black and White: the Negro and English Society, 1555–1945.* 1973.

——. *The Black Presence: A Documentary History of the Negro in England, 1555–1860.* 1971.

Willey, Basil. *The Eighteenth Century Background: Studies on the Idea of Nature in the Thought of the Period.* Peregrine ed., 1967.

Williams, Eric. *Capitalism and Slavery.* 2nd ed. 1964.

Williams, Gomer. *History of the Liverpool Privateers and Letters of Marque with an Account of the Liverpool Slave Trade.* 1897.

INDEX

Abbot, George, 23, 87, 90, 91

Abolitionist Propaganda, 18, 62–3, 67, 108–9, 116, 127, 142, 149–51, 159–60, 162–7, 172–5, 177, 178, 180–4, 186, 188–91, 194–6, 199
See also: Anti-Slavery Literature

Abolition Movement, British, ix, 11, 12, 13, 18, 30, 33, 157

Abolition Movement, in U.S.A., 14, 18, 164

Adair, James, 174, 182

Adanson, Michel, 18, 19, 43, 60, 103–4, 111, 115, 116, 140

Adomo Oroonoko Tomo, Prince, 27

Africa, Legends About, 3–4, 55, 77, 78, 121, 129, 143

Africa, Schemes for Economic Development of, 63, 151, 180, 196
See also: Gold

Africa,
See also: Names of individual places e.g. Gold Coast, Senegal, Whidah; African Culture

African Culture, 77–9, 100–19, 191–3, 195
See also: Agriculture, Architecture, Cannibalism, Crafts, Fetishism, Government, Human Sacrifice, Islam, Justice, Marriage, Music, Noble Savagery, Polygamy, Prostitution, Religion, Warfare, Witchcraft, Women

African Traders, 3, 4, 7, 8, 27, 28, 29
See also: Barter, Edward; Cabez, John; Conny, John; Corrente, John

Africanus, John Leo, 6, 17, 23, 78, 79, 104–5, 143–4, 157

Agriculture in Africa, 93, 111–14

Albert, James, 37

Albinoes, 57, 87

American Indians, 43, 61, 82, 90, 91, 92, 96, 98, 136

American Revolution, 11, 13

Anatomy, 48–9, 57, 84–8, 168–71, 198

Anderson, Adam, 173–4

Anderson, James, 25, 34, 35, 192–3

Anglicus, Bartholomaeus, 79–80

Angola, 3, 4, 113, 121, 129, 130

Ansah, Sesarakoo, William, 27–8, 36

Antigua, 174

Anti-Slavery Literature, 15–16, 19, 89, 197

Apes, 48, 51, 53–8, 122–3, 158–62, 167–78, 197, 199
See also: Chain of Being

Arabians, 84

Arabic, 105–6, 191

Architecture in Africa, 103–4

Asiento, 8–9

Association for Promoting the Discovery of the Interior Parts of Africa, 179

Astley, Collection of Voyages and Travels, 21–2, 24, 81, 84, 88, 103, 106, 110, 115, 116, 125, 134, 143, 147–8, 153

Athill, Samuel, 174

Atkins, John, 18, 23, 88, 100, 103, 106, 107, 108, 110, 116, 125, 126, 129, 131, 132, 133, 134, 140, 146, 175

Atwood, Thomas, 36

Babel, Tower of, 53, 79

Bacon, Thomas, 85

Baggs, Rev. Isham, 188

Baillie, George, 174

Baker, Henry, 85

Bambuk, 8, 108

Bancroft, Edward, 65, 71, 101

Baptism of Negro Slaves, 67–8, 72, 73
See also: Christianity and Slavery

Barbados, 64, 65, 66, 72, 165

Barbot, John, 16, 17, 23, 102, 105, 109, 110, 112, 115, 122, 123, 125, 126, 135, 137, 139, 140, 141, 146, 147, 152, 154, 182

Barrere, Pierre, 84, 87